FRAGRANCE OF THE *PAST*

A Middle Eastern Itinerary

RAANA HAIDER

tara-india research press

Tara Press
(Trade division of India Research Press)
Flat No.6, Khan Market, New Delhi - 110 003
Ph.: 24694610; Fax : 24618637
www.indiaresearchpress.com
contact@indiaresearchpress.com; bahrisons@vsnl.com

2007

ISBN 10-digit : 81-87943-92-0
ISBN 13-digit : 978-81-87943-92-1

Work of Historical Non-Fictional Writing

Cataloguing in Publication Data

Raana Haider
Fragrance of the Past
A Middle Eastern Itinerary
by Raana Haider

1. Travel - Middle East.
2. Middle East - Travel/Explore/Nomad
3. History - Travel/Exploration/Culture.
I. Title. II. Author

Printed in India at Focus Impressions, New Delhi – 110 003.

First Photo Design courtesy Ramine Haider

For my late parents
With whom I started my journey in the Middle East
And my husband with whom I made the full circle

Author with parents, Baalbek, Lebanon, 1952

Ramine Haider

Travel is the school of Man, threshold of high rank,
Treasury of wealth, master of all skills.

Anwari, twelfth century Persian traveller

ACKNOWLEDGEMENTS

My visit to Esfahan in Iran in 1999 is the *raison d'etre* of this book. It was a revisit after some twenty years. Esfahan fulfilled my expectations and more, for this jewel of a city is the culmination of all that is sublime in Persian arts. Sincere thanks are due to the staff at the Library of the Institute of Political and International Studies (IPIS), Tehran where I spent countless hours in research. Anuj Bahri of India Research Press, New Delhi, is to be lauded for the confidence he reposes in his editor Debbie Smith who simply 'took' to the Middle East manuscript. I am indebted to Debbie for the open channels of communication that we have been able to maintain. She has challenged the myth of the editor as a terror that sometimes devours and decimates a writer's efforts. *Fragrance of the Past: A Middle Eastern Itinerary* would not be in this form without the meticulous input of Jehanara Wasi. My daughter Ramine has rooted for me all the way - what more could any mother want?

Raana Haider
December 2006

Contents

Prologue

"deer ayad durut ayad."
what comes late comes well.
Persian proverb.

"I pray."
Raana Haider

A myriad of upheavals and political changes have occurred in the region since my Middle Eastern travel itinerary began thirty odd years ago.

In Jordan, King Abdullah, the son of the late King Hussein, now occupies the Hashemite throne.

In the neighbouring republic of Syria, a son has also taken over the reins of power following the death of his father: Bashar-al-Assad succeeded Hafez-al-Assad as President of Syria.

Lebanon was rocked by the assassination of its long-serving Prime Minister, Rafik Hariri. National outrage and international pressure at the event forced Syria to withdraw its military presence from Lebanon, a force that had originally come to act as peacekeepers between warring Lebanese factions during the long civil war.

Iran's nuclear programme frequently hits the headlines.

Egypt makes the news with its half-hearted plans for political reform and, happily, more often with the constant discoveries of ancient artifacts and tombs.

The tumultuous upheavals and violence in the Middle East and the snail's pace of whatever remains of the peace process, puzzles peace lovers the world over.

The volatile situation has been compounded, not least by the ousting of the Taliban in Afghanistan and the invasion of Iraq, which were undertaken to remove terror and tyranny and create a 'New' Afghanistan and 'New' Iraq. Instead, what appears pervasive today is the continuing spiral of bloodshed and the high level of insecurity in the region. Both countries lie on ancient crossroads and yet there is no authentic documentation to assess the impact of the continuing violent political events on their vast and priceless cultural heritage.

Yet for any traveller in the Middle East, the upheaval exists as a sad backdrop to a composite architectural and cultural legacy that is rivalled by few other regions and belongs to all mankind.

Ultimately, it is the people and the land that speak and it is the fragrance of the past that endures.

TRAVEL THROUGH THE AGES

"The world is a book, and those who do not travel read but a page."
Saint Augustine of Hippo, North Africa, fourth century scholar and bishop

Richard Neville (occupation noted as 'Professional Futurist') attending the 51st Annual Conference of the Pacific Asia Travel Association PATA in New Delhi in 2002 noted that following September 11, 2001 events, "Fear has entered the travel scene. Many westerners preferred to stay at home and watch the Discovery Channel, than to venture into turbulent uncertain landscapes. But, there is still a huge market out there wanting to touch, feel and experience the world as it really is." Neville furthermore - most encouragingly added - that given the global aging population, "Middle Age has been recently redefined as between 55 and 75." Whether middle-aged or not – we can all be travellers through the ages.

It is my hope that this book will induce the armchair traveller to touch, feel and experience the Middle East as it truly is – an ancient land that is both diverse in form and content and yet possesses long and distant threads of continuity. Here is a region punctuated in history by moments of splendour, glory, and some with long periods of obscurity – only to rise and some to fall again. Others enjoyed their moments in the sun, only to fade away into the sunset. Yet the magnificent diversity and remnants that they have bequeathed to us, remind us of the mortality of mankind and the immortality of our cultural heritage. On the other hand, both for the 'road-hardened been there and know it all' voyager and the 'armchair bound stay-at-home seasoned' traveller; I have hopefully captured the flavour of the place and illuminated the everlasting cultural spirit that permeates the region – where the paths of various civilisations crossed – before the concept of national boundaries were introduced.

The Middle East set between producers of silk in China and spices in India and the demands of the lands on the rim of the Mediterranean, was from time immemorial crossed by trans-continental caravan trade routes between the East and the West. It was the need for animal transport and depots for goods that linked nomads to town dwellers. The caravan route from Yemen along coastal Hejaz, through the cities of Mecca and Medina carried spices and perfume by way of Gaza to Egypt and Rome, or to Petra and Palmyra and onwards to Mesopotamia. Trade and commerce were lifelines for which merchants travelled in groups as protection against bandits along the Old Silk Road. Invaders, traders, missionaries and artists criss-crossed these commercial highways. Continental trade routes handled silver, gold, textiles, turquoise, pearls, grain, granite, shells, ivory, tin, ceramics, copper, stone, timber, lumber and salt. In addition to commodities; ideas, knowledge and customs also travelled along caravan routes and sea-lanes. In time, shifting global trade patterns reduced their importance and far-flung caravanserais and trading posts fell into decline and were eventually forgotten – only for economic epicentres to emerge elsewhere. It would be no exaggeration to state that 'to travel and to trade were almost the same.'

Importantly, there is a qualitative difference in something being old and something being timeless. Perhaps nowhere is this dictum truer than in the Fertile Crescent. This junction of empires and civilisations has a palpable resonance of the Past – echoes from the Past that sands of Time have not erased. For again and again, one comes across the vestiges of monumental prosperity and power that echo a fallen splendour that once was the heart of hustle and bustle. Perhaps John Ruskin has captured that essence in the following quote. "Nations write their autobiographies in three manuscripts: *The Book of Deeds, The Book of Words* and *The Book of Arts*. Of the three, only the last is the most trustworthy."

One journeys to the Middle East to imbibe their mastery of the sublime unification of the visual arts – be it architecture, garden design or urban planning. To a remarkable degree, the region has produced some of the world's most striking structures – all with a heightened sense of drama and power. Whether the spectacular physical magnitude of the pyramids of Giza in Egypt, the aesthetic grandeur of the Shah Abbas mosque in Esfahan, Iran or the awesome spiritual power of the Holy Kaaba in Mecca, Saudi Arabia – all rank as monumental global landmarks.

Ancient dead cities still shine with stunning remnants of architectural splendour. Luxor and Aswan and the phenomenal pyramids in Egypt continue to fascinate generations of travellers. Petra in Jordan and Palmyra in Syria were legendary commercial centres. Old, yet living cities – Aleppo, Baghdad, Cairo, Damascus, Esfahan…were built around mosques and markets thus fusing the sacred and commercial domains. The Islamic towns were often built around the *qasr* (fortress) – the seat of power and the residence of the ruler and his court. The *medina* (town-centre) was the heart of the city replete with *hamaams* (bathhouses), markets and mosques. Moving away from town were gardens, orchards and graveyards.

Geoffery Blavey in *A Short History of the World* offers a unique perspective into the development of Islamic medieval cities. His analysis is the following: "Islam is often a puzzle. The West tends to cloud its origins in mystery. It is assumed that Islam, arising out of the land of camels and nomadic pastoralists, must be a mirror of the ideas of a simple people for whom anything larger than a tent was an unfamiliar sight. In fact, Islam arose less from the desert than from walled towns. It arose less from the herders and shepherds than from merchants who were in weekly contact with the outside world. It arose less from the windblown sands and the arid loneliness of the interior than from towns shadowed by rugged bony mountains and standing close to the sea, or towns in the centre of irrigated oases."

Craftsmen travelled great distances – resulting in a distinctive decorative style. Cultural diffusion is visible. In Central Asia, artistic themes came from Anatolia via Iran and through Turkish tribal migrations with Mongol armies. Gabriele Mandel in *How to Recognise Islamic Art* elaborates. "Decoration was the main link between the various forms of Islamic art. It reflected the influence of the nomadic peoples, Bedouins, Turks and Mongols, who gave it its tendency towards abstraction, and of the settled peoples of the Middle East, Byzantium, Persia, India, and even China, with their preference for figurative art. At the beginning too, Islamic decoration made use of Greek and Roman motifs along with elements drawn from another imaginative world, the steppes of Central Asia." Ceramic tiles, calligraphy, tilework, carpets, textiles, stone and wood carvings, stucco, arts of the book, metalwork, glassware, pottery and jewellery are some sublime art forms that emerged in the region. Calligraphy is regarded as the supreme art in the Islamic world since "Writing has a sacramental characteristic since it can convey the Quran, the word of God," notes Barbara Brend in *Islamic Art.*

Travel writing is of interest for the unusual, the noteworthy and the memorable – for those who could not make the journey themselves. A successful travel book will awaken the adventurer and explorer in each of us. "Failing to get there; the next, only and best option is read a book. To really read about a country; its history, its religions, its people; its culture; its mood and mores, nothing beats a good book. Not even an on-line/web site printout." This comment comes from Fodors - the classic travel guidebook. Pico Iyer elaborates on book journeys. "Books are a form of travel as much as travels are a form of text. Books transport us around the world and travel propels us across a whole range of texts." Robert Kaplan, contemporary writer and journalist, remarked on one of his visits to Egypt that "in an age of mass tourism, adventure becomes increasingly an inner matter, where reading can transport you to places that others only a few feet away will never see." Perhaps, the wanderlust spirit is best exemplified by 95-year-old Elsie Gordon from Nebraska in the States who observed: "When I sit down with the magazine (*National Geographic*), I take a nice, long journey." Her father took out her first subscription to 'the king of travel journals' in 1909. It was renewed for two more years by her grandson.

It takes a traveller to sense another intrepid traveller's appreciation of the journey. Lord Curzon (1859-1925) accorded great value to one of the many accolades that he received. In the Introduction to his book *Tales of Travel*, he wrote, "It gave me greater pleasure to be awarded the Gold Medal of the Royal Society for exploration and research than it did to become a Minister of the Crown." For one travels in search of change; one travels for change of culture; for change of climate; for change of scenery; for change of language; for change of routine. One travels for relaxation and one travels for the sheer pleasure of it.

I am also tracing the path taken by countless other travellers who have put into writing their remembrances. I have followed in the footsteps of voyagers that have long since faded. For as the British Persian scholar E.G. Browne wrote in the late nineteenth century in his classic book *A Year Amongst the Persians*, "...he strides forward manfully on the broad interminable road which is, indeed, for the most part but the track worn by countless generations of travellers."

A pioneering tenth century traveller in the region was Al-Maqdisi of Jerusalem. His travelogue is the *Ahsan ul-Taqasim fi ma rifat al-Aqalim* (The Best of the Divisions in Knowledge of the Climes). Another poet, philosopher, traveller and chronicler is the eleventh century Persian Nasir-e-Khusrau. His writings have come down to us in *The Badakhshan.*

A statesman, jurist, historian, philosopher, scholar and traveller Ibn Khaldun was born in Tunis in 1332 and died in Cairo in 1406. He visited all major capitals and countries in his region – Bethlehem, Damascus, Egypt, Hebron, Jerusalem, Mecca and Spain. 'Muqaddimah' is his celebrated introduction to the monumental *Kitab el Ibar* Book of Considerations on the History of the Arabs, Persians and the Berbers. The earliest critical study of history was written in 1377. It is an encyclopaedia on the philosophy of history and sociology. Arnold Toynbee has declared it to be "Undoubtedly the greatest work of its kind that has ever yet been created by any mind in any time or place."

A major contributor to the early literature on travel in the Middle East and elsewhere is the fourteenth century Ibn Battuta, popularly known as the 'Traveller of Islam' and the 'Prince of Travellers'. Starting from his native Morocco in 1325 for the holy city of Mecca, he travelled for the next twenty-nine years; in Africa, extensively in the Middle East, to India, through Southeast Asia and reached China. His journeys totalled 75,000 miles–three times the distance logged by his European predecessor Marco Polo. Ibn Battuta was travelling the globe close to two centuries before Christopher Columbus. He left behind copious notes in *Tuhfa al-Nuzzar fi Ghara ib al-amsar wa aja ib al-asfar* (Rarities Seen among the Curiosities of Cities and the Marvels of Travel). He never dwelled on what drove him on. A quest for knowledge? Plain curiosity?

On the other hand, Dame Freya Stark, the twentieth century British traveller in the Middle East specified in her *Philosophy of Travel* that "The true wanderer, whose travels are happiness, goes out not to shun, but to seek...The beckoning counts, and not the clicking latch behind you." At the age of nine, she was presented a copy of *Arabian Nights* and the die was cast. A passionate nomad, she lived to a hundred years (1893-1993) and is the author of a number of classics on the Middle East. *A Winter in Arabia*, *The Valley of the Assassins and Other Persian Travels* and *Persia to Yemen* are some of her most vivid travelogues.

The Middle East attracted a steady stream of travellers in the nineteenth century – many of them British. There is Richard Francis Burton; an avid Orientalist and conversant in Arabic and Persian. Disguised as a Muslim, he went on a pilgrimage to Mecca and Medina that he described in his book *Personal Narrative of a Pilgrimage*. As British consul in Damascus, he produced an English translation of *The Thousand and One Nights* that was published in the 1880s in sixteen volumes. Gertrude Bell, an English archaeologist, diplomat and writer also contributed to the growing travel literature on the Middle East. Charles Doughty travelled through Arabia from 1876 to 1878. His *Travels in Arabia Deserta* originally published in 1888 and consisting of 1400 pages had an Introduction by T.E. Lawrence (of 'Lawrence of Arabia' fame). T.E. Lawrence's own *Seven Pillars of Wisdom* published in 1926 is a classic of modern literature and an amazing account of the Arab revolt in Hejaz and Trans-Jordan prior to the First World War and his role in the event. Scholar-turned-warrior, Lawrence described the two-year guerrilla campaign in which he served as liaison officer between British and Arab forces against the Ottoman Empire as "The Arab war waged and led by Arabs for an Arab aim in Arabia." Many critics, however, would disagree with his claim. Some would argue that the seeds of turmoil witnessed today were planted close to a century ago.

Classic cynics will argue, according to Joan Didion, a contemporary American writer that "Certain places seem to exist mainly because someone has written about them." Mercifully, only a few caustics hold this viewpoint. On the other hand, it is often said that the test of a travelogue is whether the reader has an urge to follow in the author's footsteps. A satisfying travel book provides the reader with the feeling of travelling together - hand-in-hand. While the travel writer puts pen to paper – in a manner of speaking in today's electronic age – the writer is writing for one's own pleasure. In the end - in a measure of the writer's success - the pleasure is the reader's.

GLOBAL NOMAD

'The whole circle of travellers may be reduced to the following Heads:
Idle Travellers,
Inquisitive Travellers,
Lying Travellers,
Proud Travellers,
Vain Travellers,
Splenetic Travellers,
Then follow The Travellers of Necessity,
The delinquent and felonious Traveller,
The unfortunate and innocent Traveller,
The simple Traveller,
And last of all (if you please)
The Sentimental Traveller.

Laurence Sterne, eighteenth century Irish-born writer and clergyman.
I, most certainly, belong to the last category in Laurence Sterne's list.

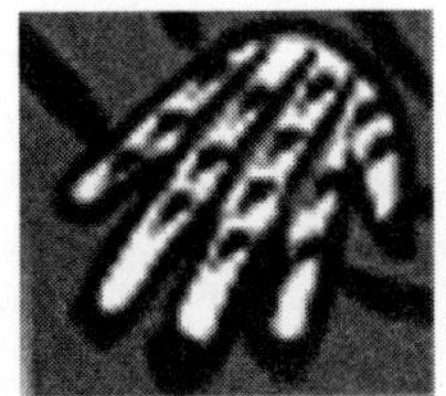

Marshall McCluhan coined the term 'global village' in 1962. I began my life as a global nomad in 1950; the beginning of a life-long global trek. That was the year I accompanied my diplomat father to Syria where he opened the Embassy of Pakistan in Damascus. In my father's thirty-three year long diplomatic service, I accompanied my parents first to Damascus, then Bonn, New Delhi, Paris, Bangkok, Karachi, Washington D.C., San Francisco; Dar-es-Salaam, Tanzania and Beirut. Following the independence of Bangladesh in 1971, I continued to visit them in their postings in Baghdad, Belgrade, Tehran and Moscow from where my father retired from diplomatic service in 1983.

My first posting with my husband Tufail K. Haider was to Moscow. We then moved to Belgrade, Tokyo, Dubai, Cairo, Paris and Tehran. My husband retired as High Commissioner of Bangladesh to India in 2003.

Half a century later - as I write this book – I am approaching the end of that long journey to foreign lands, both as the daughter and then the spouse of diplomats. I now contemplate a more sedentary life yet crowded memories linger on from my life as a global nomad..

I disagree with the view that 'going back is a total waste of time, that your journey will always end in tears.' The impulse, in part, is nostalgia and reverence for the past, and, like most recollections, the past did not exist in the form in which it is remembered. All of this does not prevent such nostalgia from becoming a heady brew and one that grows more intoxicating with the passing of time. Nostalgia appears to improve with keeping; while the past is history, nevertheless, its perfume lingers on.

The years of living in the Middle East have left their mark. I have been privileged to witness a small fraction of the passage of time in a region where time can be measured visibly in centuries, and yet the impact and memories remain vivid. "There is no past, there is no hereafter, everything is in a process of becoming," said Bedreddin, a Turkish mystic.

This region, parts of which have been termed the 'Cradle of Civilisation', has been the source of and has contributed substantially to the world's repository of architecture, art, culture, learning, and science. Egypt, Mesopotamia, Anatolia, Persia and Central Asia are lands characterised by layer-cake civilisations. The Middle East developed an extensive, sophisticated and influential culture based on contributions by the symbiotic Arabs, Armenians, Persians and Turks who were Christians, Jews or Muslims. Riverine environment gave rise to settled communities along the Nile and Tigris-Euphrates. It has produced more than its share of scholars and poets, artists and architects, philosophers and prophets. It has been prized for its natural resources and its strategic location. The crossroad of commerce and culture, it is also the hub of ancient trading routes including the famed Silk Route.

Yet the 'sands' of time, both literally and metaphorically, have dulled but not erased its infinitely rich heritage. History is brought alive in the form of ancient living and dead cities and monuments are lively manifestations of the past. While archaeology is the substance of history, it is also the evidence of mankind's past. In the volatile Middle East region, even a small loss of this material past is a great loss for humanity. It is to the rich depository of Middle Eastern cultural heritage that I have repeatedly been drawn.

A travelogue is usually a highly personal account. "The real voyage of discovery consists not in seeking new landscapes but in having new eyes." (Marcel Proust). Discovery is always personal; it does not matter that millions have made the same stop at the same spot.

I found, while writing these essays, and as I delved into the recesses of my memory that I understood so much more beyond my humble observations of the manifestations of a civilisation that had long ceased to exist. This in itself was a revelation. This book is, therefore, the expression of a voyage of self-discovery. After all is not the longest journey the journey inward? "From whatever place I write, you will expect that part of my 'Travels' will consist of excursions in my own mind." (Samuel Taylor Coleridge). The contemporary travel writer Paul Theroux put it succinctly, "Travel, is at best, a process of discovery. There is an inner experience in travel that has to do with your mood – really what you are looking for and how you are changed by the experience. It is not so much the exoticism of it." He elaborates: "For travel is the opposite of a holiday. It is about enlightenment and at its best, is a form of disappearance." Someone once asked: How to argue about the serendipity of travel? Surely, one can learn to linger. For how can one dream if there is not even time to dawdle?

The 'eye' that sees is the litmus test. "'Tis certain there are many people that pass years here in Pera without having ever seen it, and yet they all pretend to describe it." Lady Mary Wortley Montagu writing on travellers in the early eighteenth century emphasised the paramount importance of this sensitivity. 'Pera' was the European name of a suburb of Istanbul where most of the diplomats and other Europeans lived. Lady Montagu was the spouse of the British Ambassador to the court of the Ottoman Empire.

A nineteenth century French diplomat, writer and traveller, Count Gobineau had this to say on travel: "It is not everyone who knows how to travel; nor is it everyone who knows how to love, to feel, and to understand, It is not everyone who can see beneath the surface of things, and read the significance of the changing background and the novel scenes that meet his gaze, any more than it is given to everyone to interpret the inner meaning of a Beethoven sonata, or a picture by da Vinci or Veronese, or the Venus of Arles or the Passion of Bianca Capello."

Carl Sagan, astronomer and writer, has also touched on the

personal nature of travel, its private nuances. "When you make the finding yourself…even if you're the last person on Earth to see the light – you'll never forget it." And discovery is entirely a subjective exercise. There is no cardinal rule of observation; it is all in the 'Eye of the Traveller'. Some merely set out and others remain open to surprises along the way. For some it will be breathtaking, mind-blowing or simply awesome. For others – is that all there is?

Travellers through the ages who have documented their impressions in print include adventurers, anthropologists, architects, artists, cartographers, diplomats, historians, journalists, photographers, pilgrims, scholars, soldiers of fortune, social scientists, spies and traders. All of the above have contributed to the vast body of travel literature on the Middle East in varying accuracy, quality and objectivity. This literature can be found in the form of memoirs, journals, chronicles, letters, travel and scientific books. Yet travellers by definition maintain a stay of a brief period yet attempt to describe and record their experience and observations. There are, nevertheless, many who, over a longer period, never see nor hear nor feel with the heightened senses of a traveller.

Widely prevalent is the 'I have-done-and-seen-it-all' cynicism that led E.M. Forster to argue: "Then there is the prayer against cynicism which if a man forget he shall be damned, shall not even notice the sunlight in time, or that the sea is dark blue and the sky light blue, or that there are kites in Cairo and none in Alexandria. So when the old residents say to me, as they will, "There is no such country as the Orient, there is only Dagoland": I must reply to them: "You may be right, But I must gain my own disillusionment, not adopt yours; you know much, I nothing, yet I cannot learn from you."

Despite being the author of the famous *Alexandria Quartet*, Lawrence Durrell held a poor opinion of the charms of Alexandria, Egypt where he spent some time in 1944. His bitter sentiment was that "I cannot think how to write or speak to you from this flesh-pot, sink-pot, melting pot of dullness." Yet the same scenery enthralled Jean Cocteau. "I was immeasurably charmed by this road, for here the scene has not changed since Bible days…As we approach Alexandria, the air becomes lighter. Lungs can breathe in more oxygen. We go alongside the jetty with its yellow buildings facing the sea, frothing and dancing and shading into a greenish tinge as it reaches the turquoise horizon, making us forever think of Cleopatra."

Alexandria has for me the lure of a lingering memory. How can one not recall the distant presence of one of the wonders of the world, the Alexandria Lighthouse, walk the streets and recall the melting-pot of earlier civilisations and the centre of nineteenth and early twentieth centuries cosmopolitanism? Did we not spend the night at the legendary Hotel Cecil in Alexandria where Viscount Montgomery of el-Alamein battle fame has a room named after him? The offensive 'eye' of Nobel Laureate William Golding observed nothing on a Nile cruise but "Here we were, three days out of Cairo and we had seen nothing! All I had to take away with me was this close look at a river no wider than the Thames no matter how long it was!" I have made the same trip and all I can say is that the loss is entirely Mr. Golding's.

A travel writer should not, to my mind, be a passive observer but one who recreates the world travelled through. Rather than simple reportage on the sights, I wish to read of the world through the traveller's eyes. Dedicated traveller Pico Iyer voices similar thoughts, "I think that travel books of the kind you mention are the opposite of guidebooks, in that they don't tell you what to see, but how to see; in a way, they offer a pair of spectacles as subjective and distorted as any other, but allowing you to think about the world in a special way."

In a similar vein, Chateaubriand remarked, "Travel to seek wisdom. The only complete man is the one who has travelled much, and has changed twenty times his way of thinking and living. Provided that he can see! Not the length of a temple, nor the height of a pyramid nor the weight of a statue, nor the probable time needed to build a monument, would feed an imagination closed to numbers. The beauty of a work has nothing to do with age or size, it is strength that touches the heart, that allows slow progress, that brings another thought; another beauty, another light from another sun." He added, "what remains from all travels is the perfume of an open rose." On a similar note, another Frenchman Matisse declared, "the flowers are always there for those who want to see them."

The six countries covered in this book are entirely personal and arbitrary selections. I have lived in or visited the countries written about over decades. The countries cover the Arab lands of Egypt, Iraq, Jordan, Lebanon and Syria and the Persian world of Iran and Afghanistan. Lebanon is a country I am passionate about. My frequent visits to Syria from Iran from 1999 to 2001 truly denote the full circle of my life as a global nomad, a journey that began fifty years ago in Damascus. I have never visited Afghanistan, an antique land. Yet it gave to and took so much from neighbouring lands that today its forgotten cultural heritage is both the region's shared and lost past. As one can be a well-read armchair traveller; with Afghanistan, I became the well- researched armchair travel writer.

It so happened that in the late 1990s, we were posted to Iran and the saying that "a book begins as an excitement in the mind" applied to me. Ironically, it was only after leaving Iran that I came to know that I had Persian ancestral links.

While living in Iran (1998-2002), it dawned on me that surely I had origins that linked me with generations past to this area. My late father was named Mirza Rashid Ahmad; my uncles had 'Mirza' preceding their names. A prince of the former Qajar dynasty of Iran in Tehran told me the meaning of Mirza; 'Mirza' after a name signified a prince and 'Mirza' before a name a learned man or senior administrator of the realm. Others confirmed this.

When I explained this to my sole surviving uncle in Bangladesh, he said that he knew of departed elders who carried the Mirza following the name. He did not know when or how the Mirza title in the name changed position and he knew nothing of the origins of our forefathers. Furthermore, Mirza is also a Shia'a name, the Muslim majority in Iran. Over centuries, the Shia'a Mirza evolved into a Sunni Mirza in the Indian subcontinent. I was persuaded that our origins were in the region of present-day Iran and Afghanistan.

I learned from a paternal cousin that our forefather was a Mirza from the Khorasan province in what constitutes Iran today. Khorasan was a major province of the Persian Empire and included large parts of present-day Afghanistan. This forefather migrated to the eastern wing of the subcontinent, East Bengal that became East Pakistan and then Bangladesh. This genealogical information was revealed to me after he had read my essay on Esfahan.

Upon our return to Bangladesh following retirement in 2003, another paternal cousin, Mirza Shafi, much interested in genealogical research, wrote in 'In Search of Roots', "The origin of the Mirzas, as far as information goes, started with the coming to Bengal, of two educated families (both brothers) – Ahmed Mirza and Mohamad Mirza, from Central Asia and Mughal by birth. Both were educationists, widely travelled and revenue experts, whose forefathers had arrived earlier in India during the reign of Emperor Babur."

My husband was nearing the end of his diplomatic career and this brought a strong sense of nostalgia when I recollected being in the Middle East at the start of my father's diplomatic career. It seemed appropriate that my nomadic life came full circle in the Middle East. Here are my travel memoirs, drawn from the richness of memories, that explore an expanse of land that possesses a wealth of charms that include camels and caravans; carpets and cuisine, citadels and cemeteries, *madrasas, medinas* and mosques. Pivotal trade and travel produced commercial outlets whether bazaars, *khans* or *souqs*. Supreme rulers in the region went by the name of Beg, Bey, Emir, Khan, Shah, Sultan, Pasha or Pharaoh.

Katie Hickman, the daughter of a twentieth century British diplomat, explores the lives, since the seventeenth century, of British women posted abroad with their diplomat husbands in her brilliant book *Daughters of Britannia: The Lives and Times of Diplomatic Wives*. It is largely based on letters that women in distant lands wrote to their near and dear ones back home. This was an era before e-mail, fax and direct international calls. Letters could take months and a reply the same. Hickman highlights the often invisible and unacknowledged role of the diplomat spouse. She writes of a critical comment directed at the unconventional spouse of a diplomat, "You cannot organise dinners and write books."

To dispel yet another myth, I have done both.

ORIENTALISM

"Anyone who teaches, writes about, or researches the Orient—and this applies whether the person is an anthropologist, sociologist, historian, or philologist—either in its specific or its general aspects, is an Orientalist, and what he or she says or does is Orientalism."

Edward W. Said in *Orientalism*

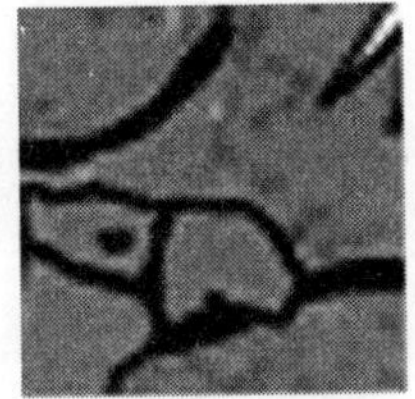

The fascination of the West for the East between the late eighteenth and nineteenth centuries culminated in a school of academicians and painters known as the Orientalists. Artists, diplomats, scholars, traders, travellers and writers in Europe fell in love with the rich expanse of the colourful scenario in the Middle East: the animals, architecture, costumes, landscape, markets and people. They were enticed by what they regarded as exotica. There were also pilgrims intent on visiting the holy sites of Islam, Christianity and Judaism. Europeans travelled to Algiers, Constantinople, Egypt, Morocco, Palestine, Smyrna and Syria. They returned spellbound with memories that some went on to immortalise on canvas. Artists contributed to the visual recording of the buildings, costumes, dress, environment and streets of the Middle East. These tableaux are a detailed and rich documentation of the region and provide, today, a vivid glimpse of a bygone era.

Orientalism in the Middle East context is the study of the Orient by the Occident. Its territorial framework is the Middle East rather than, as the term may imply, any lands further east on the Asian continent. The lands of North Africa and the Middle East are the boundaries of the Orientalists. The Crusaders first exposed the Middle East to Europe in the early eleventh century. Much later, Napoleon Bonaparte's campaign against Egypt, Palestine and Syria paved the way for French romantic Orientalism, an important contribution to the discipline in the early part of the nineteenth century. Between the sixteenth and nineteenth centuries, interest in Orientalism stemmed from the European quest for power over these foreign lands. The Portuguese, Spanish, Dutch, French and British armies and traders colonised the globe. Colonisation and increasing commerce - largely by the British and French - in the Middle East further fuelled the public's interest in Orientalism.

Improvements in modes of transportation eased the eager and curious traveller's movements. Boats and trains now covered long and previously unknown stretches of land. The renowned travel agency Thomas Cook opened in 1868. It organised tours to Egypt, taking visitors from Cairo to Aswan in Upper Egypt. Accessibility and improved facilities helped to further enrapture the public with one of the Wonders of the World – the Sphinx and pyramids at Giza in Egypt. The British Orientalist painter Thomas Seddon did justice to these immortal monuments in his work.

Ironically, not all Orientalists had ever travelled to the Orient. Some artists painted from a factual basis, while others combined reality with a fertile imagination. Richard Bonnington, a painter of rich aquarelles of Middle East notables, had never been further east than Venice. The French artist Eugene Delacroix painted 'The Death of Sardanapole' in 1827, before his travels. Later, in 1832, he visited Algeria and Morocco and painted these settings prolifically. The French nineteenth century painter Ingres's most 'sexual Oriental' paintings: 'The Grand Odalisque' and 'Odalisque with Stone' were executed not on the shores of the Bosphorus but on the hills of Rome." In the field of academics, Richard Knolles, Vicar of Sandwich and sometime Fellow of Lincoln College, Oxford published *General History of the Turks* in 1603. He knew no Turkish nor had he ever left the shores of England. He relied on the vast body of literature in a number of languages on the Ottoman Turks. His study was about "the glorious empire of the Turks, the present terror of the world."

In *Les Peintres Orientalistes*, Michelle Verrier notes, "These countries had a considerable influence over all the painters confronted by the torrid heat, the blinding sunshine, the superb colours, the gracious Islamic architecture, the decorative ornamentals, the opulent splendour of palaces and mosques, the picturesque lanes, the brilliant costumes and the foreign values of the Muslim world…They enriched their art with precise details, result of minute observations…The Orient of the Orientalist painter was and shall always remain a place of opulence, magic, beauty and mystery." The artists frequently used watercolours as they were convenient to transport and the canvases dried quickly on site.

Orientalist painters included Austrians, British, German,

Spanish and a predominance of French; to the extent that there was held in Paris in 1893, the Salon des Peintres Orientalistes Francais. Jean-Baptiste Vanmour, a Flemish artist of the early eighteenth century had spent a large part of his life in Constantinople and was a member of the Sultan's entourage. Court scenes were popular and Vanmour painted 'The Hunting Scene in Turkey' in 1711, depicting Sultan Ahmed III, a eunuch, an emir and the court. The Spanish painter Jose Cruz-Herrera lived in Casablanca, Morocco in the early 1920s and painted the local life. One of his paintings was estimated at $7000 at an auction in Paris in late 2000. He also painted the Moroccan countryside. The Orientalists theme remains very much to current artistic taste.

One of the most famous and most prolific Orientalists was the Scottish painter David Roberts. He spent almost a year in the Middle East. His etchings cover Egypt, Lebanon, Palestine and Syria. Unlike most other Orientalist artists of the period who painted in the vibrant colours of the region; subtlety, delicate contours and soft blend of colours mark Roberts' drawings. A collection of his masterpiece prints appear in *Yesterday and Today: Egypt* and *Yesterday and Today: The Holy Land.* Roberts' original prints are much in demand the world over.

By the close of the nineteenth century, both the quality and the popularity of Orientalist painters had declined. Burgeoning European tourism and the advent of the camera contributed to the lifting of the mystery surrounding the Middle East. Since exotica was now more accessible, the Europeans' romance with the East took on more realistic overtones. Orientalism did fall victim to progress.

Literature too played an active role in stoking the imagination of the European public. In earlier times, there were Chaucer and Shakespeare. Lord Byron (1788-1824) contributed much to Romantic Literature. Samuel Taylor Coleridge in 1816 wrote *Kubla Khan.* In 1859, Edward Fitzgerald published his translation of the poetry of Omar Khayyam and sparked a wave of interest in all things Oriental.

Jean-Leon Gerome (1824-1904), a French photographer, captured vivid shots of Egypt and Asia Minor. His frequent companion on his travels was Frederic Bartholdi, the creator of the Statue of Liberty in New York. Henri Lammens, a Jesuit priest of Flemish origin who died in 1937, was a professor of oriental studies at the Saint-Joseph University in Beirut. The prestigious seat of learning that exists today was founded by his religious order in 1875. Lammens is the author of *La Syrie: Precis Historique* published in 1921 by the Catholic Press in Beirut. It is a general survey of the history of Syria. According to Kamal Salibi in *A House of Many Mansions: The History of Lebanon Reconsidered*, Lammens "was a prolific and highly imaginative scholar, and ranked among the leading orientalists of his time, although he was generally criticised for giving free rein to prejudice and conjecture in his work. His students were strongly influenced by his ideas, and among them was the generation of Christians, mainly Maronites, to whom the French, in many cases upon his personal recommendation, entrusted the government and administration of Lebanon after 1920."

There has been considerable criticism of the prevailing attitudes among the Orientalists towards the culture and people they observed and depicted. Critiques refer to the Orientalist painters' disregard for Islam, to over-romanticising their subjects and portraying excessive sensuality in their perception and depiction of women, harems and court life, given that hardly any Orientalist had access to the private domains of the culture portrayed. It was often an imagination of the East; an exotic realm rather than any documented description. For many Europeans, the Orient was a fictionalised account of contrasts to their own customs and habits.

The antagonist of Orientalism was Edward W. Said, one of the most celebrated cultural critics of the post-war world and the Palestinian author of the classic *Orientalism*. In *Orientalism*, he explores at length why the West sees the East as it does and why the perspective and slant is distorted. Said debunks the creation of the myth of the exotic East. In *Studying Culture: An Introductory Reader* by Ann Gray and Jim McGuigan, Said writes on Orientalism. "So far as the Orient is concerned, standardisation and cultural stereotyping have intensified the hold of the nineteenth-century academic and imaginative demonology of 'the mysterious Orient'… Orientalism, therefore, is not an airy European fantasy about the Orient, but a created body of theory and practice in which for many generations, there has been a considerable material investment." In academic circles and in today's omnipotent media circle, there has been a continuous structured Euro-centric perspective and imagery of the Orient that persists to this day. An outspoken critic of Edward Said is Bernard Lewis, Professor of Near Eastern Studies at Princeton University. He presents an extensive counter-argument 'The Question of Orientalism' in *Islam and the West.*

At a symposium organised in Damascus in late 2000, a number of Syrian and foreign scholars debated the topic Orientalism. Dr. Abdul Nabi Steif, Syrian scholar in a lecture titled 'Towards a New Orientalism' stated that "Orientalism is a new term which refers to the knowledge known by non-Oriental people about the Orient, pointing out that this sphere of knowledge is very vast including, scientific books, journalist reports, short stories and caricatures. Orientalism did not offer anything in service of the Orient. Rather, it was employed in service of western interests." Dr. Z. Bitar noted that "the European invasion of the Arab area has paved the way for Orientalism…the Crusader's war has opened the way for European Orientalists to come to the area and taste the beauty of the art of the East through different architectural designs in the East…It resulted in the Italian renaissance in the field of oil painting…opened the treasures of old civilisation before the trends of modern European art…the culture of the West has capitalised on the product of the eastern civilisations…Another scholar, the French Director of the French Institute for Arabic Studies referred to "some grave mistakes perpetrated by Orientalists, especially their vision of the Islamic religion as opposing the development of science...Another mistake is that the Orientalists did not exert any effort to study the Islamic religion...If Orientalism was linked to colonialism at its beginning, reference should be made to the development and achievements realised by this science later on..."

In spite of considerable faulty orientation and depiction, Orientalism served to increase the information flow to the West. In many ways far-fetched in its imagery, it was influential in its impact on the European elite. Notwithstanding its Euro-centric view of colonised countries, Orientalism in its day offered Europe an alternative cultural reality. Today, it is interesting to note that a reputable international magazine on interior décor had this to describe the contents of a furniture maker in Morocco – a former French colony – "Orientalist sofas with haberdashery a la francaise." Furthermore, a 1988 publication by J. Sweetman has a title that reads *The Oriental Obsession: Islamic Inspiration in British and American Art and Architecture 1500-1920.*

EGYPTOLOGY : A GLOBAL MANIA

"Like men and passions, are not monuments exalted by memory? Is their meaning not explained by death?"

Gustave Flaubert, nineteenth century French writer

The mummy of Queen Nefertari has never been found. However, should it be found - a possibility which cannot be ruled out, given the large expanse of unexplored territory in Upper Egypt - she can surely make a legitimate claim to the superlative title 'Mother of All Mummies'. A viewing of Queen Nefertari's tomb in the Valley of the Queens in Luxor will substantiate her holding that supreme title.

On the other hand, other contenders may include Queen Nefertiti and Queen Cleopatra VII. The Big Three Queens, according to international recognition, are Nefertari, Nefertiti and Cleopatra VII. Yes, there were six Cleopatras before Cleopatra VII (of Elizabeth Taylor fame) in the Ptolemaic dynasty in Egypt, 31-44 BC when Alexandria on the Mediterranean coast was its capital. The Ptolemaic dynasty marked the end of ancient Egyptian history. Neither the mummy nor the tomb of Cleopatra VII has ever been found.

The legacy of Queen Nefertiti, 'the beautiful one who comes', has passed down to us largely because of the discovery of her exquisitely beautiful sculptured head. 'Nefer' means the beautiful one in hieroglyphics, the Greek word for sacred symbols. The head was found in Tel el Amarna before the First World War by the German Orient Company that had concessions to do archaeological work in the area. It is now to be found at the Berlin Museum. An oft-repeated tale of theft and squander over centuries has featured in the excavation and distribution of Egyptian antiquities. Nefertiti, with her oval, high cheek-boned facial structure, aquiline features, kohl-rimmed gazelle-shaped eyes, ornate headgear and elongated neck with a broad choker necklace, has captivated generations. Her tomb too has never been found.

Nefertiti was the queen of Akhenaten. A monotheist, the 'heretic pharaoh' was the first in history to worship a single god, the sun god, Aten. The Egyptians - pre-Akhenaten and following his death - were polytheists believing in a large number of deities. Queen Nefertiti ruled for a brief period following Akhenaten's death.

The magnificent monuments and artwork of ancient Egypt of 4500 to 3000 years ago are a living testament to the glory of the period and the successful quest of the rulers to achieve immortality. In their lifelong efforts to please their gods and thereby reach the After Life; pharaohs, queens, courtiers, priests, artisans and workers spent a lifetime working towards Death and the After Life. Lifetimes were devoted to a single person's search for immortality, more often than not that of the supreme pharaoh's. The purity, precision and patience of that painstaking labour has enthralled countless generations before us and will continue to fascinate many lives after us. The vision and state-of-the-art technology possessed by the ancient Egyptians created the Wonder of Mankind and one of the Wonders of the World.

These testaments to a desire for immortality, built for eternity in sandstone and granite, these temples, tombs and palaces, make amateur, armchair archaeologists out of the most blasé among us. "For here are works in whose presence it is a task for the imagination to overtake the eyesight," as one reputable guidebook has put it.

The worldwide phenomenon that is Egyptomania is not the least surprising. For discoveries are constantly being made and as knowledge increases, so does the passion. Egyptology is an endless source of discoveries and enthralment. "Ancient Egyptians also produced art and architecture not for self-expression, in the artist's sense; but for self-perpetuation into eternity. Aesthetic values were not meant for this world but for the next – a triumph over death and the certainty of eternity. And with this objective, the legacy of the ancient Egyptians has truly become eternal." I wrote these lines on the Egyptomania that swept across Paris during the 'Year of Egypt in Paris', celebrated in 1998 in my book *Paris, A Homage.*

We were on the mandatory Nile cruise from Luxor to Aswan in Upper Egypt; to be in Egypt and not undertake this journey is unforgivable by any account. We took the cruise organised by the Oberoi chain of hotels. With all meals and sleeping facilities on board, our floating hotel docked regularly along the way at major Egyptian sites of antiquities. I had brought with me Vikram Seth's magnum opus *A Suitable Boy* but it remained unread; I succumbed to the vast collection of books on Egyptian antiquities in the library and lamented the fact that I had not studied Egyptology in my youth.

"The keynote of the Nile life is peace; it is an existence placid, regular, reposeful. There is just enough variety to keep your mind awake, and just enough sameness to keep it off the stretch. There is just enough excursioning ashore to persuade you that you are not lazy, and just enough lazing aboard to assure you that you are enjoying the rest..." The mesmerising ambience has been well captured by G. W. Stevens, a journalist and war correspondent of the 1920s, who travelled in a steamer boat up the Nile. As we floated by the placid landscape on the banks of the Nile on a similar journey, I lounged on deck in a comfortable chair with an all absorbing book on the Valley of the Kings necropolis and felt as though I, too, had been transported back to the after world of the pharaohs.

On the east bank of the Nile River in Upper Egypt lies Thebes, the capital of Egypt in the New Kingdom (1567-1085 BC, the peak period of ancient Egypt) that was described by Homer as "the hundred-gated city". Its later name, Al-Uqsur means the 'city of the palaces' that has now been altered to Luxor. At the height of its glory and opulence, the New Kingdom pharaohs made Thebes their permanent residence. The city had a population of nearly one million and the architectural activities were both prolific and astounding.

The massive temple complex of Luxor and Karnak covers a hundred acres and its history spans thirteen centuries. The god Amon, depicted as a ram, is honoured spectacularly in the Avenue of the Ram-headed Sphinxes that leads to his temple and to some of the magnificent still-standing columns of the hypostyle hall. These massive columns are 12 feet in diameter and nearly 70 feet in height, each one intricately carved. The hall was 330 feet long and 170 feet deep. As you look upward, the granite structures seem to rise from the ground and disappear into space. There is little reason to dispute the claim that "there is in truth, no building in the wide world to compare with it."

The temples of Luxor and Karnak were widely shown in the movie based on Agatha Christie's famous novel, *Death on the Nile.* She wrote the book while staying at the Cataract Hotel along the Nile in Aswan. The hotel was built in 1898 and has named the suite in which she stayed 'The Agatha Christie Suite'.

Each pharaoh, in his quest for immortality (and, incidentally, Queen Hatshepsut who ruled dressed as a man; her statues show her complete with a false beard) made a contribution of their own; building their own or enlarging and embellishing temples of their predecessor so that, today, Karnak has been described as "a veritable archaeological department store - something in it for everyone," states T.G.H. James, Keeper of Egyptian Antiquities at the British Museum till 1988.

The metropolis Thebes was the 'city of the living' in keeping with the rising of the sun. On the west bank of the Nile, in keeping with the setting of the sun, is the 'city of the dead', the vast necropolis identified today, for convenience, as the Valley of the Kings, Valley of the Queens, Valley of the Nobles and the Workers' Tombs. Cut-deeply into the mountain rock are the burial sites.

The tombs in the 'city of the dead' were designed to resemble the underworld, with a long, inclined rock-hewn corridor descending into either an antechamber or a series of pillared halls and ending in the burial chamber. The walls were covered in rich-coloured drawings and hieroglyphics depicting the deceased's activities in life and imaginary scenes from the After Life. Writings from the Book of the Dead were also engraved on the walls to guide the soul in its journey to the next world.

The last tomb discovered in the Valley of the Kings was in 1922 by Howard Carter, the British explorer. He excavated the tomb of the pharaoh Tutankhamun whose 'nobody' status (he died at the early age of late teens or early twenties) has been altered forever. Tutankhamun won immortality and international fame as a result of Carter's discovery of an intact tomb full of glittering treasures.

Tutankhamun's tomb (KV 62) today receives some three thousand visitors a day according to an official of the Egyptian Antiquities Organisation (EAO). The tomb chamber is simply adorned and houses the gold-covered fourth mummy case holding the mummy of Tutankhamun in a granite sarcophagus. The other mummy cases and priceless gilded treasures and delicate artwork pieces are to be seen in the Cairo Museum. The Tutankhamun treasures remain the principal crowd-pulling attraction at the museum.

In comparison, Queen Nefertari's tomb in the Valley of the Queens is limited to one hundred and fifty visitors daily. Schiaparelli, an Italian archaeologist, discovered the tomb in 1903. However, it remained closed for much of the time since its discovery due to its poor and delicate condition, the result of accumulated debris from flash floods through the millennia, increasing water condensation causing salt build-up and erosion and rising ground water levels which lead to cracks and weakening of the surrounding rock. In recent years, the Paul Getty Institute launched a massive million-dollar renovation project of Queen Nefertari's tomb chambers. It has been opened to the public for limited viewing since late 1995. In addition to the limited numbers allowed in, a time limit of ten minutes inside is also enforced. Furthermore, a wooden walkway has been installed to prevent footsteps from raising dust, sand and debris into the air inside the tomb. For protection, glass screens are also placed in front of the elaborate engraved walls. Fans and dehumidifiers control the temperature of the tomb. Various other gadgets are also visible. These measures are designed to protect the ancient burial chambers from human pollution; perspiration, carbon monoxide, noise and numbers.

If you are one of the 'chosen few' of the allocated visitors, the first sighting of Queen Nefertari's tomb is one of breathtaking beauty.

The corridor entrance leads one into the T-shaped tomb. The ceiling of the tomb, inside the mountain-rock, is azure blue with gold star markings that appear to twinkle. The walls are covered without break in drawings and hieroglyphic writings extolling Nefertari's virtues and depicting her life. She is shown with the goddess of beauty and love, the mother-cow goddess of fertility, Hathor. We follow her hand-in-hand with the goddess Isis, the archetypical feminine figure endowed with the art of healing, the power of the Enchantress and who is often depicted as the sorrowing wife and devoted mother. We see Nefertari being received by Osiris, the falcon-headed god of prosperity. She is shown being presented, amongst ladies of court dressed in long loose white diaphanous robes, to the sun god Ra. Nefertari wears a jet-black wig, earrings and other fine gold jewellery. She has kohl-rimmed eyes and painted lips. Her long-robed belted dress consists of rich oriental colours; emerald green, saffron orange, mustard yellow, blood red and azure blue, tints that dazzle the senses. "Undying colours, colours that are still fresh, though laid on by hands that have been dust these three thousand years and more," observes an Egyptian antiquities expert. I was stunned into silence. Words simply failed me.

The twentieth century conservation and restoration work on Nefertari's tomb, her 'House of Eternity', by the Paul Getty Institute, consisted of only the immensely painstaking removal of salt and debris that had built up over the wall paintings. It did not involve repainting the drawings. The rich and vibrant colours now visible are the original masterpieces. Twentieth century state-of-the-art technology has come into full force in its task to preserve the tomb of Queen Nefertari built some 1300 years BC. In Egypt and elsewhere there is a host of evidence to show that greater damage has been done to our antiquities heritage in the last fifty years than in all times past. Encroaching civilisation and hordes of twentieth century global tourists are much at fault.

Queen Nefertari was the wife of Ramses the Second or Ramses the Great, the longest ruling pharaoh in Egypt (1298-1235 BC). The 'master builder' is the perpetrator of many of the grandiose monuments visible today in Upper Egypt. Colossal buildings were his forte and he is the subject of gigantic images cut deep into the mountain at Abu Simbel. Each of the four-seated Ramses the Great statues soars 65 feet high. David Roberts, the nineteenth century sketch artist gave the following impression: "the monuments that on its own justifies a journey to Nubia…The beauty and dimensions of this temple are exceeded by no other Egyptian monument." It is simply breathtaking. Once again, words cannot do justice to the impact of these monuments.

In the innermost sanctum of the temple are four statues of the gods Amon, Ra, Ptah and Ramses himself. In the 'miracle of the sun', the French explorer, Francois Champollion noted that twice a year during the summer and winter solstices in June and December, the sun penetrates the entire length of the temple into the inner sanctum and floods with sunlight three of the four statues. The one statue that the ray of the sun never touches and remains in darkness is the statue of the god Ptah, the god of death. The 'miracle of the sun' takes place even today. This ancient architectural masterpiece begs the question – how was this achieved?

The temple of Abu Simbel was rescued by an international UNESCO archaeological project in the late 1960s. The construction of the Nasser Dam would have flooded the rock-hewn colossal statues of Ramses the Great and his favourite wife, Nefertari. Nefertari is the only queen in ancient Egyptian history to be so lovingly honoured. Her husband, Ramses the Great built her a spectacular temple alongside his own temple. The UNESCO effort, a marvel in twentieth century technology, elevated the entire edifice piece-by-piece 150 metres above the lapping Nile waters thus preserving an irreplaceable heritage.

Since the spectacular discovery of Tutankhamun's tomb in the Valley of the Kings in 1922 by Howard Carter, there were no major discoveries of archaeological wonders until May 1995. Professor

Kent Weeks, Professor of Egyptology at the American University of Cairo and Director of the Theban Mapping Project, had been preparing a comprehensive survey of the entire necropolis area of the west bank of the Nile in Thebes. The 10.5 sq. km. area of topography and its monuments had never been systematically surveyed.

A combination of sophisticated electronics, geological sonar soundings and good old-fashioned digging led to the rediscovery of the entrance to a tomb. The tomb KV5 (King Valley Tomb No. 5) had in fact been discovered early in the nineteenth century by a British explorer, James Burton, who had entered the site in 1825 and had, with a candle flame, documented his presence on the tomb ceiling. It is clearly marked 'James Burton 1825'. He then abandoned the chambers without locating anything of interest.

Some one hundred years later, in the 1920s, Howard Carter in his excavation of Tutankhamun's tomb deposited rubble and accumulated debris at the entrance of the tomb, KV5. So KV5 lay hidden for another sixty years until the late 1980s. Expansion plans for bus parking facilities in the Valley of the Kings alarmed Kent Weeks and he sought permission from the Egyptian Antiquities Organisation to further excavate KV5.

As so frequently happens in these lands with long histories, there is the unrelenting duel between the ancient and the modern; the secret of ages lies not far below the surface. "Egypt, mysterious land, inexhaustible museum! While most European ground, except perhaps Sicily and Byzantium, is empty as soon as a few Roman coins or flint arrowheads have been unearthed, the more one asks of Egypt, the more she yields," writes Paul Morand in *The Mediterranean: Sea of Surprises.* Herein lies the source of global Egyptomania. Egypt is constantly throwing up some new discovery, some new explanation; something mysterious and exciting continues to enthral every generation.

By some accounts, Ramses the Great fathered as many as 162

children by 8 wives and innumerable concubines in his 92 years. He ruled for 67 years, the longest serving pharaoh in Egypt. Kent's foray into the tomb alerted him to the elaborate wall carvings and a reference to the names of two sons of Ramses the Great.

"We found ourselves in a corridor. On each side were 10 doors and at the end there was a statue of Osiris, the god of the afterlife," says Kent Weeks. The spectacular discovery was announced in May 1995. An upright walk-in height has now been cleared and dimly lit bulbs certainly facilitated our movements inside the tomb chambers. Earlier, Kent Weeks and his team crawled on their bellies with candles since the accumulated debris of ages past had choked the chambers.

Ducking our heads, we lowered ourselves down from the room discovered by James Burton in 1825 to the finds of Kent Weeks in the 1990s, rediscovering what may well be the largest tomb complex in Egypt deep inside the belly of a rock mountain carved some 3000 years ago. The sight evokes a gasp followed by silence; it is appropriate to say nothing.

The fragility of the excavated walls of the chambers was visible and we saw slated rock and slivers of salt formation eroding the mountain rock. The pillared hall with sixteen columns looked like a dungeon with stumps reaching from the floor to the roof of the chamber. After the sixteen pillared room (Burton's find) lay Kent Week's discovery, the corridor with small rooms leading off it and the Osiris statue at the end, its broken face at its feet. Two smaller sloping corridors branched off on either side of the Osiris statue. These corridors have small 3 metres by 3 metres chambers on either side. These mini-chambers have yielded statuettes, fragments of jewellery, bits of inscriptions and other archaeological delights. The sloping corridors then drop off abruptly a metre, strong evidence of stairways. Nowhere in this massive ancient tomb that has already yielded some eighty rooms, has been found any mummy or sarcophagus, the stone coffin housing the often gold-gilded wooden coffin and the mummified body. Yet inscriptions bearing the names of two of Ramses the Great's sons have been found and remains of alabaster canopic jars used to store the organs of the deceased - namely, the heart, liver and intestines - lead experts to believe that these chambers were used for funerary offerings.

Kent Weeks proceeds on the premise that this tomb has a unique split-level design whereby the burial chambers of the deceased are to be found in the lower level of the tomb. The anticipated stairways and ramps would allow a granite sarcophagus containing a mummified body to be lowered from the upper level of the tomb to the lower level. The direction of the expanding complex suggests the possibility that this massive tomb of the royal sons link up with their father's - Ramses the Great - tomb, not too far away as the crow flies.

The near future may yield a definitive confirmation of the belief that the mummified remains of possibly fifty-two sons of Ramses the Great are interred here. Ramses the Great is the only pharaoh known to have built a family mausoleum like KV5. The discovery of a single tomb with some eighty chambers and with more excavating to be done, leads us closer to witnessing Ramses' single-minded mission to build temples, monuments and obelisks bigger and better than anyone else. His quest for immortality and a great place in history was not to be left to chance. He ensured in his lifetime that the world would look in wonder at these immortal monuments.

The tomb structure is already an archaeological wonder. "There is nothing like this in Egypt. This one is more like an octopus, with a body surrounded by tentacles," says Kent Weeks. Most of the tombs in the Valley of Kings or Queens are syringe-like, plunging straight as a needle into the mountain rock. Further digging and examination of the piles of pottery shards, animal bones, dried fruits, alabaster jars and wall inscriptions will take years of painstaking work.

French archaeologists are working on excavating Ramses the Great's tomb. His mummy was found in a cachet in a mountain pit in the Valley of the Kings in the 1860s or 1870s. It had been removed from the tomb sometime during ancient times for protection from tomb robbers and re-buried deep into the mountain. The mummy travelled to the Louvre Museum, Paris for restoration work. Ramses now lies in state, in a prime location in the Special Mummies Room of the Cairo Museum.

There are some who believe that Ramses the Great was the pharaoh who drove away the Israelites led by Moses from Egypt; the pharaoh of the parting of the Red Sea and the pharaoh who decreed that all first-born sons, from the sons of pharaohs to the sons of slaves, must be killed - (does anyone remember the classic film *The Ten Commandments*?). Ramses the Great, the 'father of all megalomaniacs', thought big and acted big, the man who lived to the age of 92 believed in the grandiose scheme of life and death.

A journey through ancient Egypt's history of some 3500 years ago in the 'city of the dead' on the west bank of the Nile in Luxor brings to mind Gustave Flaubert's comment: "Like men and passions, are not monuments exalted by memory? Is their meaning not explained by death?" On the eve of returning to Cairo, I remarked, "now, back to reality." Someone retorted, "This is reality."

SCALING MOUNT SINAI

"Today we ascended to the summit of Sinai, which took us two hours...The view from the top is the most sublime that can be imagined."

David Roberts, *Journal*, February 19, 1839

I make it a point to remind my husband, from time to time, of the unforgettably painful trek at 2 a.m., up Mount Sinai, Egypt, in order to catch the sunrise – a 'must' according to all old travelling hands. At the start of a bitterly cold October 1996 desert night, we left our warm fire-lit cabin-room – with a view – for the real thing. We were setting out to cross the oceans of rock promontories that form Mount Sinai for the Biblical Jebel Mousa (Arabic for 'Mount Moses'). The summit is recognised traditionally as the mountain where Prophet Moses sought refuge and received the Ten Commandments. The granite peak is the principal site of the divine revelation accepted by all three monotheistic religions of the world. Muslims, Jews and Christians revere the hallowed site. In the year 2000, for the first time ever, Pope John Paul II visited the Saint Catherine monastery situated at the base of Mount Sinai.

Mount Sinai, at more than two thousand metres above sea level is the rugged, sharply serrated mountain located in the southern-central area of the Sinai Peninsula in Egypt. The Sinai Peninsula has a central plateau, tectonic era dips in its terrain and a vast desert. On an earlier helicopter ride over the vast landscape, the rugged terrain had the appearance of an eerie moonscape. The triangular-shaped Sinai Peninsula links Africa with Asia. To its north lies the Mediterranean Sea and to its south lies the Red Sea.

There we were, my husband, daughter and I, seated on three donkeys for the ascent, while more aged, and certainly more agile, Germans walked steadily past us. Far too soon, it was up to us to make the rest of the trek to the summit on foot. In complete darkness – those savvier and better informed had torches – we were often crawling on all fours, literally groping our way up a hidden stony path. The track (of sorts) was invisible; it was non-existent in places, blocked by rubble from landslides. We were feeling our way up an eroded staircase of 3750 steps – the lifetime work of a penitent monk. What the eye could not see, the mind was alert to – for on one side lay deadly depths and engulfing gorges. Between scolding and entreating, my husband managed to get us, fed up and on the verge of tears, to the top of Mount Sinai.

Hordes had preceded us onto a tiny rocky area. Before us lay waves and waves of mountain peaks shaded in semi-darkness. As dawn emerged, the crowd broke the solemnity of it all by singing 'Auld Lang Syne'. It was too funny for words – if only we were in a better frame of mind to appreciate the surrealistic scenario. I was reminded of Khalil Gibran who had said: "When you have reached the mountain top, then you shall begin to climb." However, physically we were at a low, and therefore the cacophony on the mountaintop did not lead to any philosophical height.

The trek down was almost worse. I swore I could not walk down and so we rented three camels. All too soon, my daughter and I were pleading with my husband to be let off the camels. We would walk down. My husband, having failed to negotiate 'a good price', felt that we had to make full use of the payment he was to make at the base of the mountain. That meant we had to stay seated-in-the-air on the camel. We had had more than enough. We unilaterally refused to continue the agony. The march downhill was made in silence. Moods were off and pain was on; the soreness and the memory of it remained for some days to come. This was a climb that needed a high level of commitment and it left us very raw. Travel and adventure has its downside too.

The visit to the famed Saint Catherine's monastery on Mount Catherine at the base of Mount Sinai, founded in 527 AD, became undeservedly, a ritual to get through. The sixteen hundred-year-old Greek Orthodox monastery clinging to the steep slopes of Mount Catherine houses chapels ornate with gold-leafed frescoes, rare manuscripts dating back to the thirteenth century and a magnificent and vast collection of unique icons. We, however, simply wanted to return to Cairo; home and a soaking hot bath.

David Roberts, the renowned Scottish artist of the early nineteenth century in the exquisitely-detailed and innumerable sketching of his extensive travels in Egypt, Jordan, Lebanon, Palestine, Syria, also spent time at Mount Sinai. Francis Graham Moon in London published lithographs taken from the sketches he made during that remarkable journey of exploration in the Holy Land between 1842 and 1849. The book *Holy Land* "offers an unforgettable taste of the technical and artistic virtuosity that gave Roberts a major place in the firmament of English art of the nineteenth century." Pictorial eloquence is the result of Roberts' unflagging curiosity for distant lands and his great thirst for travel and adventure.

The volume published in 1996 by the American University in Cairo Press, Egypt contains the original plates of the first edition, in large format, arranged for the first time in correct chronological order, with a current commentary and extracts from Roberts' journal and is paired with a photograph that depicts the same – a century and a half later. A most beguiling view of the distant past and the real present is the perspective that depicts so well the inexorable Passage of Time.

In 1839, Roberts crossed the vast desert between Cairo and Suez in a camel convoy. In the accompanying text to Roberts' Plate 1 (Arriving in Suez), Fabio Bourbon writes "after following for a considerable distance a track marked only by the fossilised carcasses of camel after camel. On every hand was a featureless sun-beaten desert, without a hint of tree or shrub in any direction…On the opposite side of the Gulf, in sharp contrast with the motionless surface of the great body of water, stood the mountains of Sinai, reflecting the rays of the setting sun in a red fireball." We crossed the endless horizon of the desert and heard the silence of the desert in a twentieth century invention – a car.

In his biography of T.E. Lawrence, Michael Asher provides a vivid account of a late twentieth century camel trek across the Sinai desert. In *Lawrence: The Uncrowned King of Arabia*, Asher repeats the trek across the desert that Lawrence had made in 1917. Asher writes, " It was a moonless night, and the darkness closed in around us, locking us in an endlessly long tunnel from which there was no escape but morning. A bitter wind, bone chilling as only a desert wind can be, was blasting in our faces. We were on the plateau of Sinai, the 'great and terrible wilderness', a vast shelterless plain of stone, whose great winds could freeze a man to death, and whose dust storms could suck the body dry. The breathtaking force of the wind, the weight of the darkness, numbed our senses as if we were travelling in a dream."

In Roberts' Plate 5 (The Approach to Mount Sinai), the accompanying text describes a setting that remains fixed in Time – nothing much has changed. "…an improbable and solemn setting, where nature is the only lord and, at the same time, the only witness, unchanged over the millennia, to the passage of time."

The text to Plate 10 (The Ascent to the Summit of Sinai) notes, "This was no mere outing, and the climb seems all the more daunting to a modern tourist if we consider that the path, which is extremely steep at points and quite precarious, was crumbling and exposed to avalanches at a number of points. The so-called 'Stairway of Moses' covers the most difficult portion of the climb, and consists of more than three hundred steps carved out of granite. Legend narrates that a single monk did the enormous labour involved, in order to keep a vow he had made."

Attached to the steep flank of the holy mountain - encrusted into it - lies the Saint Catherine's monastery. Pierre Lotti, French naval officer and writer described the monastery in *Le Desert* in 1896 as follows: "A Byzantine church, a mosque, small houses, cloisters, a network…the little one sees of the sky is deeply limpid…Let us climb up a flight of stairs…inside this fortress where a strange assembly of superimposed small houses merge…"

Who was Saint Catherine? Born to an aristocratic family in 294 AD in Alexandria, Egypt, Catherine received a rich and diverse education that included philosophy. She was also an early convert to Christianity. Tortured and decapitated for her belief, legend has it that she continued her defence even after she had been decapitated. Then angels transferred her body to the top of Jebel Katherina (Mount Catherine) where monks have tended her memory since the fourth century, establishing a monastery that exists today.

Emperor Justinian in 527 AD, commissioned a fortress to be built around the expanding monastery. Stephanos, a Greek architect, designed it with walls three metres thick and twenty metres high. It withstood an earthquake in 1312. In the possession of the monks at Saint Catherine's monastery is a copy of the very document that the Holy Prophet Muhammad issued for the safe conduct of all travellers in the area. The Ottoman Sultan Suleiman the First took the original, along with the Holy Prophet's banner and sword in 1515. The letter is now to be found at the Topkapi Museum in Istanbul. In the twelfth century, one of the inner chapels was transformed into a mosque and a minaret was built on top flanking the basilica tower in a symbol of the respect accorded to the holy site by both Islam and Christianity.

At the Benaki Museum in Athens in 2004, a selection of some forty artworks from St. Catherine's monastery dating from the twelfth to the fifteenth centuries were on display. It was titled 'Icons and Manuscripts from the Monastery at Sinai: A Dialogue between East and West.'

A community of some twenty-five monks today lead an extremely austere life on its premises. The Archbishop of St. Catherine's monastery has lived here forty years. Hisham Labib in *Aujourd'hui L'Egypte* outlines the rigorous and Spartan routine of the day. "They are awakened at 2:30 in the morning by 33 strokes (the age of Christ at the time of His death) of a little bell, repeated five minutes later on a larger one. At 4 o'clock, the sound of the 'Symandre' (a hard wooden beam on which one bangs with a mallet) calls them to the Morning Prayer in the basilica. After services, the monks perform their duties. At 10:30 a.m., they eat lunch together in the refectory. At 3 p.m. Vespers are announced by three strokes of the bell and, after that, three blows on the 'Symandre' announces the distribution of the evening meal, which is eaten in the cells. Starting, from sunset, the monks count the hours, and they seldom eat meat."

Joseph J. Hobbs in *Mount Sinai* (1996) writes of the revered place whose very sacredness and desert environment are threatened by excessive tourists and pilgrims. Our ascent to the summit of Mount Sinai could have been different. We were told, "The towering peaks shimmer in the emerging sunlight and eventually at the close of the day turn the crests and contours a warm golden red." For this intimate experience, an oasis of silence and space, an oasis of peace and tranquillity are prerequisites. That luxury we did not have. This is the fall-out of international tourism. A menagerie of global travellers is on the same track, the same trek and trying to make it to the same top. In this one ascent, we over-ruled the cliché that states: 'Passage is often more rewarding than the destination.' In this case, neither the passage nor sadly the destination was pleasurable; but certainly both were memorable.

CAIRO : "DESTINED TO TASTE ITS SWEETNESS AGAIN"

"He who drinks the water of the Nile is destined to taste its sweetness again."

Egyptian proverb

Every year a little deposit of mud is left by the Nile on its banks, and every year sees deposited upon the counters of the London booksellers the turbid overflow of journalising travel. Alas! It has not the usefulness of the leavings of this sacred river."

Thomas Gold Appleton, *A Nile Journal*, 1876.

My association with Cairo goes back to the distant reaches of my memory – to scattered recollections in 1959. A return visit came ten years later and a posting to Cairo followed from 1993 to 1996. We decided to spend the Millennium 2000 New Year in this city on the Nile. As for when I shall "taste its sweetness again", who knows…All I know is that, as for countless others, Cairo provides endless material for a writer.

Misr is the common Arabic name for the city of Cairo. To this day, Misr is also the name for Egypt in Arabic, Hebrew, Turkish, Persian, Urdu and Hindi. The fourteenth century 'Traveller of Islam', Ibn Battutah extolled "Misr, mother of the country, ex-seat of Pharaoh the tyrant, mistress of extensive provinces and fruitful territories, boundless in the number of buildings, peerless in beauty and splendour; the rendezvous of comers and goers and the stopping place of the powerful and the powerless." He spent a quarter of a century in the capital as a respected judge and lectured at leading educational institutions including the pre-eminent al-Azhar university.

Some centuries later, Napoleon Bonaparte also saw fit to address Egypt in superlative terms. "Egypt is one of the most beautiful, the most productive and the most interesting countries in the world; it is the cradle of the arts and the sciences. There one can see the greatest and the most ancient monuments created by the hand of man." In true Napoleonic style, he declared to his troops in Egypt: "…from the heights of these pyramids forty centuries gaze upon you." Scholars, artists, archaeologists and botanists accompanied the Napoleonic army to Egypt. The monumental seven thousand page, nine hundred plate, three thousand drawing and twenty-four volume *Description de l'Egypte* was the academic outcome.

The incomparable scale of the city has overwhelmed almost every traveller to Cairo. The Persian erudite traveller to Egypt in 1035, Nasir-e-Khusrau gave a glowing account of the wealth of that country. "I could neither limit nor define their wealth and nowhere else have

I seen such prosperity." Another fellow Persian some four centuries later swore that it was ample enough to fit the ten largest towns of his own country. In the fourteenth century, Ibn Khaldoun gushed, "What one can imagine always surpasses what one sees, because of the scope of the imagination, except Cairo, because it surpasses anything one can imagine." In the Middle Ages, for one European traveller, Cairo was four times the size of Venice. For another, it was seven times the size of Paris.

Yet these were reports recorded in relatively recent times. The Nile valley civilisation can be traced back five thousand years to the now vanished city Memphis (today, the village of Mit Rahira south of Cairo) that was the capital of Egypt and the principal residence of its pharaohs for most of the pharaonic era. Today, one of two colossal granite statues of Ramses the Great lies on the ground shaded from the elements under a roof in the old capital Memphis. The twin mega-statue (13 metres high) is curiously and most inappropriately to be found amidst a maze of flyovers in the heart of Cairo. Who, in a perverse state of mind, saw fit to place the most prolific of pharaonic builders to survey the grit and grime of an urban sprawl?

The thirty Pharaonic dynasties that ruled ancient Egypt have been divided into three periods: Old Kingdom, Middle Kingdom and New Kingdom – covering some three thousand years. It is this long stretch of history that provides us with all the form and substance of the unending global allure of ancient Egypt in all its postcard splendour. Few have remained indifferent to the immense and spellbinding beauty of ancient Egypt.

Just outside Cairo is the Old Kingdom necropolis of Saqqara that includes the step pyramid of Djoser built by the most brilliant architect of his day, Imhotep, about 2680 BC. This step pyramid – reaching a height of 198 feet - was an architectural improvement on earlier burial mounds built from mud bricks. It resembles the stepped monuments called ziggurat in ancient Babylonia. These *mastabas* proved to be the precursor of pyramids – the eternal symbol of

Egypt. According to Zahi Hawass, the dynamic Director General of Egyptian Antiquities, "The mound conceivably is the *mastaba*, the *mastaba* becomes the pyramid, and the pyramid is the staircase by which the king ascends to the Sun God."

In 1926, a young French architect, Jean-Philippe Lauer arrived in Saqqara. He is still there. His lifetime passion has been the study of the Djoser pyramid and its surrounding funerary complex. Our visit to Saqqara took place during our stay in Cairo in the early 1990s. Compared to The Three Pyramids of Giza, as we drove up to the step pyramid, it looked insignificant and unimpressive. How faulty was our first impression. Walking towards the massive mound of stone is awe-inspiring. A square base tapers into steps that form a gradual pyramid shape. Close up, the funerary citadel of mud bricks reminded me of a colossal contemporary Lego construction. Overshadowed by the famous trio of Giza, the Saqqara pyramid is still the front-ranking construction of its type.

The Giza plateau pyramids of the pharaohs Khufu, Khafra and Menkaura need no introduction. Words are inadequate to describe these ethereal structures for they are both majestic and mysterious. Every superlative cliché is correct. Yet Winston Churchill has perhaps best summed it up: "They are a riddle wrapped in a mystery in an enigma." They are the only surviving wonders of the ancient Wonders of the World; the only ones still extant of the Seven Wonders of the World exalted by the Greeks in the second century BC. The other six wonders, practically all gone, were the Lighthouse of Alexandria, the Mausoleum of Halicarnassus, the Temple of Artemis in Ephesus, the Colossus in the port of Rhodes, the Hanging Gardens of Babylonia and the statue of Zeus in Olympia.

Far back in time, Diodorus Siculus writing in *The Library of History* in the first century BC commented on the Egyptian philosophy towards life and death. He noted, "These people regard the span of life as a very short time and of little importance, and instead devote themselves to the long memory bequeathed by virtue. This is why they call the houses of the living mere hostels for a brief sojourn, but give the name of eternal abodes to the tombs of the dead."

It was in 1969 that I entered the deep recesses of the pyramid of Khufu in the Giza necropolis. I recall that we were hunched up for most of the time as we steadily climbed 'a stairway to heaven/an ascent to eternity' within a narrow and dark corridor that ended in an empty burial chamber. There was a system of lights that provided a faint glow in what was otherwise a formidable interior. Many decades later while living in Cairo, I often considered repeating the visit but the thought of bending over for any length of time (the negative age-factor) deterred me from what would now have been an even more memorable experience by virtue of my greater knowledge and my appreciation (the positive age-factor); for what is undoubtedly the most astounding construction of all time. Someone declared the Giza pyramids to be "an architectural absurdity that defies centuries." In those days, for a small amount of money, young lads would run up the pyramid and down in no time – that license no longer existed in the 1990s.

During that same visit in 1969, we attended a *Son et Lumiere* performance before the colossal and enigmatic Sphinx and the backdrop was the Three Pyramids. The history of ancient Egypt was re-enacted, with marauding invaders on horseback and camelback and the thunderous voices of long gone pharaohs which rang out in the black, still night. I vividly recall to this day the sheer magic of the spectacular setting. I was mesmerised but for one flaw; I had to keep my head averted in order to avoid the sight of small houses on which television antennas stood out - a gross twentieth century intrusion.

Today, the pyramids are to be found on the very edge of the sprawling city of Cairo. My husband and daughter loved to go horse riding there and a frequent weekend morning outing to the Giza plateau involved them riding away amongst the dunes and desert surrounding the pyramids - these castles of eternity - while I sipped endless glasses of mint tea and contemplated the endless sands and the incredible silence of the desert before me. Occasionally, I would compose lines in my head for my memoir on Cairo. The ambience was right for both rider and writer.

Founded by an Arab general Amr ibn al-Aas in 642 AD, the name of the original settlement of Cairo at its present location was 'The City of the Tent/Encampment' or Fustat. A citadel, a mosque and fortified walls were the first constructions. Under the Omayyad and the Abbasid dynasties, Fustat grew in size and stature. The name 'Cairo' dates back to 969 AD when the Fatimids swept into Egypt and named the expanding city Al-Qahir, 'The Victorious'. The Mamluk dynasty ruled Cairo for over two hundred and fifty years. 'Mamluk' is an Arabic word meaning "a man possessed by another", that is, a slave. Mamluk slaves from Central Asia and the Caucasus formed a formidable military class. Justification for importing slaves for administration had been given by Nizam ul-Mulk, an eleventh century Persian statesman and author of a classic manual of statecraft, the Machiavelli of his day. He advised: "One obedient slave is better than three hundred sons; for the latter desire their father's death, the former long life for his master."

The Ottoman Empire extended their rule to Egypt in 1517 which lasted some three hundred years. The Napoleonic invasion in 1798, while a military defeat against the British, was a French cultural and intellectual triumph. Mehemet Ali Pasha, an Albanian officer, installed himself in Egypt in the first half of the nineteenth century and made massive efforts at modernisation. In the process, his dynasty incurred massive debts that eventually led to increased British and French involvement in political and financial matters. King Farouk was ousted in 1952 and successive heads of state have been of military origin; Gamal Abdel Nasser, Anwar Sadaat and Hosni Mubarak.

The word bazaar, originally a public market, is a Persian term. Souq is synonymous in the Arab-speaking world, from North Africa to the countries of the eastern rim of the Mediterranean and the Gulf region. Bazaars or *souqs*, those labyrinths of commercial activities that form the core of every Middle Eastern city, are loosely divided into several interconnecting corridors, each specialising in a particular trade - tea, spices, leather, gold, silver, carpets, textiles, dyers, goldsmith, shoemakers - so that each business activity has its own quarter. The main bazaar has crossing extensions, each named after its founder or the craftsmen or their trade such as the coppersmith bazaar, the carpet bazaar or the silk bazaar. Such ancient covered markets are serpentine alleyways; a maze of lanes thronging with artisans, merchants, retailers and wholesalers. Designed with great architectural integrity, they are usually roofed for protection against the hot sun, either under a single roof with individual vaulted cupolas or domes or awnings. The hustle and bustle, the cacophony of humanity and the old world atmosphere are features of bazaars/*souqs* that ignite the senses for us travellers while continuing to provide a vibrant economy for the commercial community.

Commercial and cultural links were mutually reinforced. Arab, Persian, Turkish, Indian and Chinese influences intermingled while sumptuous arts flourished. This intermingling resulted in weaving of silk and linen, workshops in ivory and metal, inlaid woodwork, enamel work, engraving, gilding, braid work, silver filigree jewellery, engraved mosaic tiles, miniature paintings, block-printed textile, carpets, stonework, earthenware and ceramics. Luxurious silks and brocades and perfumes travelled to distant lands. Specialised products moved from prestigious centres of production to meet increasing demand.

It is often said that the paramount bazaars of the Middle East are to be found in Aleppo, Damascus and Istanbul. I have been to them all yet retain a particular fondness for Khan-el-Khalili in the Islamic district of Cairo. Situated for centuries within the core of the Egyptian capital - in old Cairo - its old world flavour is almost intact. Crowded, colourful and chaotic, it is the quintessential Middle Eastern market. Its narrow, dark, winding labyrinthine alleys that appear to have no beginning or end are replete with mosques and minarets, shops, cafes, drinking fountains and squares. "There remains a sensible antiquity to the rhythm of the Old City, to the worn texture of every surface and the intimate scale of public space. There is the narrow texture of every surface and the intimate scale of public space. Above all, there is a feeling of age-old territoriality to the Old City – of neighbourhoods in miniature built around a particular trade, a mosque, a café, a grocer, and the tomb of some sheikh." Max Rodenbeck in his marvellously informative book *Cairo: The City Victorious* captures the intrinsic spirit of the area.

I must admit the soft spot for Khan-al-Khalili probably arises from great familiarity. Living in Cairo – versus passing through – it became a regular haunt of mine. I have a favourite silversmith 'Saad'. There is a tiny shop that sells damascene table linen, touristy T-shirts and ordinary to exquisite kaftans. Another shop specialises in silver-plated delicate tableware that entices the pocket. The footpath stall stocks perfume bottles of every shape, size and colour – all worthy of an Aladdin's cave. There is the silver jeweller who designs stunning pieces with lapis lazuli blue or malachite green semi-precious stones. Outlets offer not only the ubiquitous papyrus roll of Egyptian antiquities but also verses from the Holy Quran. The tucked away corner shop offers exquisite gold-threaded embroidery also with verses from the Holy Quran. The paraphernalia of essential *objets d'art* that feature in the home of every true Cairo resident – red, blue, green glass decanters, delicate hand-blown candlesticks, water-pipes that go by the name of *shishah, nargileh*, hubble-bubble, *hookah* in the region beckon one persistently.

These salesmen were friends who offered me farewell gifts when we left Cairo for Paris. They bid me adieu yet assured me that I would always be welcome '*Ahlan wa sahlan*'. They know a loyal customer for I did return to them for more purchases over glasses of sweet tea and chit-chat that ended with '*Ya salaam*' which translates to 'May peace be with you'. Another favourite haunt, particularly in the month of Ramadhan, is the legendary al-Fishawi café in Khan-al-Khalili.

Dating back to 'way-back-when' (some say two hundred years ago), the 'old' Fishawi was pulled down in 1969. The 'new' Fishawi still looks characteristically old with a mirror that occupies the entire wall thus enlarging the small and dim-lit interior. There we would seat ourselves on wooden chairs, sip *cha-o-nana* fresh mint tea or a cup of strong and bitter Turkish coffee and imbibe the charisma of old Cairo. The floating waft of apple-flavoured tobacco would perfume the air from the *shishahs*. Such timeless ambience has ensured the popularity of this venue for generations of local talk, that indispensable lubricant of society.

The Egyptian Nobel Laureate and doyen of Egyptian letters Naguib Mahfouz was passionate about this neighbourhood - his birthplace – and has repeatedly captured the ambience of the old city quarter for his most important and greatest works. *Palace Walk*, *Palace of Desire*, *Sugar Street*, *Midaq Alley*, *Fountain and Tomb*, all find backdrops in old Cairo Youssef Rakha surveys a century of idleness in the form of Cairo's *qahawi* cafes in an evocative article "yet it is with Al-Fishawi that Mahfouz is most frequently associated. At the heart of Al-Hussein (district), where the octogenarian spent his first nine years, it is one of the oldest *qahawi* in Cairo and retains – if only in post-modern, tourist-oriented form – many of the *qahawis'* original traits. Opposite its elegant façade, a line of small wooden benches mimics the old seating arrangement (separate seating was not used in *qahawi* until the emergence of bars and cafes), while the corridor inside is divided into similarly arranged compartments.

Another Cairo institution is Café Riche on Talaat Harb Street whose claim to fame had more to do with politics than its cuisine. Some say that it was at Café Riche that Naguib, Nasser and Sadat and a handful of other army officers planned the *coup d'etat* that overthrew King Farouk in 1952. Cafe Riche has had under its roof the Egyptian queen of songs, Umm Kulthoum, singing in the garden in the early 1920s and Saddam Hussein, a university student then, who frequented the place for lunch.

"We proceeded to al-Hamzawi Souk, where the small shops of spices and perfumes still stand – where the *souq* still occupies the same spot it used to. It was a typical nineteenth-century Egyptian marketplace, without a counter between buyer and seller. Had this market existed in any European, country, someone would have intervened to renovate it and turn it into a tourist attraction. From there we headed to the Gold Market. Mahfouz stopped at the entrance of the Salihiya Alley. Overhead stood the minaret of al-Salih Najm al-Din Ayyub, one of Cairo's oldest minarets, distinguished by its *makbhara* or incense burner." *The Cairo of Naguib Mahfouz* is a work of love by Britta Le Va. Her evocative photographs of this sprawling neighbourhood accurately capture the lifestyle and its people. An excerpt from 'Naguib Mahfouz Remembers' by Gamal al-Ghitany in the above book on *The Souqs* provides a vivid image of the commercial site. "We left the bazaars full of tumult and light, where everything shines and where the luxury of the displays contrasts with the grandeur of the architecture and the splendour of the principal mosques, painted in horizontal stripes of red and yellow; now we are in vaulted passages, dark narrow alleys, overhung by fretted wooden windows as in our medieval streets." The Frenchman Gerard de Nerval in his travel account *Voyage to the Orient* exults in his description of the medieval quarter.

Craning one's head to sight the top of old buildings over which light filters down to the narrow, dark and meandering alleyways, one can occasionally glimpse a still protruding *mashrafiyya*-patterned wooden latticework window. These window screens provide shade, shadow and depth, often with arabesque features; decorative patterns of immense richness and complexity that ensure the feeling of space within enclosures. A characteristic feature of Islamic architecture, it allows one to look out and watch the world go by and yet excludes the outer world from intrusion into private space.

The City of the Dead has been put to use in an innovative manner. I would pass through this vast neighbourhood once a week en route to the Moquattam Hills where I was teaching at the Cairo Demographic Centre. Vividly described as 'a semi-detached suburb for the deceased', notable families through the ages have maintained a plot of land here with a central mausoleum for the burial of the family's deceased. In a city where the need for living space has been badly stretched, the sprawling cemetery of mausoleums provides a roof over the head for some three million people – living that is. Over years and over generations, the caretaker has settled down and a living community has evolved complete with shops, schools and cafes. Everyone makes a living in the City of the Dead.

Our driver took us to visit the mausoleum of the family of the last queen of Egypt, Queen Nariman. Married for a short time to King Farouk, she lives in Heliopolis, an elegant suburb of Cairo. Heliopolis is now the neighbourhood of Cairo that one rushes past on one's way to the airport. On the main highway, one passes massive elegant villas that speak of an aristocratic and wealthy past. Two villas always caught my attention. One had its upper windows sealed and the large main gate was always closed. This was the residence of the Ambassador of Afghanistan. The other was the residence of the Ambassador of Iran. Both properties, owned by the government of their respective countries, once hosted Ambassadors from the royal courts of King Zahir Shah of Afghanistan and Shah Reza Pahlavi of Iran, to the court of King Farouk. Not once during our over three year posting in Cairo did we have occasion to enter these premises and today, these magnificent properties from a different age, lie forlorn.

However, we did enter the mausoleums in the City of the Dead. We were ushered into a fairly large and solidly built room with a trap door on the floor. The caretaker raised it to show us stairs descending into darkness where the deceased is kept for years until nothing is left but the skeleton and then these remains are laid to rest in the family burial vault. The next deceased family member goes through the same procedure. After this sobering experience, we were most graciously entertained to tea and biscuits by the caretaker and his family who live on site in rooms that form extensions to the central mausoleum. They have television too.

There is also a room for mourning family members to offer prayers for the deceased and alms to the needy. "One mile from Cairo is a city that is not walled, is as large as Venice, and has tall structures and short ones...Every Saracen and townsman has a building in this city. In the short ones they bury their dead, and in the tall ones all the lords who own them give alms to the poor every Friday." An observation about the City of the Dead made in 1440 by Emmanuel Piloti, the Cretan.

Here is a city - and a country - that so honours its dead; an ancient people who have toiled all their lives in order to achieve immortality in the after-life. And it is also in this City of the Dead that a vast community lives.

A wooden cenotaph of one of Cairo's many rulers carries the following verse:

"O ye who stand beside my grave, show not surprise at my condition.

Yesterday I was as you. Tomorrow you will be as me."

PERSEPOLIS : FALLEN SPLENDOUR

"Ahura Mazda is Almighty God who created the Earth, created the Heavens and created Happiness for people."

Excerpt from an inscription at Persepolis

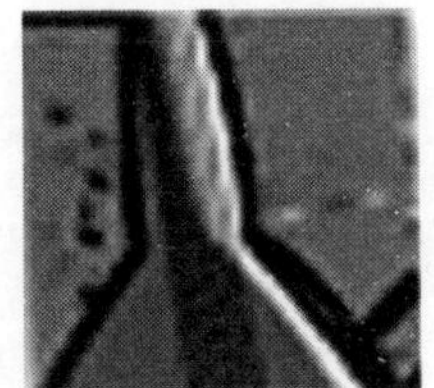

To a tent city constructed for the imperial event came the high and mightyroyalty, presidents, prime ministers, dignitaries, ambassadors and international celebrities. In October 1971 much of the world's *crème de la crème* came to Persepolis to celebrate, with the Shah of Iran Mohammad Reza Pahlavi, 2500 years of Persian history. Today, the tent city exists as a swansong of the late Shah and a rude reminder of the passing of power. The tents stand forlorn and dilapidated, bits and pieces flapping in the wind. The grand assembly of global personalities has passed into the realms of history.

Persepolis derives its name from Pars, the Greek for Fars, the surrounding province. Persepolis is the 'city of Parsa' or the 'city of Persians.' The Iranians call the site Takht-e-Jamshid, the Throne of Jamshid, Jamshid being the first, probably mythical, ruler of Persia. This archaeological wonder located on a shelf of Mount Rahmat was built over a period of 150 years. Construction began in 512 BC. At one time, eighteen metre high walls surrounded it. The showpiece of the Persian Achaemenian civilisation was the hub of the Persian Empire. However, Persepolis was more a ceremonial and spiritual capital rather than an administrative one and most of all it was a hub of power.

In those bygone days, political personalities and dignitaries came to pay homage and celebrate the vast realm of the Persian Empire. Persepolis was the powerhouse of the Persian Empire. "Wealth and visitors poured in from the Danube estuary, from the banks of the Nile, the steppes of Asia, sovereigns came to offer their allegiance, satraps (governor-generals) to make their reports, artists to participate in the embellishment of the magnificent buildings," notes Jean Hureau in *Iran Today*. Due to the severity of the summers, these representatives from every part of the ever-expanding Persian Empire frequented Persepolis only in the gentler seasons of spring and autumn. In the twenty-first century, visitors also come to Persepolis in the spring month of April. Even so, the midday sun was hot rather than warm.

The practice of having several royal capitals, some seasonal only, was common throughout Persian history. Due to the extremes of heat and cold in the Iranian plateau and the need to provide for grazing land for the flocks, there emerged a type of monarch with nomadic traditions. "He (Sultan Yaqub in the fifteenth century) was not a town dweller affected by dirty habits, as was the case with many rulers of Khurasan, Fars and Kerman, but followed the seasons wandering in open spaces going from summer quarters to winter quarters." We are informed of this fact in an interesting article 'From Tents to Pavilions: Royal Mobility and Persian Palace Design' in *Studies in Persian Art and Architecture* by Bernard O'Kane. Much later "Shah Abbas as with Sultan Uljaytu, a semi-nomadic lifestyle could coexist with the erection of palaces in new capitals...Just as the camps were mobile cities, the tents which the rulers occupied could be considered mobile palaces... The tent, together with a golden throne inlaid with rubies and other jewels, was three years in the making and took one month to erect."

Persepolis lay at the crossroad of western Asia and maintained close links with the vast steppes of central Asia. The reach of the Persian Empire for the construction of Persepolis is brought to light by the following citation in *The Land of Mehr and Mah: Persepolis, Naghsh-e-Rostam, Naghsh-e-Rajab, Pasargad.* "Cedar wood from Assyria, gold from Bactria and Sardis, lapis lazuli and agate from Sogdia, turquoise from Choresmia, silver and ebony from Egypt, ivory from India and Ethiopia, stone from Pars in competent hands of stone cutters from Lydia and Ionia, goldsmiths from Media and Egypt, masons from Babylon and decorators from Egypt and Media, all were immortalised in the construction of Persepolis. They achieved, hand in hand, and were paid with wages including silver, wine and lambs, a deed which will be remembered till eternity."

The construction of Persepolis was perceived as a symbol of the might and unity of the Persian Empire; since Persia was regarded as the nucleus of the world. The authoritative arts expert, Souren Melikian of the *International Herald Tribune* observes that "Of the three oldest civilisations that are alive – China, India and Iran – Iran had the longest continuous history under its own name. It had been used in that very form since about the second century BC and in earlier forms, long before."

First documentation of Persian history can be attributed to Cyrus II - Cyrus the Great - who founded the capital Pasargade or The Persian's Camp. In his twenty years rule that began in 550 BC, his territory covered the lands that are now Greece, Iraq, Israel, Syria and Turkey. The Charter of Cyrus the Great - a baked-clay cuneiform cylinder - was discovered in excavations at Babylon, Iraq in 1878.

Cyrus the Great was buried in his capital in a tomb whose construction was begun in his lifetime, similar to the practice of the Egyptian pharaohs. Standing stark and lonely in the vast landscape, the imposing twelve-metre-high structure is built entirely of a megalithic stone with six levels that diminish upwards and at the top stands the mammoth tomb. The clear influence of Mesopotamian architecture in the form of the ziggurat, step-pyramid, is evident in the design of Cyrus the Great's tomb.

In ancient times, inhabitants of this land attached great importance to mountains, perhaps as a means of getting closer to the Supreme Being(s). If there were no mountains then they created mountains in the form of ziggurats and pyramids, to be used as both temples and tombs. The Chogha Zanbil ziggurat in the Khuzestan province of Iran was built in the thirteenth century BC and was sacked in 640 BC by King Ashurbanipal of Assyria. Built of sun-baked mud bricks, it is an awe-inspiring construction and the finest example of Elamite architecture. A Timurid historian Abdul Razzaq Samarqandi boasts, "If you have doubts about our grandeur, look at our edifice." Originally a five-terraced concentric structure like a wedding cake, only three storeys now remain. Once reaching a height of what would today be twenty-five floors, it is surprisingly well-preserved. Unbelievably, it was lost to the world for two thousand five hundred years until 1935, when it was spotted during an aerial survey by the

Anglo-American Oil Company. From above, the terrain was marked by a series of concentric circles that, upon extensive excavation, revealed itself to be the 'vanished' Chogha Zanbil ziggurat.

Although no trace of it remains, legend has it that on the tomb was a poignant inscription: 'Oh man, I am Cyrus who founded the Empire of the Persians and was King of Asia. Grudge me therefore not this monument.' Others speak of 'Oh man, whoever thou art and from whence thou comest, for I know thou shall come, I am Cyrus who founded this vast kingdom for Persians. Grudge me not this little earth that covereth my body.'

However, Cyrus the Great's grandson Darius the Great, had no desire to continue his illustrious reign from Pasargade and founded his own capital by building Persepolis. Very little today remains of the once prosperous and powerful capital of Cyrus. An expert's insight into what might-have-been is provided by Sir Roger Stevens, British Ambassador to Iran in the 1950s and a keen Iranologist who wrote in his immensely laudable book *The Land of the Great Sophy*, "I have more than a suspicion that the Pasargade palaces were exquisitely proportioned, graceful, full of light but bare of decorative detail, while those of Persepolis were oppressively large, clumsy, drab and overloaded with ornament; that Pasargade charmed where Persepolis impressed." Today we can only be impressed for little remains of that charm. As an Italian saying laments, "Cities like dreams are made of desires and fears."

Cyrus the Great's son Cambyses II expanded the Persian Empire by heading west and occupying Egypt. Darius the Great took India and reached the Aegean Sea to the west. The Achaemenian dynasty came to an end in 330 BC when Alexander the Great routed Darius III's army at Marathon. Alexander-the-not-so-Great then proceeded to loot the immense wealth of Persepolis. The spoils were apparently transferred to Greece by a legion of some five thousand camels and twenty thousand mules over a period of many months. Dan Cruickshank in *Around the World in 80 Treasures* voices similar thoughts on the destructive role of Alexander. "Alexander destroyed one of the most beautiful products of civilisation on earth. As I look at the ruins for which he – as much as time – is responsible, I feel a shiver of anger. What irony that a man who we now associate with the high values of Greek civilisation should have committed such an act of brutality and vandalism."

The ruin of Persepolis remained a magnet for European travellers through the ages. In the fifteenth century, a Venetian ambassador to Persia, Giosophat Barbaro, travelled extensively in the country. Some two centuries later, another Italian traveller, Pietro della Valle, recorded the cuneiform script for the first time. A Frenchman, Chevalier Chardin, is credited, in the seventeenth century, with the first drawings of the ancient complex. A jeweller, he visited India and Persia as much for his love of jewellery as for his love of travel and recorded his impressions in *Lettres Persanes.*

A short distance away from the tent city of Mohammad Reza Pahlavi lies the rocky platform, 46 feet above the plain, on which was built the famed city of Persepolis. Entrance to the vast 135,000 square metres complex is made via two splendid staircases. One sweeps to the right and the other to the left and each stairway consists of 110 steps, every four or five of which are made of a single stone slab. Such is the construction that even horses could negotiate the stairs. Roger Stevens has emphatically declared "Since staircase building is an art of which we have learnt nothing and, it often seems to me, forgotten something since 500 BC, I append the measurements and other details for the benefit of future practitioners .One climbs without any sense of climbing. Massive, rugged, devoid of ornament, designed perhaps to terrify but not to tire…" The climb for us was an easy assault as Stevens declared. Reaching Persepolis on horseback, a nineteenth century French traveller Jeanne Dieulafoy wrote in *La Perse, la Chaldee, la Susiane*, "The steps are so slightly inclined that it is easy to go up and down them on horseback, and they are so broad that ten men can walk along them side by side."

Reaching the top of the terrace, we came to terms with the

vastness of the fallen city. Trumpeters would have welcomed us at the top of the stairways. The procession of guests would then have been heralded into the Gate of All Nations. We passed two massive and terrifying winged-bulls that were built to repel with their symbolic power any evil spirits that may have lurked and threatened the might of Persepolis. Elsewhere, a bas-relief depicts the king fighting a lion, a popular theme in Persian art. Winged animals were one of the heraldic symbols of the Achaemenian dynasty. However, while Man proposes, God disposes and all the mighty have fallen.

One can then choose to enter the Hall with a Hundred Columns (70 x 70 metres long) that contained, in its heyday, 100 columns 12 metres high. The few pillars that remain reveal the grandeur of their scale. Brick walls were also used extensively. However, as brick is a more perishable building agent than stone, virtually the entire royal complex has since been lost.

The fire that is alleged to have been ordered by Alexander-the-not-so-Great was believed to have started at this site. This vengeful act was a response by the Greeks for the burning of the Acropolis in Greece by the Persian King Xerxes some one hundred and fifty years earlier. When partly excavated in 1878 by Motamed Farhad Mirza, the governor-general of the Fars province, some three metres of soil and cedar tree ash was found on the floor.

You could also choose to move to the Apadana Palace built by Darius the Great. Here too, as far as the eye can see, are remnants of decorated columns and many bases. In *Pars and Persepolis* by Werner F. Dutz and Sylvia A. Matheson, we are told that the Apadana Palace had "ceiling beams of cedar, ebony and teak and were gold-plated, inlaid with ivory and precious metals." Reconstructed etchings in the above book bring forth vividly the magnificence and sheer opulence of what once might have been. A double-headed lion sculpture was the capital carved atop one of the slender columns. Today, excavated, it sits squat on the ground, remarkably intact; its state of preservation due to its being buried for a long spell. Henri-Paul Eydoux in *In*

Search of Lost Worlds speaks of "the close relationship between architecture and sculpture...the art of Persepolis is cosmopolitan and composite: it recalls the art of Assyria, Babylon and Egypt, and even that of Greece. However, Persian genius has transformed all these elements into a harmonious whole and given them a genuine originality." A tidal wave of Hellenistic style covered the entire Middle East following Alexander's conquests including Iran. The Greek architectural style then prevailed in the region for some three centuries.

Exposure to the elements over time has badly eroded one of the stairways of the Apadana Palace. However, the *pièce de resistance* of Persepolis is the eastern staircase. It was concealed for some two thousand years under a blanket of rubble until 1932. This good fortune of being buried for centuries resulted in its preservation, as burial is a natural preserver. In rock relief, we see vividly the triumphal procession of visitors who came to pay tribute to the King of Persia - loaded with gifts they travelled afar. So detailed are the rock carvings, they appear to be truly shuffling in procession as they wait to present their offerings. The figures and features are identical. Only the dress conveys the nationality of the bearer. Representatives of twenty-eight nations are identified. From far and wide came (in order): Persians, Medians, Parthians, Arians, Bactrians, Sogdians, Choresmians, Drangians, Arachosians, Sattagydians, Gandarians, Indians, Haumas, Scythians, Babylonians, Assyrians, Arabs, Egyptians, Armenians, Cappadocians, Lydians, Ionians, Scythians, Skurdians, Petasosians, Lybians and Ethiopians. So alive are the depictions of bulls, cows, camels, baskets of fruit, fabrics, folds of the dress, ornaments, bows and arrows, lances and shields, chariots and animal skins that one could spend the entire day examining this magnificent depiction of homage.

Elsewhere are found bas-reliefs of elite members of the Achaemenian army, the 'Immortals'. They were thus named for should one of them die, another soldier immediately replaced the late 'Immortal'. There they stand, one behind the other, identical in uniform, height and positioning. They appear to be marching by us.

Precedence among the delegations has been analysed by Dutz and Matheson in *Pars and Persepolis.* They argue, "None of the possible arrangements is in agreement with the sequential list of satrapies on the king's inscriptions. The delegations may therefore be received in order of their incorporation into the empire, or in accordance with travel time necessary from their homeland to Persepolis, which is not necessarily related to distance alone. The arrangement of Assyrians, Lydians, Ionians, Babylonians, Egyptians and Ethiopians excludes any arrangement in sequence outlined by numbers in the attached." Herodotus presents another convincing argument. "Of nations they honour most their nearest neighbours, whom they esteem next to themselves. Those who live beyond these they honour in the second degree, and so with the remainder; the further they are removed, the less the esteem in which they hold them. The reason is, that they look upon themselves as greatly superior in all respects to the rest of mankind, regarding others as approaching to excellence in proportion as they dwell nearer to them; whence it comes to pass that those who are the furthest off must be the most degraded of mankind…And this is the order which the Persians also follow in their distribution of honour."

The reliefs that are repeated in much of Persepolis have drawn some interesting comment. An explanation is cited in *The Splendours of Archaeology.* "We can understand commentators who have said that Achaemenian art was virtually without evolution. It never developed the concept of three dimensions, or moved away from the rigid limits of profile portrayals. However, it is important to remember that court art is always based on the archaic and has a severity considered necessary for representations intended to be passed down to posterity." 'More is better' was the motto of the age.

Also architecturally innovative was the plan of the royal complex. There are four levels; each level is two metres higher than the other. Thus the reception halls for visitors were at one level. A higher level was reserved for the nobility and their palaces. A further two metres higher were the royal living quarters. Storage rooms and administrative offices placed at the back of the buildings were at the lowest level. However, while wandering around Persepolis, these dimensions are no longer well-demarcated; time has succeeded in eroding class differentials.

Today, the magnificent Persepolis is a shadow of its former glory. Nevertheless, the ruins remain a brilliant subject for every photographer. In the backdrop of the mountains are silhouetted the lofty fluted columns and one contemplates once again about the transient nature of human civilisations and the fickleness of the passage of time. There is every reason to ponder over the enigma of a people's emergence and subsequent demise; the rise and fall of civilisations. Ancient graffiti, dated 1791, by the son of Shah Rukh Mirza on the ruins of Persepolis laments: "Where are the proud monarchs of yore? They multiplied treasures which endured not, neither did they endure."

A short distance from the dead city of the once living is the Achaemenian 'city of the dead' named Naqsh-i-Rustam, (Picture of Rustam). Rustam was the legendary Persian hero and strongman. Here is the Persian mini-equivalent of the Egyptian Valley of the Kings, the necropolis on the West Bank of the Nile where any numbers of pharaohs are buried.

Approaching the site, the rocks ahead of us reveal nothing. The place is "dominated by tall ochre-coloured cliffs, cracked and wrinkled by the wind through the ages." M.T. Faramarzi in *A Travel Guide to Iran* vividly describes the setting. Invisible to the eye, the four hypogea (rock-tombs) cut into the rocks are well camouflaged and were thus protected from desecration through the ages. Upon closer inspection, the tombs of Artaxerxes I, Darius the Great, Xerxes and Darius II appear before us cut on a monumental scale of more than seventy-two feet high. The smoothed surface of the rock is covered with intricate bas-reliefs depicting the king on a horse, vanquished enemies, and wreaths. Designed porticoes, columns and capitals face the rising sun, as do also the tombs on the West Bank of the Nile.

The carvings in the royal cemetery show representatives from the nations of the Persian Empire and bear witness to the royal deeds. The images carved into the mountain were meant to be permanent expressions of Persian might and imperial power.

The façades of all four tombs are identical in the form of a cross sixty feet by seventy-two feet. Many years ago, one was permitted to climb a makeshift frame in order to enter the tombs. Although the frame still stands there, this is no longer allowed; we could only gaze at the dark spaces marked as the entrances from the ground level. There is sufficient reason to respect the sanctity of the site. After all, they are graves and were meant to be undisturbed. There is some controversy about the public viewing of Egyptian mummies and tombs. The circus-like atmosphere and the raucous crowds that prevail in the Egyptian halls of museums are sacrilegious to many.

Roger Stevens has provided us with a description of the interior of the tomb. "The tomb chambers are bare, save for the plain sarcophagus itself; they are difficult to access, being approached only by two metal ladders against the face of the rock. The legend goes that Darius the Great's parents fell to their death when visiting his tomb…The scale, the symmetry and the simplicity are profoundly impressive." A stone tower dug deep into the ground before the rocky necropolis is subject to differing ideas on its origins. The square structure of white hewn limestone is thought to be a fire temple, a depot for the holy books of the Zoroastrian faith or the tomb of an Achaemenian king prior to Darius I; the debate continues inconclusively. And so we left the desolate and majestic site of bygone ages.

SERENE SULTANIYEH

"Here is a dome which simply stands by virtue of a perfectly conceived and constructed profile. The cross-section of its construction is as great a delight to an architect as the vision of the splendid blue dome is to the traveller on the Tabriz-Kazvin road."

Andre Godard in *Survey of Persian Art*, Vol. 2 by Arthur Upham Pope

The Safavid dynasty ruled Persia from 1502 to 1736. In 1598, the Safavid ruler Shah Abbas the Great transferred the capital from Qazvin to Esfahan. Roger Stevens in his mesmerising travelogue *The Land of the Great Sophy* observes, "Today Kazvin is a shrunken town with an unmistakably old-fashioned air. I know of no better place in which to get the feel of nineteenth century Persia – long-standing neglect, dignified decay side by side with seedy respectability, life running on among the ruins and grinding gradually to a stop, the sort of hopelessness which pervaded provincial life after a century of indifference." Stevens adds that although Kazvin is no *ville monumentale*, it can still boast some outstanding monuments. A time-gap of more than fifty years had lapsed between Rogers Stevens' keen observation on Kazvin and our year 2000 visit. Today, the city poses as an average modern minor Iranian city. Not much remains of its glorious past except for the vast Friday mosque.

Near Kazvin at Sultaniyeh is the fourteenth century mausoleum of Sultan Oljeitu built entirely of brick that has "long defied architectural analysis." The word 'mausoleum' derives from a magnificent tomb named after the Carian king Mausolus (fourth century BC). The vaulted ceilings and walls contain such an intricate wealth of designs that they prompted Arthur Pope to declare them "a series of masterpieces of architectural ornament capable of holding its own with anything ever achieved in Persia." Arthur Upham Pope and his wife, both twentieth century American scholars, wrote an authoritative six volume series, the *Survey of Persian Art.* They maintained a house in Shiraz for fifty years that is, today, part of the Narejestan Museum. Some of their slides and photographs on Iran are kept at the museum. They are buried in Esfahan.

The ardent British traveller of the nineteenth century E.G. Browne in *A Year Amongst the Persians* also recorded his sighting of the Sultaniyeh mausoleum. He wrote, "Nearly three hours before reaching the latter place we could plainly see the great dome of the mosque for which it is so celebrated." The Sultaniyeh mausoleum is an outstanding example of Byzantine-Arab architecture; a massive dome superimposed over a cubic base. In this case, it is a colossal dome over an octagonal base. The dominating dome of the mausoleum recalls the Dome of the Rock of Jerusalem built in 691 by the Omayyad Caliph Abd al-Malik. The Haram al-Sharif in Jerusalem was built over the sacred rock from which the Holy Prophet was believed to have made his ascension to heaven - the Miraj or Night Journey.

Roger Stevens minced no words in his description of the huge edifice. "It is difficult to describe the mausoleum of Sultan Oljeitu at Sultaniyeh except in superlatives. Though plundered, shaken by earthquakes, partially ruined (and now in 1971 under repair), its massive construction is so admirable that it remains one of the great architectural wonders of the world. No photograph can convey an adequate idea of its magnificence, still less of the genius which inspired its decorations..."

Sultaniyeh takes us on a journey to the distant past – of more than 700 years – and leaves a strong impression. There we were, on a bleak, grey and overcast morning, in a capital city of the Mongols of Central Asia. Set in a vast plain between two mountain ranges and once a major trading centre in Persia, the city boasted mosques, *madrasahs* (theological schools), caravanserais, hospitals, royal court buildings, theological discourse centres and monuments. Sultaniyeh became the second largest city, after Tabriz, of the Mongol-Ilkhanid Empire in the fourteenth century and one of the major trade centres of the region until the end of the Timurid dynasty. Like many a once thriving metropolis it, in time, passed into oblivion.

The wonder of Sultaniyeh and one of the wonders of Iran is the mausoleum of the Mongol king Oljeitu who reigned from 1304 to 1316. He was a descendant of Genghis Khan and an ancestor of Tamerlame. Sultan Oljeitu was, interestingly, baptised a Christian but thereafter became a Buddhist, then a Sunni Muslim and, in 1309, he converted to Shia'ism within the Islamic faith. Oljeitu commissioned the building to house the remains of Hazrat Ali, the son-in-law of the Holy Prophet. Hazrat Ali had been buried in Najaf in present-day Iraq. Oljeitu wanted to expand the importance of Sultaniyeh in the empire by making it a place of pilgrimage that would also augment the city's income and reputation. His goal to transfer the body of Hazrat Ali from Najaf to Sultaniyeh was never realised. Although it is commonly believed that Oljeitu himself was then buried there, no body was ever found. It seems highly unlikely that a mausoleum built to house the remains of such an important religious personage would then be used by the man who had commissioned the construction.

What of the mausoleum itself? Neither E.G. Browne, nor Roger Stevens nor Arthur Upham Pope exaggerated their testimonies. It can be seen from miles away, the dome jutting out over the vast plains surrounding it. This mighty dome reaches a height of more than fifty metres. On approach, it is enormous in bulk and stands solidly, notwithstanding its 700 years plus age, with parts of the turquoise-plastered dome still intact. Today, it has the third largest interior following the church of Santa Maria in Florence and the Aya Sophia mosque in Istanbul. Extensive restoration work is now underway. The entire interior of the mausoleum is criss-crossed by intricate scaffolding that is in itself impressive. The dome is 48 metres high and 25 metres in diameter. The area under the dome is an octagon with eight bases of some 50 square metres each made with mud-bricks and cemented with clay and gypsum. The dimensions and aesthetics are stunning. A risky climb over steep blocks of stairs to the first and then second floor permits one to appreciate both the beauty and dimension of the mausoleum. In many places the brick-works covered in plaster are intact with ceiling decorations of an exquisite design created by the inscriptions 'Allah', 'Mohammed' and 'Ali'. The repetition of these names, singly or in combination, provides the sole ornamentation of this colossal monument. It is striking in its simplicity and serenity.

Close by is the tomb of an *ulema*, an Islamic scholar. He was buried in the thirteenth century but a Safavid ruler built the mausoleum over the tomb in the sixteenth century. A climb to the rooftop revealed pockets of snow nestled in the crevices of the dome, the turquoise plaster still remarkably intact. The scenario was memorable for its setting with a harsh biting wind, a flurry of snowflakes, the greyness of the sky and the touch of warmth created by distant specks of turquoise-coloured domes. Nearby, a second tomb is that of a Sufi dervish, a grandson of the Persian mystic poet Mevlana Jalaludin Rumi. A high-walled building encloses a central courtyard off which lie the rooms of study and repose of the followers of the dervish. Behind it stands his mausoleum.

We were present at a crossroad in history.

ESFAHAN "IS HALF THE WORLD"

"A city as brilliant as the thoughts of a wise man, in which the whole world is reflected. A city as beautiful as the beloved one's face in which you many find anything you wish."

Khaghani, tenth century Iranian poet

"Isfahan is a city built on a plain. It has a fine climate. They reach cold pure water anywhere they dig for about 30 feet. The city has strong high walls. There are streams of water and beautiful tall buildings in the city; with a large and beautiful Friday mosque… All across the land where Persian is spoken, I have not seen a city better than Isfahan."

Nasser-e-Khosrau, eleventh century Iranian scholar and poet.

"Nowhere else in the oriental territory can be compared to Isfahan. Even as to Constantinople, Isfahan is not only a match from several respects, but one can dare say that it is even better."

Pietro della Valle, sixteenth century Italian traveller.

"Isfahan, the capital of Persia, with its suburbs, is one of the biggest cities of the world."

Jean Chardin, seventeenth century French traveller.

"Everywhere there were gardens which for grandeur and fragour, are such as no city in Asia outvie..withal so sweet and verdant that you may call it another Paradise."

Thomas Herbert, seventeenth century English traveller.

"Who can claim to have seen the most beautiful city of the world without having seen Isfahan?"

André Malraux, twentieth century French politician and writer.

"Isfahan is half the world they say. For me, it is the world."

Alain Bailhache, twentieth century French artist and frequent resident of Esfahan.

In my humble opinion, there was no bravado on the part of the sons of the soil nor was there any exaggeration on the part of foreign observers. Esfahan was and remains enchanting and merits the early Farsi declaration *Esfahan nesf-e Jahan* (Esfahan is half the world).

There is poetry in the name 'Esfahan'. It rolls smoothly off the tongue, evoking fabled crossroads of culture and commerce. Here is a meeting-place of manuscripts, miniatures, monuments, mosaics and mosques, artifacts from centuries of civilisations. Esfahan is the heartland and the epitome of Persia as one imagines it to be. The origin of the name, however, is mundane. The Farsi word for army is *sepah*. There was a garrison base in this area in early times that gave birth to the city's name.

There are art cities in the world that blend grace and harmony in their architecture and cityscape. Esfahan is one such metropolis, a living museum that just happens to be inhabited. Esfahan is not in a ruined condition, nor is it anywhere near a shadow of its former glorious self. There is only a certain faded glory. There is more than enough to satisfy the most demanding and jaded traveller and to enthral the first-time sightseer. My introduction to Esfahan belongs to the latter category and my repeat visit to the former.

My first visit to Esfahan was in August 1978. My father was the Bangladesh Ambassador to Iran and I flew by Kuwait Airways from London to Tehran for a two-week visit to my parents. This was six months before the 1979 Iranian Revolution. Twenty-one years later, in November 1999, I once again flew into Esfahan. This time I was accompanied by my husand, who was now the Bangladesh Ambassador to Iran, and our daughter. At Esfahan airport, a board greeted us.

"The Islamic Revolution like a volcano is everlasting." Representative of the Public Relations of the Esfahan Airport.

The name Iran is derived from Aryan, meaning 'Land of the Aryans'. However, Iran, in history, has been widely known as Persia, a name derived from Pars or Fars, one of the southern provinces of Iran. Esfahan is located along the Zayandeh Rud River in the west-central part of Iran, 340 kilometres south of Tehran, and can trace its history back 2500 years. During the Caliphate of Omar, it was established under Muslim rule that continued for 300 years. It was a major city of the Seljuki Turk dynasty in the eleventh and twelfth centuries. Today, Esfahan is sister city to Florence, Kuala Lumpur, Lashi in Romania, Saint Petersburg, Xian in China and Yerevan in Armenia.

The Mongols invaded the city in the thirteenth century. Kamaleddin Esmaeil, a renowned thirteenth century poet of Esfahan despaired about the catastrophic impact on the city. He wrote "There's no one to cry for his homeland or for the souls that have been wasted. Yesterday, there were two hundred crying over a dead body. Today, there is none to cry for a hundred dead." There are areas all over the world that have been soaked in blood with monotonous regularity. Settlements have been besieged, burned, desecrated and rebuilt numerous times over the ages. Newcomers have then gone on to reshape the city in their image, leaving their own stamp of identity.

Early in the fourteenth century, Marco Polo, the Venetian voyager, passed through Iran. Globalisation was a phenomenon even then. Bernard O'Kane in *Studies in Persian Art and Architecture* confirms "a resurgence in trade with China via the Silk Route, as a result of which a new taste for chinoiserie had been established in the Middle East, influencing Persian painting and manifested in the appearance on glazed tiles of Chinese motifs such as the dragon, phoenix and lotus."

In the seventeenth century under the Safavid dynasty, Esfahan reached the zenith of its fame. Its Golden Age came under the reign of Shah Abbas, born in 1571 in Herat in present-day Afghanistan. Shah Abbas ascended the throne in 1587. His grandfather, Tahmasp, is alleged to have commented on his grandson: "He will be the light of our dynasty." According to various Iranian historians, Shah Abbas, Cyrus and Darius were the only rulers to be endowed with the suffix 'The Great'. The same ruler who, in 1609, issued a royal ordinance giving women the right on Wednesdays to move freely without veils in certain streets of the capital, Shah Abbas also had his son, the crown-prince, assassinated in 1615 and another son, a second crown-prince, blinded in 1621. Upon his death in 1629, loyalists transported his body some five hundred kilometres all over Iran. In a bad state of decomposition, the body was finally buried in a simple tomb in Kashan. However, because of political intrigue in the capital city of Esfahan and a fear that Shah Abbas's burial place would become a centre for gathering and reverence, his successor had four identical funeral corteges sent out. One headed for Ardebil, the other to Mashad, the third to Qom and yet another to Kerbela.

The population of Esfahan then stood around a million, making it one of the world's largest cities of its time. Here was a cosmopolitan city, a melting pot of Muslims, Armenians, Zoroastrians, Indians, British and Dutch East India companies, Swiss watchmakers and Chinese potters. The legacy of conquerors over the ages fused with the traditional skills of artisans in decorative arts and culminated in creating a magnificent city; a centre for the arts and architecture, calligraphy, culture, miniature painting, philosophy, religion and science. The thriving metropolis attracted architects, carpenters, calligraphers, engravers, painters, philosophers, potters, theologians and tile-makers. Jean Chardin in his travels in Persia in the seventeenth century reported that in 1666, Esfahan already had 162 mosques, 48 *madrasahs*, 1802 caravanserais and 273 *hamaams* (elaborate bathhouses). Chardin's *Travels in Persia (1673-1677)* is a splendid prose portrait of an ancient land and its people.

John Fryer in *A New Account of East India and Persia* in the seventeenth century summarised his impression of Esfahan: "The magnificently arched bazaars which form the noble square to the

Palace; the several public inns which are so many seraglios; the stately rows of sycamores which the world cannot parallel; the glorious summer houses and pleasant gardens, the stupendous bridges, sumptuous temples, the religious convents...are so many lasting pyramids and monuments of Abbas's fame ; and people are wont to say 'Shah Abbas', as we should say, 'well done.'" The cityscape and image of Esfahan was and remains one of tree-lined boulevards, spacious squares, magnificent mosques, palatial palaces and wide expanses of greenery.

For a man born and brought up in arid Herat, the more fertile lands in Esfahan provided ample scope for greenery. Bernard O'Kane in 'From Tents to Pavilions' in *Studies in Persian Art and Architecture* observes, "one can imagine what an impression the multitude of gardens in the city which were available for his leisure would have made on him...The garden complexes with pavilions, verdure, numerous canals, and open spaces with the flexibility to accommodate a multitude and variety of tents represented the ideal compromise between nomadic and urban life." Ancient practices of a new land were adopted and cherished by Shah Abbas.

The longest ancient urban axis in civilisation is to be found in Mexico. It is the 'Street of the Dead' of the Teotihuacan civilisation. That was exceeded in the seventeenth century by the Naqsh-e Jahan (Design of the World) *maidan* (central square) in Esfahan. This core of urban planning measures 510 metres long and 165 metres wide, with an area of more than 80,000 square metres. It is twice as large as Moscow's Red Square and seven times the size of the Piazza San Marco at Venice. The other famed urban square of spectacular beauty is the Place de la Concorde in Paris. The largest urban open space in the modern world is the Tiananmen Square in Beijing according to our excellent guide, Agha Mahmud Reza Shayesteh, a civil engineer who both enlightened and enthralled us with his elaborate explanations of the delights and merits of Esfahan's many architectural splendours. I told him that our next visit to Esfahan would have to be according to his convenience, since we insisted that he once again accompany us. In the recent past, he had accompanied the Sultan of Brunei and Kofi Annan, United Nations Secretary General, on their excursions to Esfahan.

Entering the Naqsh-e-Jahan square, the focal point of the capital city, where should one first rest one's eyes? The square itself is formed by a quadrangle of brick buildings of two storeys of recessed arches and arcades containing some 200 rooms, all built equal in size and form. In the middle of each flank of the square, stands an architectural marvel, a unique monument that mirrors the pinnacle of human creativity. The culmination of Persian Islamic architecture and its finest and purest expression is Esfahan.

"The heavens often rain down the richest gifts on human beings, but sometimes with lavish abundance they bestow upon a single individual beauty, grace and ability, so that, whatever he does, every action is so divine that he surpasses all other men and clearly displays how his genius is the gift of God, and not an acquirement of human art." So remarked Giorgio Vasari, architect of the Uffizi Gallery in Florence in the mid-sixteenth century about Leonardo da Vinci.

Such a profound declaration is applicable to the architect Ustad Mohammed Reza Isfahani of the Sheikh Lutfullah mosque and the architect Ali Akbar Esfahani of the Imam mosque (previously known as the Shah Mosque and even earlier Shah Abbasi Mosque) that grace the Naqsh-e-Jahan square. The Sheikh Lutfullah mosque was a private mosque for Shah Abbas, built over a period of eighteen years, early in the seventeenth century, by Ustad Mohammed Reza Isfahani, son of Ustad Hussain, builder of Esfahan. The architect's name appears in two tablets installed in the *mehrab*, the prayer niche inside the mosque that indicates the direction of the Holy Place of Mecca towards which Muslims pray. It says 'a poor humble man in need of God's blessing, Mohammad-Reza son of master mason Hussain Isfahani, 1208 Hejira (1793 AD).' The mosque is named after Sheikh Lutfullah, a Lebanese preacher.

A single *café-au-lait* dome, as seen from a distance, minus any minaret stands in splendid isolation. The Lutfullah mosque's unique yellow-dominated tiled dome with turquoise inlaid petals in intricate arabesque and floral design, is a jewel in the crown of mosques to be found in Esfahan or anywhere else in the world. The yellow turns gold in the sunlight and presents a sublime composition in the backdrop of a clear azure sky. A frequent feature of Islamic architecture is the 'infinite pattern', "an abstract or repetition pattern repeated in continuous sequence." It has achieved perfection in the dome of the Sheikh Lutfullah mosque. "In Islamic art the decorative element is of such importance that the term arabesque is now applied to an enormous range of surface decoration using fanciful motifs of foliate elements. Its earliest Islamic form, depicting patterns of grapes, foliage and tendrils was derived from classical Greece, Rome and above all, Byzantium and was developed by craftsmen working under Omayyad and Abbasid patronage," we are informed in *How to Recognise Islamic Art.* The Omayyad and Abbasid caliphates ruled much of the present-day Arab region from 661 to 945 AD.

Ali Akbar Esfahani is the Iranian Michelangelo of the Masjid-e-Jam'e Abbassi (Abbassi Mosque) built between 1611 and 1616 with expansions continuing up to 1638. He was an artisan of the soul. The opulent yet extraordinarily simple mosque is the crowning achievement of Shah Abbas. He died before its completion despite exerting considerable pressure on its architect and builders. The structure staggers the visitor with its inventiveness and magnificence. It "represents the culmination of a thousand years of mosque building and a magnificent example of architecture, stone carving, and tile work in Iran, with a majesty and splendour that places it among the world's greatest buildings," rightfully proclaims *A Travel Guide to Iran* by M.T. Faramarzi. It is, understandably one of UNESCO's World Heritage Sites.

An architectural marvel it is. The main portal in the middle of the southern flank of the Naqsh-e Jahan square was built in order to maintain the symmetry of the central square. However, the axis of the mosque itself has been built at a forty-five degree angle so that it can face the direction of the Holy city of Mecca. An exterior viewing of the building from the square will not reveal any of this accomplishment. Much of Islamic architecture excels in balance and symmetry. Yet Nature itself is asymmetrical and imbalance is reality. Roger Stevens raves about "the vast pile at the southern end of the *maidan*, that is in design and conception the most majestic expression of Persian Islamic architecture at the crown of its most sumptuous and triumphant era. The scale is stupendous, the plan ingenious." Noteworthy is the simplicity, an elegance that is enhanced by rich ornamentation and colour. In *Islamic Art*, Barbara Bender summarises that the two mosques of Esfahan "enshrines one of the Islamic ideals of architecture as the art of surface decoration." The new congregational mosque was more than spacious enough to accommodate the burgeoning population that now inhabited Esfahan. Rulers also encouraged the public to frequent the extensive bazaars adjacent to the mosque thus combining the commercial and sacred precincts.

Entering the vast portal, one is struck by its sheer magnificence. Someone who has captured my sentiment as I took in the simple splendour is Roger Stevens. He writes: "Once inside the great portal, whose massive dado of Ardistan marble with finely carved corner column leads the eye upwards to glistening stalactites of mosaic, the enchantment takes effect and critical faculties are dulled. Only prejudice bred of too much knowledge could fail to succumb to those encircling walls of dazzling blue, those soaring minarets, their reflections in the tank of the great court, or the deep shade of the ivans which reveal man's pigmy stature. For all its reckless riot of colour, the Royal Mosque, by sheer weight of mass and contrasts of light and shade, is awe-inspiring; the hand may be the King's but the glory, there can be little doubt about it, is to God." As I read of Stevens's enchantment, the words of Giorgio Vasari regarding Leonardo da Vinci came to mind. Yet another analogy with the 'Other

World' comes from Dan Cruickshank in *Around the World in 80 Treasures.* "The Emam Mosque in Isfahan, one of the greatest mosques in the world, is a vision of paradise on earth. The geometry of the mosque is dramatic – in form it is simple and elegant while the surface decoration is lavish."

Persian Islamic architecture perfected the construction of the ivan. In *Iran Today,* Jean Hureau states, "An ivan has the aspect of an apse open off the internal courtyard of the mosque or forming a porch with on each side, high vertical walls like those bordering a theatre stage. There are usually minarets on each end. The entire complex is covered with mosaics or bright-coloured ceramic tiles, and occasionally by mirrors arranged into geometrical compositions... The southern ivan is 38 metres high and 26 metres in depth." As you walk under the construction of dazzling perfection, you enter a great prayer hall that is covered by two domes: the outer dome is 52 metres high and the inner dome is 38 metres high – that leaves an empty space of 12 metres between them. Here is another architectural feat.

The Persians also raised the art of cupola building to a peak. André Godard wrote in his book *Art in Iran* "that cupolas have become once again splendid brilliant bubbles in the sky. They are really the world's most magnificent expression of enamelled architectural decoration." Gazing upwards at the cupola, one is moved by the vast display of floral design, all in golden-yellow and dense-blue enamel tile craftsmanship and the entire surface is illuminated by sunlight - creating a wonder between the cupola's gold and the blue of the sky. A Persian master ceramist of the fourteenth century called for domes to be covered with tiny specks of gold leaf so that the domes "might shine like unto the resplendence of the sun." I am witness to that impact.

The unique combination of double cupolas of the Abbasi mosque has produced a sound miracle, a pure resonance that is heavenly. The acoustics produce both amplification of sound as well as replication of sound. We tried it and it is astounding. The purpose of this sound miracle was to relay the words of the *Imam* (leader of the prayers) to the congregation. The echoes must have produced within the gathered assembly a heavenly feeling.

The embellishment of facades held its own as the vogue for architectural ornamentation in the form of tile mosaics, created glory for Persia for three hundred years and put Persia at the pinnacle of this form of decorative art. In *Colour and Symbolism in Islamic Architecture – Eight Centuries of the Tile Maker's Art*, Michaud and Michael Barry tell us that mosques were adorned with thousands of ceramic tiles bearing the 'Seven Colours of Heaven' – turquoise, night-blue, black, green, red, ochre and white. Islamic architecture transformed geometry into a major art form using principles of symmetry, repetition and change of scale to create a bewildering variety of effects. Highly developed artisans and technical expertise combined their endeavours to create star-shaped patterns of 4,5,6,8,12 and 16 points that resulted in abstract geometric patterns adorning public buildings.

On the west side of the central square lies the Ali Qapu palace known as the Sublime Gate. Shah Abbas built this as a reception and entertainment palace early in the seventeenth century in order to symbolise the power and prestige of the Safavid dynasty. The Ali Qapu palace is the first skyscraper built in Iran, consisting of six floors and rising to a height of forty-eight metres from ground level. A large porch with a central pool built of copper and marble is to be found on the second floor. This expansive veranda has twenty slender columns over twenty feet high, each column made of a single chenar tree-trunk. The columns were originally encased in glass in order to give the impression of a roof floating in the air. These mirrored-columns would have reflected the water of the fountains and pool creating a visual impact. The open space was used to watch polo playing, sporting events and processions in the Naqsh-e-Jahan *maidan* by the ruler, his court and his guests. The sixth floor has niches shaped like bowls worked into the ceiling for both aesthetic purposes and acoustics. This floor was the music room. Making it to the top floor allows one an aerial view of the maidan and beyond. The entire construction and its decorative arts constitute an architectural marvel. Chardin declared, "This is the biggest palace that can be found in any capital."

Another palace built for official entertainment and ceremonies was the Chehel Sutun palace or the palace or forty columns. The name is derived from the pillars that dominate the large first floor open space. Twenty of them are laid out in three rows of six with two additional ones on either side of the main entrance. The remaining twenty are reflected in the water in the rectangular pool with a pavilion at the far end of it. It is an exquisite and ingenious play of the substances of solidity and liquidity. Thus the name Chehel Sutun since forty in Farsi is *chehel* and forty is also considered an auspicious number. The inner door portal had been covered with chipped Venetian glass. Necessity is the master of masterful invention; the glass came all the way from Venice and the broken bits were artfully put to good use. The ceiling has large expanses of Venetian glass mirroring the ornamental arts to be found in the rest of the building. The detailed and large expanses of frescoes inside the inner reception hall are superb. Sadly, many have been chiselled and badly defaced by subsequent dynasties. In 1721, the Bishop Barnabas of Esfahan described the Chehel Sutun *talar* (column porch) as follows: "The palace where the King held his reception is not a room or covered hall, but a very large open porch, handsome and more majestic than that of St. Peter's though not so big. It is completely full of large and small mirrors, marvellously interlaced, and some pictures with fine frames…"

A small museum contains an intriguing item, a 'Tear Holder' in turquoise glass from the tenth century. It was used to collect tears of the wives of the ruler. They had plenty to cry about. My daughter and I were not amused at this idea of adding insult to injury. Once discarded, we wondered if the wife had to prove her sense of loss by publicly demonstrating her sense of shame and pain.

The building of bridges was another architectural forte. The two most impressive ones are the Khaju *pol* (bridge) and the Si-o Seh *pol.* The Khaju Bridge was built between 1642 and 1667 under Shah Abbas II. The name is derived from the district of Khaju on the northern bank of the Zayandeh Rud River. The bridge is 110 metres long and little more than 20 metres wide in places. A two-tiered arcade is the simplest way to describe this remarkable construction. It serves as a bridge, a dam and a walkway that contains pavilions. An amusing observation in *A Travel Guide to Iran* notes that "This famous tea-house under the bridge used to be one of the most atmospheric places in Iran to sit and drink tea or smoke the ghalian surrounded by slumbering Esfahan manhood."

We made two visits to the tea-house, now open in the evening twilight, and in a small space richly decorated with tribal rugs and other traditional Persian ornaments, we partook of glasses of tea, slivers of caramel sugar and dabbled in the art of the *ghalian* (water-pipe). A Farsi poem states: "Take your seat beside the running water and observe how is the trend of life passage, life is passing like a moving boat but it seems as if standing still."

Arthur Pope in Volume 3 of his *Survey of Persian Art* enthuses in his comments: "Efficient, luxurious, poetical, this bridge is a typical product of the Iranian imagination and proof that Persia was capable of sound and original architecture long after degeneration had begun to compromise the building art in other countries of Islam." Pope and his wife, life-long specialists of Iranian architecture, chose to be buried on the banks of the river. For Roger Stevens, the Khaju Bridge "is an astounding construction, ingenious, practical in the highest degree and at the same time lovely to behold." That it is. A photograph taken at night of the bridge gives it the appearance of a string of pearls illuminated in the black of the night.

The Si-o-She Bridge is the Bridge of Thirty-three Arches since it has thirty-three openings. It is also known as the Allahverdikhan Bridge after Shah Abbas's Commander-in- Chief of his army. The lower level of thirty-three (Si-o-She) arches is surmounted by a second layer – thus, giving the bridge its name, beauty and rhythm. The bridge is now open only to human traffic and like the Khaju Bridge serves as a prime spot for rest and recreation. These two bridges add immensely to the charm of the city.

Arthur Pope described the dome and minarets of the Madraseh-ye-Chahar Bagh as "perhaps the last great building in Iran." It was built between 1706 and 1714 in the reign of Shah Soltan Hosein, the last Safavid monarch. The *madrasah* was financed by the Shah's mother after whom the building is also known; Madrasah-ye Madar-e Shah, the theological school of the Mother of the Shah.

The adjoining caravanserai also provided the *madrasah* with funds for the welfare of its students and teachers. According to *Abbasi Hotel: Museum within a Museum*, "at first, the main motivation for constructing the market and the caravanserai was to benefit from its income for maintaining the school and provide for the living of people involved in the management of the school..." Furthermore, we are told, "Along with economic prosperity in the Safavid age, the construction of utilitarian monuments such as bazaars, bridges, dams, pigeon towers, water supplies, inns, mosques and schools was the vogue of time. Yet the most distinguished monument of that era, is the complex of caravanserais, some of which, although ruined and deserted, are still extant here and there. The caravanserais did not just provide lodging for the passengers and passers-by or were not centres of loading or landing of the caravans. The urban caravanserais were appropriate places for storing goods and for commercial exchanges." Chardin, the seventeenth century traveller, estimated some eighteen hundred caravanserais in Iran in the Safavid dynasty. The ancient Esfahan bazaar houses, to this day, a wide range of traditional artisans and their trade. Here we find masters in inlaying, enamelling, calico, engraving, illuminating, mosaic, wood inlaying, braiding and brocading.

That ancient caravanserai is today the world famous Shah Abbasi Hotel. In 1978, my parents and I had stayed at this sumptuous rest house. Pope noted in 1966, "The glorious decoration of Abbassi Guest House is one of the distinguished products of art. The splendid art of the Safavids is so dextrously and elegantly revived in this mystic enchantment of A Thousand Tales. These decorations demonstrate both the dynamism of Persian artistic conventions and the continuity of modern supplement to other precious historical monuments of Esfahan." The interior décor of the Shah Abbasi Hotel is renowned for its exquisite and highly detailed mirror-work, wooden latticework, painting on wood, miniature painting, plaster moulding and illumination.

In our visit to Esfahan in 1999, it was closed for restoration work. The renovation in the teahouse facing the central garden courtyard had a plaque noting that the work was undertaken by the Iran Insurance Company. Its name was also to be found on a large plastic clock - very twentieth century - hanging on the wall. The rectangular laid-out garden of today's hotel was the open courtyard sheltering animals and goods of the earlier caravanserai. An annexe, the 'new' Shah Abbasi Hotel, was built in 1964.

Gilles Lambert in *Connaissance des Voyages* wrote in 1970, "When you return to Shah Abbas after an excursion, you are certainly not plunged into the standardised universe of the tourist…Persian and French architects worked together on this undertaking, particularly Mr. Siroux, a specialist in traditional Iranian architecture and Mr. Foroughi, Director of the Iranian Art Institute, Mr. And Mrs. Paul Augier (from the famous Negresco Hotel in Nice, France) supervised the interior decoration. Most of its decorative features – windows, stained glass, sculpted doors and engraved wood – are ancient. The reception halls are decorated with Persian miniatures. Iranian painter Mehdi Ebrahimian took his inspiration from the Chehel Sotoon (Forty Columns) pavilion…and recalls that Esfahan – Nesf-e-Jahan (Half of the World) – was, long before organised tours were invented, a dream spot for the forerunners of long-distance tourism: the desert caravan-drivers."

Ebrahimian's first sighting of the interior of the ancient caravanserai led him to comment: "When I saw the building, I confronted a gloomy and dull atmosphere, but entering the courtyard, one was enchanted by so much beauty and harmony which had surrounded me from all sides. I found that the only way to reconcile the old and the new styles and to achieve an equilibrium was to adopt a Persian decoration and preferably the Safavid era."

A drive outside the city centre reveals intriguing structures or what remains of them. Upon questioning our well-informed guide, we were told that these were pigeon-towers. These huge mud-brick buildings once housed several thousand pigeons. They were built mostly during the seventeenth century when the expanding city required higher output from its farmland to feed the increasing population. The pigeon-droppings collected within these towers were used as manure to increase the fertility of the land. The largest grouping of them - some twenty - lie ten kilometres east of Esfahan on the Nain-Yazd road. The other, even more intriguing structure is a desolate mass of ruins perched on a rocky promontory enhanced by the scenic beauty; an oasis featuring ancient pigeon-towers, mud-brick houses, orchards and streams. These lie at the base of the granite rock where a sixth century BC five-storey high Zoroastrian fire temple-cum-palace is to be found. The now craggy ruin, on a moonscape of granite and well-camouflaged by its rock base, sits eighty-five metres above street-level. A grotesque cylindrical water tank, built some 50 years ago, has successfully marred the view of the ancient fire temple. The water tank was built at considerable cost, never used and is now to be broken down – a perfect example of short-term, inappropriate 'modern' planning.

Fire is an essential element in life. As Stephen Pyne once noted, "We are uniquely fire creatures on a uniquely fire planet." For Zoroastrians, fire is sacred, a source of awe and supplication. It also provides basic needs: food, light, protection and warmth and is thus a factor in community building and unity. 'Towers of Silence' were the traditional Zoroastrian burial sites. In Iran, they have not been in use for over three hundred years. In these 'Towers of Silence', eagles and vultures disposed of the bodies, thus preventing earth, water and fire - the divine elements – from being contaminated; the soul of the deceased already having been received by Ahura Mazda, the Supreme Being. Contrary to popular belief, Zoroastrians do not worship fire but regard fire as an essential element in Life and thus a symbol of worship. Zoroaster founded the religion some 3700 years ago in northwest Iran that is today west Azerbaijan. We visited a functioning fire temple in Esfahan that was built thirty years ago and donated to the city by an Armenian couple.

Shah Abbas persuaded or ordered some 30,000 Armenians from mountain-dwellings and the city of Julfa in Azerbaijan, close to Iran's border, to move to Esfahan early in the seventeenth century. Better opportunities or strategic coercion? There are differing views. "By this authoritarian move, the Persian sovereign ruined a commercial centre then under Turkish influence, and settled in his brand-new capital hard-working and skilful citizens," notes Jean Hureau. In *Shah Abbas : Empereur de Perse* by Houchang Nahavandi and Yves Bomati, the Iranian and French authors write of the 'scorched-earth' policy that Shah Abbas wrought in the 'Old' Julfa region as a political move against the Ottomans with whom the Armenians were not at peace anyhow. Such a 'burn and rule' tactic was also much favoured by Shah Abbas' grandfather, Tahmasp. Regional rivalry between the prevailing power – the Ottomans – and the Safavids, led Shah Abbas to forcefully move the Armenian population to Iran using a 'carrot and stick' strategy.

According to Nahavandi and Bomati, an Armenian delegation asked Shah Abbas for help against the Ottomans in 1602. In 1604, Shah Abbas made his move. Subsequently, the migrants from 'Old' Julfa who settled into 'New' Julfa in Esfahan were accorded religious freedom, land and commercial advantages. The Armenian community flourished. Of the many Armenian churches – there were once twenty-eight - the largest, much gilded and most ornate is the Vank cathedral. Built between 1655 and 1664, it is richly decorated with exquisite murals depicting scenes from the Old Testament. In the cathedral museum there are Armenian manuscripts, Safavid charters, even a sketch by Rembrandt and a rich collection of paintings and tapestries. Hosts of Americans of Armenian origin are to be found wandering around in search of their roots.

Esfahan truly has something for everyone. There is enough diversity in the city to satisfy the most demanding of travellers. For in Esfahan, the imagination has soared and beauty has assumed crescendos of perfection.

SCENTED SHIRAZ

'Pars is a very beautiful district having both plains and mountains both sea and land. Everything found in cold and warm regions is found in Pars…"
Ebn-e Balkhi, Farsnameh

"The visitor forgets his homeland
When in May he comes to Shiraz."
Saadi, thirteenth century poet

"Right through Shiraz the path goes
Of perfection
Anyone in Shiraz knows
Its direction."
Hafez, fourteenth century poet

"Suddenly, we turned a corner and in that moment – a moment of which the recollection will never fade from my mind – there burst upon my delighted gaze a view the like of which (in its way) I never saw…lay the home of Persian culture, the mother of Persian genius, the sanctuary of poetry and philosophy, Shiraz."
E.G. Browne in *A Year Amongst the Persians*

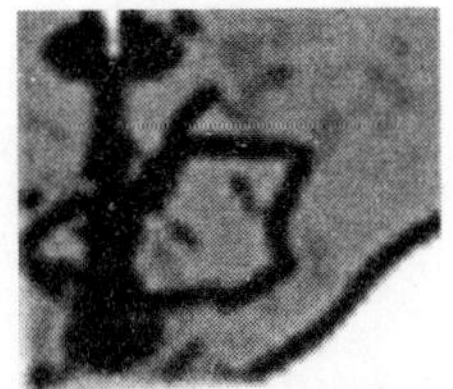

What first struck me in our mid-April 2000 visit to Shiraz was the sweet, rich floral fragrance permeating the balmy evening air. Criss-crossing the city from one site to another, one breathes in the black exhaust fumes from surrounding cars. Yet a step into any of the mandatory gardens surrounding the many palaces or mausoleums of the immortal Iranian poets Hafez and Saadi and floral scents emitted by the pansies, snapdragons and beds of roses in every colour of a rainbow, regale one's senses. After all, Persian gardens were created as earthly forms of paradise and heaven. However, since Shiraz is known as the 'City of Roses, Nightingales and Poetry', I had expected to see the many wide boulevards fringed with the famed roses or other floral displays. That is not the case: floral arrangements remain largely to be found behind walled private domains. As for the nightingales, they have passed into historical extinction, existing only in the verses of the city's illustrious poets and on the distinctive decorative tile-work in mosques and palaces.

The province of Fars, the cradle of Persian civilisation, has as its present capital, the city of Shiraz, a city that pays homage to birds, flowers and love. The language of ancient Fars (Pars) Farsi or Parsi became the official and literary language of Persia or Iran. A former epithet of Shiraz and justifiably so was Dar ul Elm, House of Learning, since Shiraz is the birthplace of two giants of Persian poetry. Fars is also the root of the nation's historical name, Persia. The country became Iran only in 1935 when it was officially adopted as the country's appellation.

By the twelfth and thirteenth centuries, Shiraz had developed into a large and populous city, as prosperous as Baghdad. Roger Stevens describes the city in *The Land of the Great Sophy*. "Shiraz, by tradition the city of roses and nightingales, cypresses and wine, bulbous domes and terraced gardens, has I suppose been more extolled in poetry and prose than any other city of Iran."

Under the Safavid dynasty, Shiraz flourished in the seventeenth century. The Governor of Fars, Imam Gholi Khan, brought peace and prosperity to the province. The city acquired avenues shaded by tall cypresses, a characteristic feature of Shiraz - canals, gardens, monuments, mosques and palaces. However, the capital of the Safavid Empire remained Esfahan. Shiraz only became the capital of the Persian Empire under the Zand dynasty in the eighteenth century and reached its zenith during the reign of Karim Khan Zand. He never took the title of Shah (King). He called himself Vakiil (Advocate) of his people. Although Karim Khan Zand wanted to create an Esfahan out of Shiraz with architectural achievements similar to the Safavid splendour, he had neither the power nor the purse to realise his desire.

However, under the Zand dynasty, artistic levels reached new heights in the interior decoration of the many opulent palaces of princes and prosperous merchants. Roger Stevens picks out the particular features of Shirazi aesthetic features. "The new style is particularly evident in tile-work and wall and ceiling decoration where the designs have become more naturalistic and the colours softer, the Safavid preponderance of deep blue giving way to greens, pinks or pale blues often used on a white ground. Increasing use was made of oil-painting and also of rich mosaic mirror work, both popular under the later Qajar dynasty."

The profuse use of decorative tile-work in Shiraz catches the eye. The designs of the tiles include flowers, leaves, plants, birds, peacocks, animals, hunting fields and calligraphic inscriptions. Scenes from legendary epics and depictions of mythological tales from the immortal poet Firdausi in his *Shah Nama* are also popular subjects of the tile art form. Predominant are the Shirazi tiles, exquisite arabesque and delicate floral designs of the city's symbols - the rose and nightingale. The richness of Persian tile-works has been well extolled by Mahmoud Maheronaghsh in his article 'The Art of the Tile-work in Islam'. "Any design can be created by cutting and trimming the tile. A tile is not flexible as long as its shape is square or rectangular but when it is turned into smaller pieces it reaches to an astounding flexibility that it can be used on any surface and in any arch." Favourite motifs in Iranian art include geometrical shapes and patterns such as medallions and meanders; grapevines and other floral patters, often highly intricate and complex. Also popular are highly stylised real or imaginary animals such as lions, griffins, peacocks, elephants and phoenixes. We managed to buy a contemporary tile-work mosaic composition of the famed Shirazi Gul-e-Bulbul, Shiraz's Rose and Nightingale.

Another feature of Islamic architecture that attained heights of beauty and perfection was the art of calligraphy. Akbar S. Ahmed in *Living Islam: From Samarkand to Stornoway* remarks that "Calligraphy, which derived from and reflected the Quran, was particularly prized. Quranic verses as decoration are found everywhere, on tombstones and textiles, on tiles and even on weapons. Calligraphy adorns buildings and books and is a highly respected art form. The words of God reflect the spirit of the Quran and they beautify everything that a Muslim creates. "Good Writing," said the Holy Prophet, "makes the truth stand out."

Shirazi residents acted as cultural emissaries both internally and externally by beautifying Samarkand and many of the Mughal cities in India. Most noteworthy was Ustad Isa, a seventeenth century Shirazi architect who provided the design for the Taj Mahal at Agra, according to the guidebook *Lonely Planet: Iran.*

The most impressive Zand monument in Shiraz is the Vakil mosque completed in 1773 and restored in 1825. The mosque is designed with two-pointed arches (ivans) located on the northern and southern sides of the central courtyard. The facades of the ivans are tiled in Shiraz's characteristic style with hafte-rang tiles, tiles in seven colours. The spacious winter prayer hall shabestan behind the south ivan is supported by forty-eight monolith pillars carved in spirals. It is impressive. Such carved spiral columns were first designed for use in hammams where the built-up steam would trickle down the spiral grooves, adding to the beauty of the columns. The aesthetics of it caught on and were subsequently incorporated into the interior design of the Vakil mosque. The *minbar* chair used for sermons is cut from a solid piece of marble with an approach of fourteen steps, in honour of the Holy Prophet, his daugher Bibi Fatima and the twelve Imams named by the Shia'i sect of Islam. Shia'ism was declared the official religion of Iran by the Safavid dynasty in the sixteenth century.

An interesting square-cut opening about two feet deep in front of the *mihrab*, a semi-circular prayer niche directed towards the Holy city of Mecca, is where the Imam preacher would stand. A feature started in the Safavid period in the seventeenth century in Iran and continued till present, it provides security for the Imam leading the prayers. At a level lower than the amassed gathering, while standing or while prostrating, the Imam would be less vulnerable to strikes from opposition figures and, thus, would have less chance of 'being stabbed in the back'.

The Vakil citadel was used as military quarters and as a private residence and is, today, in a sorry and dilapidated state. Unlike many a ruin elsewhere, it is far from being in a state of 'exquisite but faded' disrepair, a condition that echoes past grandeur. A general prison till 1932 and then a prison for political prisoners till 1971, it has suffered badly under plaster cover-up. Entire walls, facades, ceilings have been defaced. Two ramparts were built around the citadel, the outer one for external security and the inner rampart wall to provide internal security for the Vakil's family and harem from the peering security guards and soldiers perched above. One of the four massive towers of the Vakil fortress has a substantial tilt. It has emerged over the years due to subsoil movement. Now reinforced, the awkward tilt nevertheless remains. Two of the three porches facing the courtyard had two single stone columns. One pair was shifted to Golestan palace in Tehran by the subsequent ruling dynasty, the Qajars, and replaced with two wooden columns.

Karim Khan Zand, the Vakil, had been buried at the pavilion - now the Pars Museum - in Shiraz but the founder of the Qajar dynasty moved his remains to Golestan palace, Tehran. The new ruler had the mortal remains of his predecessor placed beneath the entrance stone to his apartment at Golestan palace so that he and others could relish walking over his predecessor's remains.

The Qajar tribe succeeded the Zand tribe as rulers of Iran. "The shift of power was not made on the basis of logic, mutual agreement, regulation or lawful handling of power according to a constitution, but came about as a result of massacre, suppression and the spread of terror," argues Mahmoud Sariolghalam in an article "Tribal Sources of Iranian Political Culture."

Democratic transition was not the rule of the day.

The four-room *hamaam* of the Vakil citadel is impressive. Built underground, marble columns with smooth, spiral, rope-shaped carvings support the roof. Small domes with large glass-covered holes in them were designed to allow natural sunlight to penetrate the steam-filled *hamaams*.

The most elegant of palatial houses is the Afifabad or Golshan palace. The Ghavam family, an artistocratic Shirazi family, built it in 1863 during the Qajar dynasty. Roger Stevens described it in the 1950s, "It is being restored as an officers' mess and is difficult to get into, but a glimpse through the classical Persian gateway down to the principal pavilion reveals a surprising contrast to the other houses. The façade is comparatively sober, and has an arcade-running all around it, reached by a flight of steps up to a double-column portico."

Acquired by the former Queen Farah Diba of the Pahlavi dynasty, it has been beautifully renovated and restored. The ground floor was converted into an army museum with an impressive collection of guns and rifles of the eighteenth and nineteenth centuries. Many had been made in England and Germany. A two feet high tiled-skirting with trailing trellises and roses is to be found all around the museum floor. The ceilings are covered in hafte-rang paintings on wood of floral designs and boxed scenes of Shiraz. Carpets from Tabriz in coral blue and dusky pink, adorn the two card rooms - now conference rooms. These were Reza Shah's and Queen Farah Diba's card rooms for entertaining bridge players. A large frame holds some twenty sepia-coloured photographs of Shiraz – its palaces, gardens, mosques and other monuments. Startling is the one showing a public hanging.

Another renovation undertaken by Farah Diba was the Qajar palace, Saheb Qaranieh palace within the Niavaran palace grounds in Tehran. A number of exquisite burnt-orange varnished doors covered with Persian miniature art paintings from Shiraz are installed at this palace in northern Tehran. Some other items of Shirazi decorative arts were also transferred to this palace in the form of painted alcoves and ceilings.

There is a definite stamp of the feminine touch at both the former Qajar palaces in Shiraz and Tehran. Farah Diba was a second year architectural student in Paris in 1958 when she married the Shah of Iran. Her lifelong association with France remained constant. Following the Iranian Revolution, their exile from Iran and the death of the Shah, Farah Diba took up residence in Paris. A large number of French architects and interior designers worked in Iran during the Pahlavi era. French furniture and French decorative arts were in vogue. In Paris in the late 1990s, we had the honour of meeting, on three occasions, the former Farah Diba (or Shah Banu as she had earlier been called), an extremely chic and beautifully elegant woman. These were memorable occasions at banquets hosted by the Aga Khan.

A perfectly restored dream-house of a *chai-khanna* (teahouse) is to be found along the outer wall of the Golshan palace in Shiraz. Restored in the 1960s by Farah Diba, huge seating alcoves are carpeted and cushion bolsters are lined-up against the walls for resting and partaking of tea. The walls are covered in striking and detailed mosaic tiles depicting Rostam and Sohrab, epic figures from classical Persian literature. The Shirazi symbols - roses and nightingales – feature frequently on the tiles. These Persian-style cafés were perfect venues for poetry recitations, discussions and matters of intellectual pursuit while taking time off for more leisurely lounging and slumbering. Unfortunately, we reached the *chai-khanna* just as they were closing for the evening. Otherwise, we could have engaged in lazing and lounging while taking in the Persian ambience, since poetic pursuits are well beyond us.

Two French artists, Eugene Flandin and Pascal Coste, documented Iran in the mid-nineteenth century in drawings and engravings. They travelled extensively in Iran, also visiting Persepolis, Shiraz and Esfahan. Their sketches appear in a contemporary compilation *Qajar Iran (1839-1841)*. Their original research and drawings form the monumental two volumes *Voyage en Perse* published in 1851.

Shiraz is also a poetry capital since it gave the world two of its greatest poets, Hafez and Saadi. Wordsworth once defined poetry as "Emotion recollected in tranquillity." Persia's literary output has been mainly in verse whose language reached a climax in the imagination of the classical Iranian poets. Persian poetry from the pens of Firdausi, Nasr-e-Khusrau, Nemazi, Omar Khayyam, Maulana Rumi, Hafiz and Saadi have delighted people the world over and are available in any number of translations. Omar Khayyam's *Rubaiyyat* or quatrains are most familiar to English-speakers through the Victorian translation by Edward Fitzgerald. Yaqoob Azhand in his article 'The Global Impact of Iranian Culture' writes "...Farsi poetry flourished in the local courts of local dynasties, so much so that the people danced to verses from Hafiz. Farsi poetry spread even to the Bengal region."

The greatest Iranian lyric poet and literary giant of the fourteenth century was born in 1324 in Shiraz and died in his home-city at the age of sixty-three. Hafiz is the penname of Shams ad-Din

Mohammad meaning 'he who knows the Holy Koran by heart'. A student of Arabic literature and humanities, Hafiz also studied theology and theosophy.

A master of ode, couplet and quatrain, his fame is due to his writing of sonnets. These sonnets are considered the soul of Persian *ghazals* (verses). His masterful use of allusions, parables, metaphors and other figures of speech reached great heights. According to Nahavandi and Bomati writing in *Shah Abbas*, "He celebrated like never before, wine, love, beauty, tolerance and fraternity among mankind." Among Persian poets, wine has been known as the 'daughter of the vine.' Hafiz's poetic heritage includes some 4000 to 5000 verses, 400 to 500 lyric-poems, several long elegies and short couplets. His lyrics are attributed to divine grace and his expertise of the Holy Quran. The poet Jami, his near contemporary, considered the poetry of Hafiz virtually untranslatable. Jami raved "with all its sweetness, delicacy, freshness, ease, elegance, flow, agreeableness and unaffectedness, it is something very near a miracle; it is a just object of pride and not only for Persians: it is a glory for all mankind."

V.S. Naipaul in *Among the Believers: An Islamic Journey*, relates the following conversation with his Iranian guide, Behzad, in his visit to Iran in 1980. "Behzad, whose father was a teacher of Persian literature, said, 'Persian poetry is full of sadness.' I said, 'But tears for the sake of tears, Behzad?' Firmly, like a man who wasn't going to discuss the obvious, and wasn't going to listen to any artistic nonsense, he said, 'Those tears are beautiful.'"

A collection of poems by Hafiz fetched 1.1 million pounds sterling at an auction by Christies, London early in 2000. The *pièce de resistance* was a sixteenth century oriental manuscript of the 'Diwan' illuminated with 873 illustrations of birds in small square panels painted by an anonymous master. The volume of collected poems by Hafiz had been copied by the Iranian calligrapher Abd al-Rahim of Herat. It was the prize item of the lot of Islamic arts that fetched a stunning total of 7 million pounds sterling. The rare manuscript was dated 1587. Shiraz, by mid-fourteenth century, was known as the principal centre of commercial manuscript production in Persia.

Hafiz was buried in a garden known as the Hafezieh. His mausoleum is visited and venerated by all in Shiraz and beyond. The cupola resembles a dervish's hat and is covered in copper that changes colour over the hour and has been transformed over time. The alabaster tombstone is delicately inscribed with two of Hafiz's ghazals. Karim Khan Zand had an open-air hall with four tall columns in stone built over the grave. Ali Asghar Hekmati and André Godard conducted the last renovation in the 1930s under the Pahlavi rule. Numerous tombstones surrounding Hafiz's grave were then removed – a few still remain – to create space and provide a courtyard for the many admirers and visitors who throng the site. The garden in April was a delight for any horticulturist; roses of every colour and fragrance struck one's senses.

The earthly 'Garden of Gardens' in Iran has to be the Prince's Garden, Bagh-e-Shahzadeh in Mahan, Kerman province. In 1880, a Qajar prince and governor-general of the province, Farmanfarma, created a spectacular stepped 50,000 square metres garden on the slopes of the Tigran range of mountains. The uniqueness of design and landscaping is enhanced by the contrast between the aridity and ruggedness of the environment and the lushness of greenery and abundance of water in the garden. Perched on top of the slope is a princely palace. Leading from the entrance gatehouse, two parallel stone-paved pathways gently ascend to the palatial edifice. Symmetrical rows of cypress, pine and poplar trees stand along the sides of the pathways. In between lie slender fountains, pools and water cascades that ripple down. And the roses…discreet lighting and a full moon created a magical setting as we climbed the gentle slopes to the top and to a sumptuous dinner with the governor-general. The other comparable garden, to my mind, is the Versailles garden outside Paris.

Fortunately in Shiraz, we were able to enjoy tea in the *chai-khanna* in a small courtyard with a central small pool and the evening-air waft with the fragrance of roses and the delicious aroma of apple-scented tobacco emanating from the bubbling ghalians water pipes. There were niches built into the brick-walls for putting one's feet up and relaxing. Unfortunately, lights were all too soon dimmed (a universal signal for their closing down and our need to move on) and the magic of the evening came to a close.

At the adjoining table sat six young Polish students from the University of Cracow, Poland. Students of Iranian studies, they were in Iran for six months at the University of Rasht in northern Iran, near the Caspian Sea. Like us, they too were on their first visit to Shiraz. All of them spoke fluent Farsi. We were most impressed and they were most engaging.

The next port of call was the mausoleum of the other Immortal Poet of Persian poetry, Saadi born in Shiraz in 1194. His proper name was Maslih u'din or the 'Umpire of the Faith', but he was better known as Shaikh Saadi Shirazi. A Sufi of profound learning, he studied at the Nizamieh College in Baghdad, a regional seat of learning. He performed the pilgrimage to the Holy City of Mecca some fifteen times by the only means available in the thirteenth century; largely on foot in the company of camels and caravans.

A much-travelled man in his day, Saadi visited "Europe, Barbary, Abyssinia, Egypt, Syria, Palestine, Armenia, Asia Minor, the three grand divisions of Arabia, and every province of Iran and many parts of Turan, or of Persia and Tartary, from Busrah and Baghdad to the Scythian Wall, and at Rudbar, Deliman on the Caspian Sea, Cashghur beyond the Jihun, or Oxus, across the Sindh'h, or Indus, and into many parts of Hindustan, etc.; and, from a poem in his book of Fragments, it appears that he had a practical knowledge, for he quotes a line in each, of eighteen idioms, dialects, and languages, as spoken in the many regions into which he had thus travelled." James Ross in his translation of Saadi's *Gulistan* quotes this from the Introduction. Saadi's best-known works are the *Gulistan*, *The Rose Garden*, and the

Bustan, The Orchard. The masterpieces are collections of anecdotes and moral tales couched in verse and rhymed prose.

Gulistan translated into English by James Ross, an Englishman, was published in 1823. It was dedicated to the Chairman and Directors of the East India Company. Ross was a surgeon with the East India Company and a dedicated and devout student of Persian literature. In his Introduction to the translation, Ross makes a passionate plea for the Persian language. "A company of British merchants have established an empire of the finest provinces of Asia, nearly equal in population and extent to all Europe, where Persian is the language of law, religion, commerce, and in fact of all civilised usage; and instead of falsifying and abusing this language, our duty, as well as interest, as Englishmen, point out the justice of righting and supporting; and let our scholars, now brought up to a classical knowledge of it at the East India Company's colleges, endeavour to weed what they will find the current language of Hindustan of its vicious metaphors, immoderate hyperbole, silly conceits, prettinesses, bombast and idle verbiage of the last three centuries, or since AD 1450, and restore it to the sublime and pathetic imagery, and the just diction of its golden age from Dakiki and Rodaki, AD 950, to Jami and Hatifa; and rescue it from being mangled by men learned and respectable in their knowledge of Greek and Latin, but vulgar and illiberal in their ignorance and prejudices in whatever respects the languages and literature of the East, and in particular of this scientific, diplomatic, financial, legislative and commercial dialect of a hundred millions of our fellow subjects!".

Dowlat Shah writing about Saadi's life, observed "that the first thirty years of Saadi's long life was devoted to study and laying up a stock of knowledge; the next thirty, or perhaps forty, in treasuring up experience and disseminating that knowledge during his wide-extending travels; ...he spent the remainder of his life, or seventy years, in the retirement of a recluse, when he was exemplary in his temperance and edifying in his piety."

The following two lines of poetry by Saadi greet us as we pass under the gate of the mausoleum of Saadi:

> *"The tomb of Saadi of Shiraz with the scent of love*
> *Even a thousand years after his death."*

The garden in the month of April was abloom with the rich fragrance of roses. The portico has tall columns of pink marble topped by a turquoise-blue dome. To one side is a colonnade of columns. The mausoleum now stands where the poet had once lived. It was rebuilt in the early nineteenth century by Karim Khan Zand and then again in the mid-twentieth century by the Pahlavi dynasty.

Steps lead one down into an underground pool filled with fish in the garden surrounding Saadi's tomb. As in pools of water the world-over, we threw in a coin for good luck. We soon came across the Polish students we had earlier met at the *chai-khanna* near Hafiz's tomb. A young man in the group immediately coined the following poem:

I became a poet, I made a wish
I threw in a coin, And killed a fish.

THE PERSIAN CARPET : "ART THAT IS TROD ON"

"Where thy carpet lies is thy home."
Persian proverb

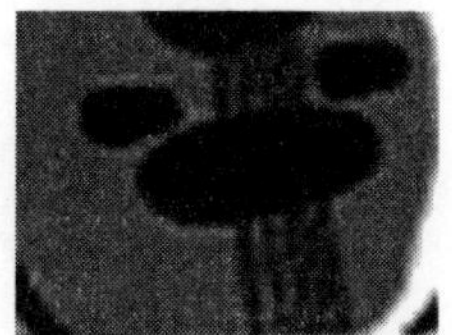

Few earthly items epitomise the joy of art and beauty than a Persian carpet. After all, even Cleopatra had herself rolled out of a carpet before Julius Cesar. These mirrors of creativity, these masterpieces are art forms uniquely made to be trod on. Carpet-making is a channel for expressing the craftsman's talent for controlling exuberance and imagination in both design and colour. It is an exercise undertaken by a genius. It is also a popular art and to a great extent, a tribal expression of art.

A Persian carpet has been defined as a hand-woven carpet or rug produced in Iran and characterised by fine warps and filling yarns, unusually tight, even pile made with the Sehna knot and a variety of floral, foliate, animal and avian designs woven in rich, harmonious colours. The word carpet is derived from *carpere* meaning 'to pluck or seize' in Latin; implying the plucking of wool. The word reflects the fact that for centuries wool has traditionally been used for making carpets.

Out of necessity was born art. The numerous nomadic tribes that once wandered the great expanse of land created floor and wall coverings to protect themselves from the bitter winters of a forbidding landscape. There are mountains with snow-covered peaks and rocky slopes accompanied by fierce winds. There are also areas of parched wilderness where nomads roamed from oasis to oasis in search of waterholes for themselves and their flocks of sheep, goats and camels. Warm colours and artistic designs provided some relief in an otherwise harsh environment. Carpets in the tents were sat on, slept on, used as door coverings and wall hangings and used to keep warm. Carpets were also used as barter in exchange for other necessities of life. They were essential items in a constant battle for survival.

A most prized possession, it was treasured for the immense measure of beauty and warmth that it brought to surroundings of harsh extremes.

Carpets evolved over time from being an item of basic necessity to one of wealth, conspicuous consumption and investment. Persian carpets are popularly known as an Iranian's 'stocks and shares'. In times of need, they can be sold off. Persian carpets - a matter of the purse - have also become an integral part of affluent interior décor globally. From the tents of nomads to the palaces of potentates, Persian carpets have a colourful history.

Persian carpets were regular features of the caravan trade that passed through the region. A major centre of the flourishing commerce was Tabriz in Azerbaijan in the northwest of Iran. Tabriz was a gateway to the West, since it lay on one of the principal trade routes from Persia to Turkey and then onwards to Europe. To the East lay the towns of Mashad in the Khorasan province and Herat, oasis towns en route to Turkestan and China. This was the famed Carpet Route that for centuries passed through ancient Persia.

There are two major traditions in the carpet industry, Oriental and Western. The older is Oriental including carpets from Central Asia, Middle East, the subcontinent, China and North Africa. The Western tradition is derived from the Oriental and was established much later. Marco Polo, the Venetian traveller of the thirteenth century, judged that Asia Minor produced "the best and handsomest carpets in the world." The carpet trade with the West took off in the sixteenth century. In the West, carpets were originally used as coverings for beds, chests, tables and other furniture. Only since the early eighteenth century were carpets associated with floors. The reasoning appears to be that these works of art were too precious to be left on the floor to be walked on. They deserved to be shown off as objects of art.

During archaeological excavations of burial mounds in the Altai Mountains in Siberia, Professor Rudenko discovered, in 1949, the earliest known Oriental carpet. The carpet dates back to the fifth century BC. Robbers raided the tomb but left aside the carpet. Through the opening, water froze and the carpet was mercifully preserved. This ancient carpet is known as the Pazyryk carpet. It has a wooden pile and is knotted with the Turkish Chiordes knot. Its central field is a deep red colour and it has two wide borders, one depicting deer and the other Persian horseman. The Pazyryk carpet hangs at the Hermitage Museum in St. Petersburg, Russia.

Historical records show that the Persian Achaemenian court of Cyrus the Great at Pasargade was decked with magnificent carpets. That was over 2500 years ago. Alexander the Great is said to have been dazzled by the carpets in the tomb area of Cyrus the Great at Pasargade. By the sixth century, Persian carpets of wool or silk were renowned in court circles throughout the region. The 'spring or winter' carpet of Khosrow was made for the main audience hall of the palace at Ctesiphon, now in Iraq. It depicted a formal garden. With the defeat of the Persians by Arabs, Ctesiphon changed hands. It is alleged that Arabs cut the carpets into small fragments and divided the booty among the victorious soldiers.

The Mongol invasion of Persia in the thirteenth century wrought havoc in every artistic domain. Carpet-making went into sharp decline. Yet in a subsequent era, Mongol rulers attracted, with lavish royal support, the best artisans for their palaces in Central Asia. The apex of the art of carpet-making occurred in the sixteenth century in Iran under the Safavid dynasty. Shah Abbas established a royal carpet factory in Esfahan and hired master craftsmen. Esfahan was then 'a paradise of art and beauty'. A unique carpet of the period is known as the Ardebil carpet dated 1539. It was the handwork of Maqsud Kashani, an inhabitant of Kashan. The masterpiece was made for Sheikh Safi-ud-Din from Ardebil. It is recognised as the oldest Persian carpet in the world. A detailed star medallion dominates an elaborate system of stems and flowers on a vivid indigo field. Roger Stevens in *Land of the Great Sophy* rejoices in the beauty of this woven masterpiece. "The great Ardebil carpet is in the Victoria and Albert Museum (in London) whose splendid sunburst with its subsidiary satellites is like a vision of the firmament framed in an enormous window..." Another smaller similar carpet is housed at the Los Angeles County Museum. While the carpet industry dates back more than 2500 years, only fragments remain of carpets woven earlier than the seventeenth century.

The Venetian traveller Barbaro mentioned the existence of a carpet industry in Cairo in the 1470s. This is thought to be the production of Mameluke carpets. According to Barbara Brend in *Islamic Art*, "These beautiful works of highly sophisticated design seem to make a sudden appearance in the late fifteenth century, and it has been suggested that they were made by émigrés craftsmen from Iran. The knot used is indeed the asymmetrical type, favoured in later centuries by Persians rather than by Turks...Mamluk carpets have a lustrous pile in red, green and light blue, with small quantities of cream and tan in the more refined examples." As the seventeenth century wore on, there was increasing demand for more luxurious and refined carpets both in Iran and abroad. The peak of artistic attainment then petered off. By the mid-nineteenth century, quality was sacrificed for quantity. Cheap artificial dyes, low quality wool, chemical washing and poor design combined to affect poorly the carpet industry.

Traditionally, sheep wool, but also camel and goat hair, was used for the weaving of carpets. Luxury carpets were later woven with silk pile. Simple tools are needed for the hand-manufacture of carpets; *Persian Rugs and Carpets* informs us, "They are a knife, a beater and shears. The knife is used to cut the threads of the knot. It is made entirely of metal and may have a hook at the end of the blade to assist in the formation of the knot. The beater consists of a series of metal blades, the points of which are splayed to form a set of teeth. It is used to tighten the threads of the weft against a line of knots. The wide-bladed flat shears are used to clip the pile of the carpet."

Traditionally, only natural dyes were used for the colouring of wool. Dyeing materials included mineral pigments, insect and animal derivatives and vegetable and plant products, such as, leaves, bark, root, fruits, flowers and plants. These dyes were much in use till the nineteenth century for the colouring of weaving yarns, although synthetic dyes came slowly on the scene from as far back as the sixteenth century. Resistance to the use of chemical dye for wool exists to this day. Present-day Persian carpet buyers frequently ask whether the wool is natural vegetable dye or chemical dye. Synthetic dyes became popular for their low-cost and brilliant colour. However, their durability is limited, the colours fade and deteriorate fast. The use of artificial dyes marked a decline in the time-honoured quality of carpets.

It has to be recognised that the origins of carpet-weaving lay with nomads as a product of necessity - in this case truly the mother of invention. It was only over time that the utilitarian nature of the carpet was superseded by its aesthetic value. As both appreciation and market prices rose significantly, slowly some of the production of carpets moved to urban, organised workshops. Earlier all carpet-weaving had been carried out in scattered nomadic communities. While carpets are both an urban and a nomadic expression of art, *kilims/gilims* (floor-rugs) are purely nomadic pursuits. Each carpet-weaving family is known for its carpet designs; motifs, patterns and weaving skills using gentle roses, brilliant sunshine, resplendent flowers, green leaves, birds… all 'divine blessings'. The designs are closely guarded family secrets. Months and even years of painstaking work go into the creation of a single carpet.

There are two classifications of carpet-making. One is flat-woven including tapestry, brocading and embroidery and secondly, knotted pile weaving. The earliest carpets were always flat-surfaced weaves. The earliest pile carpets from the Middle East date from the middle of the thirteenth century. Geometric designs of squares, octagons, tendrils are found in all carpet art of Asia Minor and Central Asia. An essential characteristic of Oriental carpets is hand-knotting. Such knots are either *Senneh*, the Persian knot or *Ghiordes*, the Turkish knot.

"The miracle which attends the birth of every Persian carpet begins therefore at the knotting stage. Millions of differently coloured knots are patiently aligned one against the other to form the patterns and motifs – sometimes geometric, sometimes floral – but always full of imagination and style. Among the nomads, colours and designs often grow instinctively out of the basic tradition. There is no preordained plan – just a general idea which takes into account the shape of the carpet to be made, the symbols which are to appear on it, and the colours available. All the rest is imagination, whim, skill and the innate creativity of the nomad," states Djavad Yassavoli in *Persian Carpets and Rugs*. It is critical to consider three factors in the creation of a carpet: the person who orders it, the person who creates it and the person who uses it. This dimension of carpet-making referred to in *The Sofreh of Kamo* by Parviz Tanovoli was a revelation.

Oriental carpets share characteristics that have remained constant over centuries. Most carpets are rectangular but some are round or square-shaped. Within the majority rectangular carpets, all designs are divided into border and field. The field may have an *eslimi* (a central element), or a repeating pattern. "A repeated pattern which seemingly has no limits and an endless variety of floral shapes and colour shades gives the impression of the pattern's endless development in space," notes *Treasures from Central Asia* published by Arts and The Islamic World. Khatai, the floral design, fills the empty spaces in between the *eslimi* and the border. Prayer rugs illustrate a woven arch at one end, the *mihrab*, a prayer niche adopted from early eighth century Islamic mosque architecture. Patterns of Persian carpets are based on balance and symmetry and mastery and perfection. Thus while Nature may be asymmetrical, Man's creativity is portrayed in symmetrical terms.

According to *Persian Rugs and Carpets* by Erich Aschenbrenner, "Persian carpet patterns are intricately drawn and precisely executed. Floral shapes and arabesque tendril work predominate as well as realistically drawn birds, flowers, palmettes and rosettes. Carpets have central, multi-lobed medallions, or less frequently, repeat patterns…Field and borders are clearly separated, often by between two and five minor borders and guard stripes." These carpets are deep rich in colour and magical in design while giving a glow and a vibrancy of extraordinary dimensions.

In a marvellously illustrated book *Flowers Underfoot: Indian Carpets of the Mughal Era* published by the New York Metropolitan Museum of Art, Persian carpets are categorised into two groups. There are pictorial scenes adopted from book illustrations and patterns comprising networks of scrolling vines and palmettes sometimes symmetrical and overlaid with animals or a central medallion. The scrolling vines may be linked to animal patterns or blossom patterns or even to both.

The fine arts have also inspired carpet designers. The flourishing of arts in Persia lends itself to an exchange of creativity among artisans. Manuscript illuminator, silk embroiderers, miniature painters and metal workers all inspired carpet weavers. The rich tile-work, structure and geometric shapes of ancient monuments and cupolas of mosques also provided food for thought. The "new art styles led to stylised, vegetal, geometric and calligraphic compositions," states *Treasures from Central Asia.*

There are nineteen basic groups of patterns with sub-patterns of Persian carpets. They are named by Djavad Yassavoli in *Persian Carpets and Rugs* as the following: Patterns of Historic Monuments and Islamic Buildings, Shah Abbassi Patterns, Spiral Patterns, All-over Patterns, Derivative Patterns, Interconnected Patterns, Paisley Patterns, Tree Patterns, Turkoman/Bokhara Patterns, Hunting Ground Patterns, Panel Patterns, European Flower Patterns, Vase Patterns, Intertwined Fish Patterns, Mehrab Patterns, Striped Patterns, Geometric Patterns, Tribal Patterns and Composites.

I am now able to look at a Persian carpet and not only appreciate the immense technique and vibrancy of the piece of art but actually identify the motifs, the symbols, the setting, all of which add considerably to an amateur's appreciation and understanding of this object of sublime beauty.

Eight months had passed in Tehran, before I entered a carpet shop. We already had Afghani and Central Asian carpets, acquired in the Soviet Union. We did not need more – or so I thought. Accompanying a guest on her purchase of a Persian carpet, I fell head-over-heels in love with a Qom, all-silk prayer-niche carpet with its roses that appeared to be embossed on the silken surface. An object of such softness that I could pleat the carpet into folds like that of a sari! Sensing my increasing desperation, the carpet dealer suggested I take it home to 'see how it fits' in our home. Not yet familiar with this sales strategy, I agreed reluctantly. Of course, it 'fitted perfectly'. The magic carpet lay on our floor as if it had been waiting to belong there.

At the end of three years of living in Tehran, and sporadic forays to carpet shops, we easily succumbed to the beauty and complexities of these Persian works of art. A carpet-dealer would bait us with a shimmering object that came alive before us and then he would go 'for the kill' and elaborate on the motifs and the colour scheme and its provenance. With infinite adeptness he chipped away at our firm resolution not to succumb to temptation and in no time sold us another vision of beauty.

The power of symbols in the design of Persian carpets is reflected both in the use of colours and designs; "The 'tree of life', an ancient Mesopotamian design, insures the eternity of the soul; the 'pomegranate' brings abundance; the 'camel' promotes wealth; the 'dog' protects from sickness and from the malefic influences of the evil eye; the 'cock' heralds victory in battles; the 'carnation', a favourite symbol for weavers, brings happiness; the boteh a sort of palm or cyprus tree with a curved top, represents fecundity; 'columns on both sides of a garden' are the doors to Paradise". This interpretation of carpet symbols appears in *Iran Today* by Jean Hureau.

Among the many patterns, four in particular have enjoyed great success on the world market. So states *Persian Rugs and Carpets*. These winners are the 'garden design', in which the field is divided into small squares like flowerbeds, containing different flower motifs and figures. The 'striped design' consists exclusively of stripes in different colours and ornamentation running with the length of the carpet. The great throne-room in the Golestan Palace in Teheran is covered with striped carpets of this kind, of varying provenance and 70-80 square yards in size. 'Illustrative carpets' can depict birds, winged lions, dragons, ancient Persian hunting scenes, historical scenes, etc. In this respect, the imagination of the artist appears inexhaustible. The birds and animals are usually of silk yarn. The 'prayer niche' is also immensely popular.

Among the carpets of the Middle East and Asia Minor, one can broadly categorise four regional groups; Caucasus, Turkoman, Turkish and Persian. For eight hundred years, Caucasus, a vast mountainous region between the Black and Caspian Seas, retained great cultural, ethnic and religious diversity. Caucasian carpets are identifiable by highly stylised and geometric form, usually on a red background.

Turkoman carpets were under the early influence of Mongols and Turks. No weavings were done before the eighteenth and nineteenth centuries. A predominance of red, brown and gul an octagon motif, stylised flower motif or tribal symbolic heraldic form is to be found among Turkoman carpets. The Anatolian carpets from present-day Turkey were, in their purest form, traditional, medieval and longest lasting. The earliest Turkish pile carpets date from the thirteenth century.

Produced by the unparalleled mastery of Persian carpet makers are the classical and sublime 'garden' carpets. In these carpets, an inner field of the carpet resembles a typical Persian garden, an ideal dating back to the Achaemenian dynasty. The word 'paradise' is derived from the old Farsi word *pairidaeza*, an enclosure or garden. Iranians have always sought to create a luscious, secluded, walled haven in contrast to the harshness of the outside desert, mountains and plains. Persian carpets are also known as 'Windows to Paradise'.

The largest hand-woven Persian carpet in the world was exported to Oman in December 2000. This masterpiece has a dimension of over 5000 square metres, is made up of 1.7 billion knots and was woven over a period of three years by 500 weavers. A central medallion set in a larger medallion is found within a square of floral art. Four borders with differing floral patterns then complete the gigantic work of art. Experts have estimated a price of $5.3 million for this Persian carpet. The square carpet is actually comprised of 42 pieces, the largest of which is 1200 square metres in area and the smallest 24 square metres. A group of Iranian experts moved to Oman for a period of three months to put together the pieces. This magnificent handiwork is to find a home at Muscat's Azam Mosque.

A visit to the Arabzadeh Carpet Foundation in Tehran is an eye-opener. An artist, a carpet designer, a man versed in literature and a philosopher, Rasan Arabzadeh is known as the father of modern carpet design. He died in 1996 at the age of 84 and left a legacy of 66 masterpiece carpets to the city of Tehran. Born in 1914 to an artistic family in Tabriz, Arabzadeh received his early training in the arts – calligraphy, literature, music, poetry, sculpture and tile design - from his father. His unique carpets reflect this rich artistic background. "By combining tradition with artistic innovations in carpet patterns, he brought philosophy and literature into the realm of carpets and so changed a thousand-year-old style…The borders of literature, philosophy and mysticism were opened to him through the creation of new masterpieces. Shams and Mevlana (Sufi mystics) inspired him like the moon and the sun, and began to speak through his artistic fingers in the form of carpets," states the brochure of the Arabzadeh Carpet Foundation. Every carpet in the museum has a plaque listing the number of hours worked, the number of knots woven, the number of colours used and the dimensions of the carpet.

The Foundation displays 38 diverse and extraordinary carpets. The master artist trained prisoners - as vocational training - in the art of carpet-weaving. In a surprising move, the late Shah of Iran pardoned four prisoners who had achieved the status of accomplished carpet-weavers. Prisoners wove Arabzadeh's 'Birds in a Cage' carpet. It depicts birds perched on rods. Four birds in open cages are the four prisoners who were reprieved. The carpet hangs on the wall complete with shadows of the birds woven into it. For a second, I thought it was the play of light. It is a superb and moving masterpiece of art.

A sublime carpet is the 'Door to Heaven with the Mosque Lamp'. The two panels of the door invite one to push it open. At the top of the left panel of the door hangs a mosque lamp, lighting the way. The door appears to be woven in varying shades of brown. Yet, the plaque informs us that there were 32 colours used in the weaving of the carpet. The divine carpet took 5102 hours to weave. There are also 1,803,200 knots in the carpet.

How about a carpet of autumn leaves? Exquisite. Then there is the carpet canvas of Firdausi, the poet reciting his poems in court. The design is that of miniature art. The details achieved in facial images and dress details in the medium of carpet-weaving are entirely captivating. Arabzadeh's portrait of 'The Girl from Qasem' used 380 colours and it took 2053 hours to make. You have to remind yourself that it is a carpet, for it looks like a photograph.

If ever carpets have been made to come alive, then the carpet maestro Rashan Arabzadeh was a principal conductor of this form of traditional art. His carpets actually have the power to move you. We left behind a realm of unimaginable beauty where women put their hearts and soul into the carpet weave. The creation of the Persian carpet is testimony to its heritage. Thus it is no exaggeration when Hooshang Amirahmadi, President of the American-Iranian Council states, "More than caviar or pistachios, the Persian carpet is part of Iran's identity."

On a visit to Turkmenistan's Carpet Museum in the capital Ashkabad, we gazed at the large repository of magnificent traditional carpets. The guide spoke to us eloquently of an object that is commonly and dismissively trampled upon:

"It is easier to dig a well in the desert by a needle, than make a carpet."

"A carpet can be tender as a rose and yet stronger than a stone."

"Water is life, a house its wings and a carpet is the soul."

"Spread your carpet and I will read your soul."

BAGHDAD : CRUCIBLE OF CIVILISATION

"The most elegant country is Iraq. It is the one which most lightens the heart and sharpens the mind and in which the soul is most at ease and thought is most refined, if means suffice..."

Al-Muqaddasi, late tenth century Arab traveller.

"Among the cities of the world Baghdad stands out as the professor of the community of Islam."

Yaqut al-Rumi, thirteenth century Muslim geographer and author of the standard geographical dictionary on Islam.

"This city, called into existence as by an enchanter's wand, was second only to Constantinople in size during the Middle Ages, and was unrivalled for splendour throughout Western Asia, becoming at once, and remaining for all subsequent centuries, the capital of Mesopotamia."

*Guy Le Strange in *Baghdad During the Abbasid Caliphate*, 1900 at the earliest.[1]*

Sir Henry Rawlinson, the archetypical diplomat/scholar of the nineteenth century, suggested that Guy Le Strange write this book on the history of Baghdad in1883.

[1]* Although there is no date of publication, it was published by Clarendon Press, Oxford and the preface notes the following: Athenaeum Club, Pall Mall (London), August 1900. Furthermore, this book has passed through many hands and in itself has a remarkable history. Within the book, are the names of a 'P.M. Holt, Department of Education, Sudan' (British colonial administration); another signature with the date 'July 1917'; yet another name Mohammad Ali Aghassi , signature and date '1956' (Iranian ownership); and a date '20 August 1979' printed on an inside page that was a few months after the Iranian Revolution of February 1979. I borrowed the book from the Library of the Institute of Politics and International Studies (IPIS) in Tehran in 2001.

We were a group of seventeen Bangladeshi pilgrims from Dhaka, Dubai and Tehran who made the trip to Baghdad from Tehran in the summer of 2000. We flew from Tehran to Kermanshah, the Iranian city closest to the Iraqi border. At a hotel in Kermanshah, we transferred to an Iranian tourist bus and took the three-hour trip to the Iran/Iraq border. Following Iranian immigration formalities, we walked across to the Iraqi side for more of the same. Upon clearance from the Iraqi authorities, we boarded another bus and we were on our way to Baghdad. It was quite an uneventful journey through sparse scrubland and desolate desert under a dry hot July sun.

I had first visited Baghdad in 1973 when my late father was appointed the first Ambassador of Bangladesh to an Arab country. My second visit was in 1991 when my mother and I visited Baghdad. At the time, my husband was Bangladesh Consul-General in Dubai and we flew in from Dubai. The overland trip to Baghdad from Iran took place in July 2000 while my husband was Bangladesh Ambassador in Iran. Our group was on a pilgrimage to the shrine of the great Sufi saint, highly revered in the Indian subcontinent, Hazrat Abdul Quader Gilani, who was born in Rasht in the Gilan province of modern-day Iran but left for higher studies to Baghdad where he eventually died in1253.

Visiting the city after nearly ten years, Baghdad appeared to move at a slower pace. On my visit from Dubai in 1991, I was struck by the presence of numerous large cemeteries along the highways out of the city. These presumably were the final resting places of the large number of casualties of the long Iran-Iraq War of the 1980s. The cemeteries seemed to have been walled up since and were not visible from the highways. The wide boulevards and buildings of Baghdad were covered in a film of dust, the colour beige being the primary tone. The seasonal *khamseen* sand storm, so regular in this part of the world, would cover anything and everything in dust.

The other overwhelming presence was the innumerable banners, posters and paintings of President Saddam Hussein that plastered Baghdad. He was to be seen suited in battle fatigue dress and in naval uniform, with a pipe/without a pipe, sitting or standing. Some of the banners covered a couple of floors. However, there is something regional about this aspect of publicity. I recall seeing similar banners of Kemal Attaturk, the Founding Father of modern Turkey, hanging down the façade of a building in Ankara in the late 1970s and also of President Hafez-el-Assad in Damascus in 2000. In Syria, what were remarkable were the 'trio' photographs/posters of the President, his surviving son Bashar and his deceased son that were found pasted on walls, doors, gates, attached to public garden railings and fluttering in the breeze. A comment on this exhibition was the following: 'Here we have the Father, the son and the holy ghost.'

The former Sheraton Hotel was in a shabby state. It had most certainly seen better days. The furnishings, food and quality of service were far from ideal and was reflected in the low occupancy rate. Almost all of the few occupants at the hotel were Iranian Shi'ias who were in Baghdad for pilgrimages to the many sites of reverence including Najaf, Kufa and Kerbela. We were also there to make car journeys for *ziarats* pilgrimages to the holy sites.

What was striking was the quality of restaurants outside the hotel. We ate very well, regardless of the fact that I am extremely fond of Arab cuisine. The quality and quantity of the food was admirable. The two or three restaurants we ate at were consistently full for lunch and dinner, frequented by men and women and families. We had a memorable open-air dinner on the banks of the Tigris River. The restaurant, renowned for its *mushguf* grilled fish, was packed. I recalled a similar culinary outing in the summer of 1973. Coming from Iran, we felt the cool evening air passing through our hair, an experience we had not enjoyed for a long time. In Iran, the law of the land dictates that all females over the age of nine must observe *hejab* (mandatory head-cover) by covering their hair and by the wearing of a long coat or a *chador* over their clothes.

We briefly visited the mausoleums of the former Iraqi royal family and the National Museum. Privy to great civilisations, Islamic and Abbasid, both the form and content of the museum left much to be desired. Two long recent wars, the Iran and Iraq War in the 1980s and the Gulf War in the early 1990s, have taken their toll. Notwithstanding these two wars and others before that and for a variety of reasons, much of Iraq's bountiful cultural heritage is to be found in the collections of the most renowned museums in the world. The Louvre in Paris along with the British Museum in London have the most impressive Mesopotamian artifacts, including mega-stone statues depicting the Assyrian human head of a winged bull from the famed ancient cities of Nimrud and Nineveh in northern Iraq near the city of Mosul. Sadly, I never managed to visit the northern reaches of a country that possesses an astounding array of archaeological riches.

I had first visited Babylon in 1973, one of the most famous of the many ancient sites in Iraq, when the only visible structure was the Ishtar Gate named after an ancient god. The guide, I remember, pointed to some barren, rocky hilly terrain and informed us that this distant site was where, once upon a time, 'The Hanging Gardens of Babylon' existed - one of the Seven Wonders of the World. Apart from this, there was very little to see. In retrospect, I realise that at that time I demanded concrete evidence or I was not interested. Today, my imagination soars and I can bring the non-evident past to life. Such are the benefits of age.

This time on our visit to Babylon in 2000, I was amazed to see extensive reconstruction. Large expanses of reconstructed buildings now exist – without the benefit of the patina of age. The complex looked like a period setting for a film location. Many more years are required for the recent 'period' buildings to be enhanced by the desert winds. In the distance, was a massive building. In response to my query as to its identity, I was told it was a palace being built for President Saddam Hussein – and no photographs were allowed. I clearly recall the vista that presented itself on my first visit some three decades ago. I also recall that in the small museum that existed on site, the guide kept pointing to an object and repeating, "this is the coby, the original is in the London Museum...the Berlin Museum...the Louvre Museum". Many Arabs are unable to pronounce 'p' and substitute it with the 'b' sound.

King Hammurabi of Babylon founded the Babylonian capital. Hammurabi is most renowned for his Code of Law, forerunner of contemporary law. Some two hundred years of Assyrian rule then followed. Babylon reached its zenith during the reign of Nebuchadnezzar II. Babylon was renowned for its high-fortified walls and for the magnificence of its temples and palaces. Nebuchadnezzar built the splendid Hanging Gardens of Babylon for his wife Amytas (a Medean girl from the mountains) to allay her homesickness. Herodotus, who is believed to have visited Babylon, admiringly proclaimed, "It surpasses in splendour any city of the known world." It was Assyrian-Babylonian literature that produced the renowned 'Gilgamesh Epic', one of the most evocative epic tales of the ancient world.

Lieutenant William Heude of the Madras Military establishment wrote his travelogue in 1819 about his return journey from India to England, *A Voyage Up the Persian Gulf.* While passing through Babylon, he captures the same sentiment in a language far more eloquent, "In tracing the site of those long lost cities, of which the name only now remains to the superficial observer; the man who applies the powers of reasoning to the aid of extensive learning, will naturally associate the recollection of their former state, with those faint, yet speaking traces of a past existence which they still exhibit."

His impressions of Baghdad are also worth mentioning. "Such is the present state of this great capital: it presents something in the novelties of the scene, but more in those recollections which are allied to the memory of its former condition. Its bazaars are splendid beyond any thing we have ever seen in other parts, even, as we might almost assert, in the capital of the Turkish empire itself; its fruits as delicious and highly flavoured as any of the East; its people as highly civilised, and perhaps more courteous in their demeanour towards Europeans than those of any other Muslim city we are acquainted with. It possesses many advantages both of climate and situation, and enjoys a considerable trade; still, if it were not Baghdad, the city of wonders and romance, it might not be so highly spoken of as it generally is."

At the Bastan National Museum in Tehran is a boundary stone found in 1966 by archaeologists in Babylon that dates 2000 BC and is credited to the reign of the last ruler of the Kassiti dynasty. Also on display at the museum is a copy of the original stela pillar of black granite that has inscriptions of 282 articles of government dated 1800 BC in the reign of Hammurabi. The French architect Jacques de Morgan found the pillar in Susa (now in Iran) in 1901. This explains the current location at the Louvre Museum of the original Hammurabi stela. Alexander the Great, legend has it, died in Babylon in 323 BC. Interestingly enough, during our posting in Cairo, there was an archaeological find near Alexandria, Egypt in the mid-1990s, which Greek archaeological experts then ruled out as being the long-lost tomb of Alexander.

Baghdad, located in the fertile land of Mesopotamia, lies between the two mighty rivers, the Tigris and the Euphrates. This land is known as the 'Cradle of Civilisation' for it was this region that produced the first cultivators, early form of the calendar and the cuneiform writing. Low plains and the marshes of Mesopotamia produced the rich and fertile soil and farmland that gave rise to a sedentary lifestyle and Man's first urban settlement. The Sumerians of Mesopotamia introduced cuneiform writing in the form of pictographs. Written texts on clay tablets were accounts of grains and cattle. The best-preserved copy of cuneiform text is to be found at the Ashmolean Museum at Oxford. The etymology of the name Baghdad appears to be from two ancient Persian words Bagh (God) and Dadh (founded or foundation) thus, Baghdad would signify the city 'founded by God'. To the Arabs, Baghdad was known as Madinat-as-Salam 'the City of Peace'. It was also known as the Round City, as a result of the double wall and four gates that were built in a circular manner and equidistant.

Surrounded by a double brick wall, a deep moat and an inner wall rising to ninety feet, the newly founded city of Baghdad took four years to build. The four gates of the Round City were the Kufah Gate (SW), Basrah Gate (SE), Khorasan Gate (NE) and the Syria Gate (NW). The Gates were positioned in the direction of the named city or territory. In the centre of the Round City stood the Palace of the Caliph and the Great Mosque. Caliph Mansur decreed that the architectural plan of the new city should ensure that the Ruler should live equidistant from his citizens. Within the city was to be found the Street of the Water-Carrier, the Street of the Horse-guards, the Basrah Street or the Khorasan Street. For the most part, construction was in the form of sun-dried mud bricks that over the passage of time lapsed into its original form, "...a fact which must account for there being now hardly any ruins of the ancient city," observes Le Strange. The scarce if not non-existent remains of the Abbasid civilisation are explained by the relatively short life of the construction material. However, Baghdad has been immortalised in numerous chronicles, travel writings and historical records left by men long gone.

Today, we have only an imaginary 'old' Baghdad to fall back on. The city of Baghdad was largely built from 762 to 768 AD. Baghdad existed as the capital city for two periods with an interim capital established at Samarra for fifty-eight years. Caliph Mansur built Baghdad on the western bank of the Tigris River and it remained the capital from 762 to 836. Samarra then became the new capital – a hundred kilometres away. All that remains of Samarra today is the 50-metre high freestanding minaret set on a square plinth, composed of an anti-clockwise spiral tower, a ziggurat. The massive walls are all that is left of the mosque built in 848, according to some accounts the largest in the Islamic world. On our visit to Samarra in the summer of 2000, the wind in the open plain was fierce and the sun was scorching. We took in the height of the ziggurat while huddled along the walls of the mosque and then sought quick refuge in the car. From 892, the Abbasid capital returned to Baghdad, this time expanding significantly on the eastern bank of the Tigris.

Le Strange in *Baghdad during the Abbasid Caliphate* puts forth an assessment of Islamic dynasties. He remarks "...for in the East, it would appear to be almost a necessity of the case that every new dynasty should found a new capital." He then elaborates the founding of Islam in Mecca, the Hijrah Flight to Yathrib (later named Medina), and the departure from the Hejaz peninsula northwards to establish the expanding Muslim capital at Kufah (modern-day Iraq) by the Caliph Ali, the subsequent shift to Damascus by the Omayyads and then the move to Baghdad by the Abbasids.

The Abbasid dynasty descended from an uncle (Abbas) of the Holy Prophet and thus claim lineage with the clans of Hashemites, Kureishis and of the Holy city of Mecca. The first Abbasid Caliph Saffah defeated the last Omayyad Caliph in 750 and spent the next few years putting down every male descendant of the house of Omayyad, except for one who escaped to Spain and founded the Cordova branch of the Omayyad Empire. In 754, Saffah's brother succeeded as Caliph and in 762 moved the capital of the Abbasid rule from Damascus to Baghdad. Baghdad was destined to be the seat of power on the banks of the Tigris River for some five hundred years, from 762 till 1258, when the Mongol Hulagu, the grandson of Genghis Khan, razed it to the ground. Hulagu breached the walls of Baghdad in eight days, ransacked the city and, for good measure, had the last Abbasid Caliph Mustasim put to death. Baghdad lost its libraries, universities, mosques, treasures and hundred thousands of inhabitants. Never again would Baghdad serve as the crown of medieval Muslim civilisation.

The Mongols had earlier also ravaged Baghdad. The 'scorched

earth' policy occurred between the years 1220 and 1225 under the helm of Genghis Khan. Ala al Deen al Juwaini, the Persian historian writing in *History of the Conqueror of the World* despaired. "In the Muslim countries devastated by Genghis Khan, not one in a thousand of the inhabitants survived...If from now until the day of the Resurrection, nothing hindered the natural increase of the population, it could never reach one-tenth of its density before the Mongol conquest." In 1401, the Mongols once again attacked Baghdad. This time Tamerlane levelled the city in true Mongol tradition. The repeated razing to the ground of Baghdad led an Egyptian historian to lament "The very word civilisation is no longer applied to Baghdad."

The choice of the banks of the Tigris for the new Abbasid capital was a strategic decision based on the new empire's orientation further eastward towards Persia and Central Asia, the source of Abbasid power. Damascus was, in the new equation, too westward in its location and stance. The Romans, Greeks and Byzantines had directed earlier power play in the region. The shift was now definitely eastwards and this was reflected in the location of the new capital city of Baghdad. It was in an advantageous position on the Tigris River, close to the Euphrates and not far from the Persian Gulf.

John Bagot Glubb, more popularly known as Glubb Pasha, in his classic book on the Arabs, *A Short History of the Arab Peoples* argues: "The movement of the capital from Damascus to Baghdad thus resulted to a large extent in the orientalisation, not only of the Arab empire, but of the world of Islam itself... While the Roman Republic had been ruled by Italians, the empire was an interracial, Mediterranean commonwealth. The Arab Revolution of 750, in the same manner, transformed the purely Arab empire of the Umaiyads into a Muslim state. The Abbasids were, of course, Arabs, the official language was Arabic, as the language of the Roman Empire had been Latin, but advancement was henceforward open to all races." Henceforward, growth and prosperity of the Islamic world veered eastwards. Baghdad was to be that window opening towards the east.

Along with Byzantine/Constantinople, Baghdad, in its Golden Years, was the largest city in the known world with some million inhabitants of various nationalities. It was the celebrated centre for statecraft, judiciary, administration and defence of the Abbasid Empire. The Golden Age of Islam lasted from 750 to 1050. The Abbasid realm, in its commercial prosperity, touched the present territorial boundaries of Iran, Iraq, Syria, Egypt and the Maghreb countries of North Africa. Trade relations existed with the Horn of Africa and the Saharan region, Central Asia, the Far East, India and the Persian Gulf. The Abbasid long reign and its progress in the areas of art, culture and intellect contributed to the Renaissance of Islam declares Yves Thoraval in *Dictionnaire de Civilisation Musulmane.* According to Philip Hitti in *Capital Cities of Arab Islam*: "Political prestige, financial supremacy and intellectual activity were the three features of the age." While Hitti termed Damascus 'the 'Imperial Capital', he named Baghdad the 'Intellectual Capital'.

To the markets of Baghdad flowed glassware from Lebanon, pearls from Bahrain, brocade and carpets from Persia, metalwork from Syria and gold, silver and marble works from Khorasan. There was a vibrant regional trade in olive oil, honey, sugar, rose water, wheat, barley, dates and cattle. Under the Abbasids "Arab merchants did business in China, Indonesia, India and East Africa. Their ships were by far the largest and the best appointed in Chinese waters or in the Indian Ocean. Under their highly developed banking system, an Arab businessman could cash a cheque in Canton on his bank account in Baghdad," declares John Bagot Glubb in *A Short History of the Arab Peoples.*

Even much later, according to J.J. Benjamin II in his description of trade in Baghdad in the mid-nineteenth century, the commercial hub that was Baghdad did not appear to have waned. "The importance and extent of the commerce of the town are universally known; enormous caravans, some more than 2000 camels strong, come and go daily in ceaseless change from and to all parts. I was told that twice a year a caravan of more than 6000 camels went to Damascus. The trade with India is completely in the hands of the Jews, who possess manufactories in Calcutta, Bombay, Singapore and even at Canton. The most important articles of trade in these countries are indigo, spices, silk stuffs, some kinds of rare fruits and dyes, which come from different provinces of China. From Persia come chiefly carpets, shawls, silk, tombako (a kind of tobacco), wines and almonds. From the same country are also obtained precious stones, rubies, emeralds and corals; and from the Island Rein in the Persian Gulf beautiful pears are procured."

At its apogee, Baghdad "had a thousand physicians, an enormous free hospital, a regular postal service, several banks (some of which had branches as far a field as China), an excellent water-supply system, a comprehensive sewage system, and a paper mill. Indeed, it was in Syria that the Occidentals, who until their arrival in the Orient used only parchment, learned the art of manufacturing paper from straw," elaborates Amin Maalouf in his highly evocative book *The Crusades through Arab Eyes.*

Ibn Khaldun, writing in the fourteenth century, recognised the movements of artisans from city to city. On the transfer of artistic expertise, he remarked, "When the realm of a dynasty is large and far flung with many provinces and subjects, workers are very plentiful and can be brought together from all sides and regions and superior social organisation and engineering skill are present." Caliph Mansur brought in workmen and artisans from Babylonia, Persia, Mosul and Syria. One of his four chief overseers was Imam Abu Hanifah, the founder of the Hanifites, the earliest of the four schools of orthodox Sunni theology. The mosque built in his honour is, in its present state, one of the finest mosques I have seen anywhere. In fact, it reminds me of the late twentieth century built Jumeirah mosque in Dubai. Both are simple, serene and sublime in their off-white arabesque stuccowork exterior. The Arab traveller Ibn Batutah, who visited Baghdad in 1327, described the shrine of Abu Hanifah noting that food was here distributed daily to all in want and that this was the only place in Baghdad that such charity existed.

The earliest tribute to Baghdad came from the writers of the ninth century namely, Yakubi, Ibn Rustah and Ibn Serapion. They described the fortification walls, the canal system, roads, suburbs and topography of the city. Masudi the historian wrote in the tenth century chronicle *The Meadows of Gold.* Khatib wrote the *History of Baghdad* in 1058. Khatib described the Greek Embassy in Baghdad and the Palaces of the Caliphs. On a pilgrimage to Mecca in 1155, the Persian poet Khakani visited Baghdad en route and in eloquent poetic terms described "the gardens as equal of those of Paradise; the waters of the Tigris, which are only comparable in their pellucid ness to the tears of the Virgin Mary, the river surface is everywhere covered with boats which liken to the cradle of Jesus for their grace of build." The Jewish traveller Benjamin of Tudela visited Baghdad in 1160 and described the Jewish community resident in Baghdad. Much later the well travelled French jeweller J.B. Tavernier passed through Baghdad in 1632 en route to India and stopped in Baghdad again in 1652 on his return journey from India.

A building boom in the tenth century in Baghdad, resulted in a palace being built at the cost of 500,000 pounds sterling, at a price quoted in the early 1900s. A number of dykes were built to halt inundation from the over-flowing Tigris River. The Park of the Wild Beasts was the zoo of the day. The Palace of the Tree had a tree made of silver that weighed some 50,000 ounces. The tree stood in the midst of a tank of water. The branches of the silver tree had mechanical birds in gold and silver that sang. Adud-ad-Dawlah built the great hospital Bimaristan in western Baghdad. According to the Spanish Arab traveller Ibn Jubayr, who visited Baghdad in 1184 while returning from his pilgrimage to Mecca, the Bimaristan "was an immense palace, situated on the Tigris bank, with many chambers and separate wards furnished like a royal abode. Every Monday and Thursday, the city physicians attended there to visit patients, for whom both food and medicine were gratuitously prepared by servants especially appointed for this office. The building was plentifully supplied with water from the river."

Ibn Jubayr has provided the most vivid accounts of his impressions of the famed city and in one he states, "In the whole of Baghdad, Ibn Jubayr further counted eleven mosques where the Friday prayers were said, and of hamaams, so many that none could tell their number, one person assuring him that there were over two thousand, and he adds that in these the halls were so finely plastered with bitumen, brought from Basrah, that the visitor imagined the walls to be lined with slabs of black marble. Of colleges – each more magnificent than a palace – over thirty were to be counted, the greatest being the Nizamiyah."

In 1065, the Wazir Nizam-ol-Molk established the Madrasah of Nizamiyah. He was a friend of the astronomer and poet Omar Khayyam. Among its celebrated lecturers was the renowned theologian Ghazzali and Bahadin, the biographer of Saladin. In 1185, Ibn Jubayr described it "as the most splendid of the thirty and odd colleges when then adorned the city of East Baghdad." Hamd-Allah, the Persian geographer raved about "the Mother of the Madrasahs' in Baghdad in 1339. However, by the mid-eighteenth century, Danish traveller Carstein Niebuhr found no trace of the once illustrious learning centre.

Abbasid Caliph Mustansir built the Madrasah of the Mustansiriyah. In a phrase aptly coined by Jason Goodwin in 'Lords of the Horizon' in which he analyses the wide administrative reach of the Ottoman Empire, Goodwin refers to "the spirit of imperial benevolence" practised by the Ottomans but also equally applicable to other Islamic reigns. By all accounts, it surpassed anything previously seen in Islam; in terms of architecture, ornamentation, furnishings, library, wealth of its charitable foundations and reputation. It contained four separate law schools for the four schools of Islamic theology: Hanafi, Maliki, Hanbali and Shafii schools. Two of the four founders of the Islamic theological schools were buried in Baghdad. Ibn Batutah described the *madrasah* (as did Hamd-Allah) as "the most beautiful building then existing in Baghdad." In 1750, Carstein Niebuhr visited Baghdad on his way from Arabia and also provided evidence of its existence and splendour. In the year 2000, we wandered through a central rectangular courtyard with arched doors leading into rooms of the *madrasah*. Much of what we saw was reconstructed, leaving its famed splendour to our imagination.

Baghdad evolved over time into a capital city attracting the best of the region's human capital. Philip Hitti declares in *Capital Cities of Arab Islam*, "In brief, hardly an intellectual movement appeared in early medieval Islam without Baghdad's sharing in it." Artists, philosophers, traders, intellectuals, architects, theologians and scientists flocked to this radiant city. The Persian-speaking Al-Khawarizmi born in Kheva (in modern-day Uzbekistan) was drawn to Baghdad in the late eighth century during the reign of Caliph Al-Mamun. Al-Khawarizmi became a major contributor to astronomy, geography and mathematics. He developed the decimal system – algorithm or algorism – that is named after him. His *Suratul Ard* (The Outlook of Earth) served as a major textbook in geography in Arab and European academia. Hunain Ibn Ishaq was born and died in Baghdad in the ninth century. Historians regard him as the most noble of all Arab physicians and medical scholars. His renowned *Al-Masa'il fi at-Tib il Muta'alimeen* (Treatment of Diseases: Guide to Medical Students) served as a major textbook in the field of medicine in the Arab world and Europe. *The Compendium of Astronomy*, an Arabic work, was in use as a textbook in Europe until the sixteenth century. It is to Ibn-al-Furat, a tenth century vizier of the caliphs of Baghdad, that we owe the following Machiavellian-genre saying: "The basis of government is trickery; if it succeeds and endures, it becomes policy."

The development of paper in the seventh century facilitated the diffusion of knowledge and contributed significantly to the establishment of libraries as centres for learning. A copy of the Holy

Quran that was copied and decorated in Baghdad in the year 1000 can be found at the Chester Beatty Collection in Dublin, Ireland. It is written in very fine Arabic *naskh* lettering. Such calligraphers were regarded as 'jewellers with words'. Through Sicily, southern Italy and Andalusia, the contributions of Islamic civilisation filtered through to Europe. The fifth Caliph was Harun El-Rachid (766-809) whose name is familiar through the ages through the epic tale 'A Thousand and One Nights'. "With its myriads of mosques, palaces and government offices it was a centre of power, wealth and piety. With its gardens pavilions and patios it was also essentially a city of pleasure – 'a Paris of the ninth century' in Richard Burton's phrase," observed Peter Mansfield in *The Arabs*. The Abbasids contributed significantly to the flourishing of Islamic art that went on to bloom to unparalleled heights in Turkey, Egypt, Iran, Afghanistan and Central Asia.

A few years before the Mongols ravaged Baghdad in 1258, Yakut, a native of the city, wrote *Geographical Dictionary* which "forms perhaps the greatest storehouse of geographical facts compiled by any one man during the Middle Ages," declares Le Strange. Describing Baghdad, Yakut wrote, "Immense streets, none less than forty cubits wide, traversed the city from one end to the other, dividing it into blocks or quarters, each under the control of an overseer or supervisor who looked after the cleanliness, sanitation and the comfort of the inhabitants." A few years after the destruction of Madinat-as-Salaam, the Persian historian Tabakat-i-Nasiri wrote an account of the Mongol siege of Baghdad in 1260. Wassaf wrote another account of the Mongol invasion. He was a Persian historiographer of the Mongol Il-Khan dynasty of Persia.

It is worth noting that the tombs of the Abbasid Caliphs lie scattered throughout the realm of their wide-flung empire. Their presence can be found "from the pilgrim road near Mecca to Tus in Khurasan, or the gate of Tarsus in the north-west for the burial-place of the Caliph was where he had died, on the road, so to speak, journeying in the affairs of Islam," concludes Le Strange.

In an eloquent tribute to the contribution of Mesopotamian culture and thought to western heritage, George Roux in *Ancient Iraq* observes, "Classical scholars, long dazzled by the so-called 'Greek Miracle', have now come to realise the full impact of oriental influences upon the formative phase of Greek thought art and ethics – and the Orient, throughout most of pre-classical antiquity, was to a great extent culturally dependent upon Mesopotamia."

On our brief visit to Baghdad in the summer of 2000, we discovered a nation with a glorious past that is little known. The historical 'Intellectual Light' of the region receives scant recognition today. Undoubtedly, Iraq is a crucible of civilisation.

PETRA : GOLDEN SILENCE

"Match me such a marvel save in Eastern clime
A rose-red city half as old as Time…"

John W. Burgon

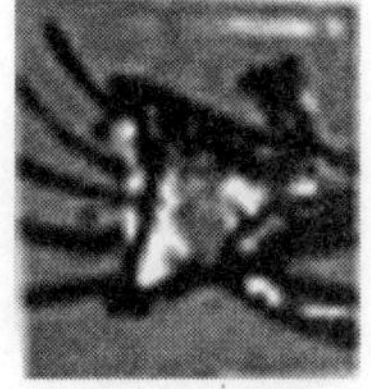

Nothing prepares one for Petra. No photographs in dated *Life* magazines, no double-spread pictures in *National Geographic*, no vivid accounts by seasoned travellers though the ages can initiate one to the spectacular power of Petra. At the first glimpse of the ancient city of Petra I was mute with awe and amazement; I actually gulped with emotion. In these days of exaggeration and over-kill, to have an experience and not be disappointed, to have an encounter that is greater than one's expectations, to possess a feeling that literally takes one's breath away is tremendously powerful and memorable.

The Nabataeans, an ancient people of northwest Arabia, built Petra. Their capital, east of the present village of Wadi Musa, is situated in what is now southwest Jordan. The Nabataeans were originally nomads from the Arabian Peninsula who settled and evolved into a monarchy and, through extensive trading, achieved prosperity and power. The stronghold and treasure-city of the Nabataeans is referred to as Sela (Hebrew for rock) in the Bible. The Arabs called the city Wadi Musa, the Valley of Moses. Petra is Greek for the 'city of rock'.

Petra was chosen as the Nabatean capital for its almost inaccessible retreat in a spot sheltered from the desert. Once secure, Petra accumulated its riches and subsequently its power. Philip Hitti, the eminent historian wrote in *Syria: A Short History*, "Arabic in speech, Aramaic in writing, Semitic in religion, Hellenistic in art and architecture, the Nabataean culture was synthetic, superficially Hellenic but basically Arabian, and so it remained."

The strategic location of Petra has been explained in *Yesterday and Today: The Holy Land: Lithographs and Diaries* by David Roberts. Fabio Bourbon writes in the accompanying text: "Petra developed as a rock city at the intersection of three gorges. Later it became a centre for offering haven and defence for the local nomadic populations. The decision by the Nabataeans to choose Petra as their capital was therefore based on considerations of security. Hidden as it was in the mountains, with very few easily guarded points of access, Petra constituted a secure safeguard for the wealth that the Nabataeans had accumulated with their caravan trade."

Petra lay in the land of Edom between the Dead Sea and the Gulf of Aqaba at the crossroads of the great caravan routes from Gaza on the Mediterranean Sea and Damascus, from Eilat on the Red Sea and the Persian Gulf. From the fourth century BC until the second century AD, Petra was the capital of the Nabataean kingdom, a unique trading nation. By the first century BC, the empire included a large portion east of Palestine – from Damascus in the north to the Red Sea in the south, including ancient Philadelphia now the modern city of Amman. The commercial city dominated the silk, spice and slave routes from Damascus to Aqaba. The Greek historian Diodorus of Sicily wrote of the Nabataeans who were shepherds and caravan traders "carrying to the Mediterranean Sea incense, myrrh and the most precious aromatic herbs delivered to them from so-called happy Arabia." Strabo, the ancient Greek geographer, also mentioned products imported from Petra: copper and iron, purple raiment, styrax and statues.

Petra was situated at the crossroad between Arabia, Egypt, Palestine, Phoenicia, Syria, India, China and the Mediterranean Basin. In 106 AD, Petra was annexed by Rome and it became the Arabia Petrae province of the Roman Empire. At its peak (509 BC to 330 AD) the Holy Roman Empire extended from the British Isles to the Caspian Sea. In time, as all empires in decline, the empire was reduced to being neither Holy, nor Roman, nor an Empire.

New trade routes bypassed Petra that led to its commercial decline. Palmyra - (in present-day Syria) and another architectural and historical gem in the Middle East - emerged as a major trading centre at another junction of caravan routes, under the powerful reign of Queen Zenobia. Petra's rival, Palmyra took away most of Petra's trade. Jerash, another stunning city testimony to a glorious past which lies to the north of Amman close to the present-day Jordanian/Syrian border, also emerged as a rival major trading caravan capital. The power of Petra slowly diminished and it was conquered by the Muslims in the seventh century and captured by the Crusaders in the twelfth century. Two natural calamities in the form of earthquakes in 363 and 749 AD contributed to Petra's demise. The 'city of rock' fell into ruins.

Jealously guarded by local Bedouin inhabitants, Petra lay 'undiscovered' for centuries. The commercial value of its once thriving existence passed into history. Following the rediscovery of the 'secret city' by the Swiss explorer Johann Ludwig Burckhardt in 1812, the 'new' appreciation of the 'dead city' by generations many times removed – visitors – evolved slowly. Burckhardt studied Arabic for three years in London and Cambridge. He was a member of The African Association, a body formed to fight slavery and study the hitherto unknown economic opportunities presented in a little known continent. He was sent to Syria by the African Association to study the Arab and Muslim ways before proceeding to the Sahara. According to Henri-Paul Eydoux in *In Search of Lost Worlds*, "He travelled in Arab dress and practised all the Muslim rites. In fact his knowledge of Islam was so profound that some time later he was able to stay for four months in Mecca without arousing the slightest suspicions about his nationality." After his visit to Petra, he proceeded to Cairo but never made it to the Sahara. He died of dysentery in 1817 and was buried in a Muslim cemetery in Cairo under his assumed name, Ibrahim Abdullah. His visit to Petra resulted in a sketchy study of the area and its ruins. His fear of discovery was a major constraint.

The next recorded travellers to Petra were two Frenchmen, Leon de Laborde, an architect and explorer and Maurice Linant, an engineer. In the late 1820s, fuelled by curiosity and enthusiasm and in local dress, they reached Petra. More fortunate than Burckhardt, their observations, sketches and studies have come down to us in the form of three volumes published in Paris in 1830. The book is *Voyage de l'Arabe Petree* by Leon de Laborde and Maurice Linant. According to

Henri-Paul Eydoux, "the illustrations, down to the minutest detail, are as accurate as photographs." Laborde went on to become a member of the parliament under Louis-Philippe and a senator under the Second Empire. Linant later became chief engineer of the Suez Canal. Leon de Laborde raved in his writings about the city of Petra. "The most extraordinary spectacle, the most magical picture of nature in its grandiose creation that men in their vainglorious ambition have bequeathed to the curiosity of generations to come."

David Roberts, a Scot and renowned Middle Eastern lithographer, reached Petra on March 6, 1839. Upon the payment of a handsome amount of money, Roberts was allowed to stay in Petra for five days to sketch and take notes. His extraordinary lithographs, with their minute attention to detail, have come down to us along with his informative diary. He wrote in his journal: "6th – Petra. Today we encamped in the centre of the remains of this extraordinary city, which is situated in the midst of mountains, surrounded by desert, but abounding in every vegetable production…"

In a superbly descriptive summary of El Khasne, the monumental mountain-cut building in Petra, Fabio Bourbon writes, "Just as soon as camp had been made, Roberts decided to go and see the Khasne, certainly the best known monument in Petra, as well as one of the wonders of the ancient world. In order to better understand the profound impact which the sudden appearance of this superb creation of human genius has upon the visitor, it should be noted that Petra is located in an extremely secure location, since the only easy access to the place is set to the east, and consists of a narrow stream bed, enclosed by two cliff walls that are separated in certain points by no more than twelve feet one from the other. This passage, now known as the Sik, is about two and a half miles in length… About halfway up, at a point where the Sik suddenly changes direction, carved into the cliff, one can see the Khasne, a funerary temple that has no rivals on earth. The contrast between the delicate pink façade of the building and the shadowy Sik is quite impressive, while the symmetry of the façade is absolute, the proportions are exquisitely tasteful, and the degree of conservation is practically perfect." (*Yesterday and Today: The Holy Land: Lithographs and Diaries* by David Roberts.)

Further on in the book, Bourbon enthuses once again about Petra. "...they certainly constitute one of the most singular and enchanting monumental complexes of the ancient world. There are two sets of reasons: first, the exceptional quality of the architectural creations themselves and second, the odd and perhaps unique location of the city, clamped between volcanic hills, set deep in narrow gorges, enhanced by the remarkable colour of the rock from which the buildings have been carved..."

In his journal David Roberts wrote: "6th - Our first stroll was to the Khasne, and I cannot say whether I was most surprised at the building or its extraordinary position. It stands, as it were, in an immense niche in the rocks, and the fine colour of the stone, and perfect preservation of the minute details, give it the appearance of having been recently finished..." His following entry reads: "7th – I am more and more astonished and bewildered with this wonderful city, which must be five or six miles each way in extent; and every ravine has been inhabited, even to the tops of the mountains. The valley has been filled with temples, public buildings, triumphal arches, and bridges, all of which have been laid prostrate, with the exception of one arch, and one temple, and of this temple the portico has fallen. The style of the architecture varies from all I have ever seen and in many of its parts is a curious combination of the Egyptian with the Roman and the Greek orders. The stream still flows through it as heretofore; the shrubs and wild flowers flourish luxuriantly; every crevice of the rock is filled with them, and the air is perfumed with the most delicious fragrance."

At one point in his stay in Petra, David Roberts expressed dismay and felt discouraged and inadequate to the challenge of depicting such marvellous creations on paper. Yet Roberts has most certainly captured the extraordinary beauty of Petra and has devoted thirteen evocative sketches to it. People vanish and leave behind their works of art. Is not culture that which remains when all else is gone?

An eager visitor to Petra in the early twentieth century was T.E. Lawrence. In 1914, Lawrence of Arabia was appointed to make an archaeological survey of the Negev Desert and northern Sinai under the aegis of the Palestine Exploration Fund. Others have suggested that the real reason for the mission was to study the area under Ottoman rule in the eventuality of war breaking out between the two powers, the Ottoman Empire and Britain. Britain had a major stake in the Suez Canal, the Red Sea and the Indian Ocean, the naval route to its 'Jewel in the Crown', India.

In the immensely readable biography of T.E. Lawrence, Michael Asher describes Lawrence's trip to Petra. Lawrence succumbed to the magic of the rock-city. He too was mesmerised and "unprepared for the overwhelming effect of the place." Asher writes, "Lawrence decided to march north up the Wadi 'Araba to Petra, the ancient Nabataean city carved in solid rock, which he had wanted to reach since his first expedition in Syria in 1909. Photography was forbidden, but despite his escort he managed to get half a dozen photographs by pretending to be suffering from diarrhoea and taking frequent leave. He sent his twelve camels and five camel-men on to Wadi Musa at the entrance to Petra and he and Dahoum stalked off around Mount Hor. While alone, they discovered a route through the hills which Bedu raiding-parties used when heading for Sinai. Lawrence found Petra to be a feast. Though he had read a great deal about it previously, he was unprepared for the overwhelming effect of the place. It was not the rock-cut tombs and temples which awed him but the natural beauty of the site with its marbled colours of red, black and grey, its great cliffs and pinnacles, and its gorge or Siq, like an undersea cavern, abrim with oleanders, ivy and ferns. For once he felt his powers of description inadequate. "Be assured," he wrote to Edward Leeds, "that till you have seen it you have not the glimmering of an idea how beautiful a place can be."

Agatha Christie was inspired to set her 1938 novel *Appointment with Death* in Petra. She dedicated the book to 'Richard and Myra Mallock to remind them of their journey to Petra'. Andre Parrot, a French archaeologist working in the Middle East in the 1930s and 1940s, was moved to say, "It seems that one has entered a world in which only Titans could live and, moreover, one expects that they may at any moment materialise."

"There are few places in the world, especially those easy to reach, whose impact on the visitor can be compared to the emotions aroused when, after rounding a bend in the narrow gorge called the Siq, he finds himself face to face with the tall façade of the 'Treasury' the most famous monument in Petra. At every return, the emotion presents itself anew..." *Art and History of Jordan* (2000 edition). All references to Petra belong in the superlative category.

Our journey to Petra started from Amman at an auspicious time, January 1, 2001, a new year in the region of the 'cradle of civilisation' and the birthplace of the three monotheistic religions.

In a hired car, we drove across beige slate soil on which a few scattered sheep were well camouflaged. Gradually, the mainly flat plains turned into rolling dunes in a desert, the landscape bereft of man or habitation. We were moving through winding, rock-strewn valleys and stretches of windswept desert. What lay before us was a vast expanse of inhospitable land. The January sun was warm and comforting in the enclosed space of the car. I wondered what it would be like in the heat of July or August. We were in the middle of nowhere; a trip in the height of summer would have plunged us into a world of scorching sand and searing sun. The rolling dunes were left behind as we now slowly roller coasted over mountains and curved around bends in our approach to the place I had wanted to see since childhood.

We passed the touristy 'support-city' of Petra with its hotels, hostels, cafes, restaurants and souvenir shops. We then descended into a valley, the valley of Wadi Mousa, and left our car at the Visitors Centre parking lot. A plaque marks Petra as designated by UNESCO on the World Heritage List "as a universal value of cultural or natural site that deserves protection for the benefit of all humanity." Petra received this recognition in 1984. Accosted by a number of men offering donkey, horse, camel or carriage rides that we resolutely managed to avoid, my husband, our daughter and I started off on the trek of a lifetime.

The first sight of the monumental rock façade carvings that is characteristic of Petra came within a few minutes of our walk. The area that we were walking through was wide, with differing heights of cliffs surrounding us. To the left stood a majestic row of columns with openings at ground level with obelisk-type pinnacles at a higher level. These monuments were several storeys high. These were some of the oldest tombs in Petra, dating to the third century BC. Hellenistic and Egyptian artistic features mark them. One had to remind oneself that what we were seeing were sandstone cliffs carved to appear as buildings complete with rooms inside.

Gradually, the path became narrower and the cliffs appeared more like mountains. The earlier beige colouring of the ground and cliffs started turning a darker shade of beige, bordering on pink and brown. To our right we could see the mouth of a man-made tunnel carved within the mountain, six metres wide and eighty-eight metres in length. This is known as the Wadi Muddhlim Trail and was made to channel water to the inhabited area.

We then entered the Siq, the natural gorge of spectacular geological formation; the result of a natural calamity that split the mountain into two. It is the dry bed of an ancient stream that is some two kilometres long and the width narrows to some three metres in places. The jagged cliffs soar into the sky. In places, the colours of the sandstone cliffs veer from beige to dark pink to reddish-brown to moss green, shadows where sunlight never touches the rocky façade. At the entrance of the Siq, constructed way above our heads we saw the base of a triumphal arch that had once graced the mouth of the gorge. This was the path for religious processions and the gateway to Petra. There was a relief sculpture carved into the rock depicting a caravan of camels. The hydraulic skills of the ancient Nabataeans are further demonstrated by the carving of a channel for the transport of precious water along the two sides of the gorge. The clearly visible rock-cut channel is at about waist-level height.

As we ambled along the path of the Siq, we took in the incredible natural creation moulded by the forces of wind and rain. The elements had in themselves turned into artists. There were even stripes of black streaking the contour of a pinkish-brown rock. Our heads kept turning and our eyes kept lifting to try and catch sight of the seemingly never-ending height of the enclosing cliffs. In the peak season of tourist travel, we were still fortunate enough to be the sole travellers on the route. We were alone to enjoy the experience of a lifetime; it was unreal and unforgettable.

We were so immersed in taking in this natural wonder that we were suddenly stunned to find ourselves out of the gorge and we stood speechless, gaping at a vast opening in the midst of mountains. We were standing before El Khasne, The Treasury. All my earlier research had not prepared me for this. I now understood the fierce emotional impression felt by countless others through the ages.

This superb creation of human genius moved me to tears. Probably built by Aretas IV between 85 and 84 BC, the façade of El Khasne is 40 metres high and 28 metres in width. A stairway leads to three Corinthian columns, each over forty feet high, on each side of a portico. Another stairway leads us through a large doorway into a large cool vestibule measuring 46 feet long and 18 feet deep. There are small chambers on both sides. We were now well inside the mountain! The exterior façade of the building has a second floor-level where three elegant pavilions have been carved out of the mountain. The conical roof has an urn perched on the top. The Bedouins believed that a pot of gold was to be found within the urn. There are a number of bullet marks on the surface, the result of attempts to break the urn and be showered with its riches. These attempts were not successful and the urn retains its position of splendour and looks down upon us mortals.

The multi-level façade of this unbelievable architectural achievement is sprinkled with fine sculptures of eagles, lions, horses and human figures - some intact and some broken. The delicate architecture is enhanced by the warm pink-rose tint of the excavated areas of the building that contrasts sharply with the dark brown colour of the intact surface of the mountain. This building, cut deep into the mountain, speaks of pure elegance and refinement. There is not a jarring or disproportional spot anywhere.

There has been ample debate about the purpose of El Khasne. Although the Arabic El Khasne means 'The Treasury', there is speculation that the more likely purpose of the construction was a funerary temple or a tomb or even a burial place for a number of people. No such remains, however, were ever found. Mystery only adds to the allure of this sumptuous building. Tearing ourselves away from this magical spot, we continued our walk along the only path out of El Khasne.

A short while later, the narrow ravine once again opened into a broad space. We were now in the middle of the 'Street of Facades'. To our left was a beehive of tombs carved into the mountains at various levels. This was a veritable Valley of Tombs. These tombs were not simply holes cut into the mountains with decorative interiors but openings cut into the rocks with intricate and painstaking decorations on the external surface.

At specified spots along the way were a number of boys and men offering rides on donkeys, horses or camels. A particularly imaginative salesman called out; "Want an air-conditioned-ride in a

Ferrari?" We walked on. There were also tattoo-marked Bedouin women selling beaded necklaces, T-shirts and 'new' antiques.

The next awesome sight was the Theatre. Carved entirely into the facade of the mountain, it has thirty-three terraces and can accommodate some three thousand people. The thought of individuals hammering away at a mountain in order to create a magnificent amphitheatre in the first century AD (or any time for that matter) was simply mind-blowing.

Sitting in the Theatre, we paused and took in this amazing site. We were surrounded by sandstone cliffs with sculpted facades of columns and friezes that housed tombs, some of them placed high up in the mountain range. The tomb known as the Tomb of Silk or Rainbow Tomb rose above us. The columns cut into the mountain have been eroded by wind and time. The names of the tomb have been given in recognition of the incredible colour range of the rock. "Extremely eroded by atmospheric agents, a series of four attached half columns can be barely made out of the façade, while the name comes from the blue, white, yellow and bright red striations on the horizontal bands of sandstone which recall watered silk", is the vivid description provided by *Art and History in Jordan.*

Continuing our walk in a daze, we passed on our left a large broad terraced construction that at street level contained the ruins of shops. USAID was involved in some restoration work here. We were now on the main street in downtown Petra. Here lay the remains of baths, *agora* (marketplaces), squares and the gymnasium. We were walking on the ancient paved road in Petra. We walked under the ruin of a triumphal arch with three gates of considerable size. Fallen blocks of stone indicated that the once triumphal arch was richly decorated with Graeco-Roman art. Further ahead, UNESCO was restoring the Qasr Al-Bint Temple. Within the ruins one could make out the courtyard with its central altar and stairway leading to a columned building. Subsequent inhabitants, the Romans and Arabs, used the site as a quarry.

We were then in the middle of a vast space where the remains of a stream were visible. Here was a modern-day refreshment spot with cafes and restaurants and, importantly, clean toilets. The surrounding mountain range still bore evidence of the monumental Nabataean facades with their harmonious blend of Assyrian, Egyptian, Hellenistic and Roman features. What remained to be seen was El Deir, The Monastery. However, we decided to give it a miss since it meant a further trek following an extremely rough trail which would then become a steep stairway, nearly a mile long, cut into the side of the mountain. A climb of nearly a thousand feet was involved as well. Up to now, we had been more than three hours on our feet on more or less level terrain. We had also reached a saturation point in our ability to take in any more of this wondrous spectacle.

David Roberts has described El Deir in his journal: "8th March 1839 – Today we wound our way up a steep ravine, a broken staircase extending about a mile. We reached a building, rarely visited, called Deir, or Convent, which is hewn out of the face of the rock...The view here is magnificent, embracing the valley of El Ghor, the mount Hor (the tomb of Aaron crowning the summit), and the whole defile, leading through rocks which make you giddy to look over, while the ancient city, in all its extent, is seen stretching along the valley..."

We made a U-turn and headed back via the same and only route out of the ancient city of Petra. My daughter and I made the way back to the car park on foot. My husband succumbed to the temptation of a camel ride from this point to El Khasne. Sitting in between the two humps of the camel with one leg folded across the other and the *keffiyeh* Arab headdress, he sauntered off into the setting sun. I suddenly recalled Peter O'Toole in the film *Lawrence of Arabia.*

JERASH : RECALLING 'BEN HUR'

'The ruins present the most imposing view of its kind that I have ever seen.'

Guillaume Rey, nineteenth century
French traveller in the Middle East

Our daughter was suffering from ruin-fatigue. How many more three-quarters of a wall, half a column and an imaginary roof could one see? She wanted to get back to the twenty-first century – Internet and MTV. However, the will of the mother prevailed and we stopped at Jerash in Jordan on our drive back to Damascus from Amman. How could we be so close to one of the largest and most densely built ancient Roman colonial cities and simply drive away from it?

Jerash was another important regional trading capital of its time. At its zenith, Jerash had close commercial ties with the Nabataean city of Palmyra in modern-day Syria. Henri-Paul Eydoux in *In Search of Lost Worlds* makes an interesting analogy. "Trade carried on across deserts can be compared with maritime trade. Posting stations and land bases are necessary. Gerasa was one of these: silks, spices, incense, precious stones, ivory and other valuable goods changed hands there, enriching both those who brought and those who forwarded them." Jerash was inhabited virtually without interruption for over one thousand years. Hellenistic, Nabataean, Roman, Byzantine, Omayyad, Abbasid reigns were flourishing periods for the city.

There is some evidence that Jerash was inhabited in Neolithic times. However, it was during the time of Alexander the Great in 332 BC that the Hellenistic settlement became prominent. The Roman emperor Pompey conquered the region in 63 BC. Entrance to the ancient Roman city is via the obligatory triple-gated Triumphal Arch. A generous donor, Flavius Agrippa built it in order to commemorate a visit to Jerash by the Roman emperor Hadrian in 129 AD. Far-flung reaches of the empire demanded periodical visits by the ruler to stabilise and protect colonies and establish Roman suzerainty. Such visits ensured perpetuation of power via tactics of divide and rule and a system of check and balance. Interestingly enough, it was Julius Caesar who declared, "I am not king but Caesar." 'Caesar' became 'Kaiser' as the term used for the Germanic Prussian ruler and 'Czar' for the Russian emperor.

Romans were also ambitious in their civic embellishments and motivated to display, via their public works, a sense of majestic presence, thereby leaving the mark of the Roman imperial order. Vestiges of the power and glory of the expansive empire are reflected in scattered indelible images of ruins of temples, for a amphitheatres, and agora marketplaces.

The *National Geographic* travel journal has termed the Roman Empire the West's first true superpower. Furthermore, it notes that it was in many ways the precursor of the European Union. "A single currency, a single code of laws, a single army and a single emperor held sway over a vast swath of the Western world, including the heart of Europe, a large chunk of western Asia, and the northern tier of Africa, from the Atlantic to the Dead Sea. This was the Roman Empire, which pacified and unified the entire Mediterranean rim – a signal achievement in the art of governing. Long before anybody thought of automobiles, airplanes, or email, the emperors efficiently maintained their famous Pax Romana over a 3000 mile-wide territory that today includes parts of more than 40 different nations. They did it with a genius for organisation and a tolerance for cultural diversity that was interrupted now and then by bursts of utter ruthlessness."

As in the case of many other ancient cities in the Middle East, Jerash lay lost and forgotten for many an era. The earth revealed neither dead monuments nor the glories of the past. The one-time living sites were buried deep under sand and debris over time and forgotten. The Arabs have a proverb to express utter desolation 'like the ruins of Gerasa'. Many vestiges and legacy of ancient times were resurrected and revealed by painstaking archaeological work in the nineteenth century. Yet paradoxically, it was the burial over time that was the ideal form of conservation - that on rediscovery has yielded incredible ancient treasures. So was Jerash once again brought to light by the German traveller Seetzen in 1806. However, excavations began only in the 1920s. On our visit to Jerash in 2001, we found densely packed monumental ruins that lie in the midst of the equally densely packed modern city of Jerash. Within minutes, we had crossed multiple ages of time.

Entering the old city, to our left lay the ruins of a massive hippodrome. We climbed over the remains to gaze at a scenario recalling Charlton Heston furiously riding his chariot in *Ben Hur.* People flocked to the hippodrome to watch a most popular sport of the day, the death-defying sport of chariot racing. Riders were out to win by means fair or foul. Victory knew no morality. They were required to circle the elongated ellipse-shaped racecourse seven times. At each end were two semi-circle posts that had to be passed through. Some fifteen thousand spectators could be accommodated in the hippodrome.

We were now approaching the unique and immense, completely paved oval forum that still has sixty of its slender Ionic columns on the periphery. The expanse of space is grand, simple and elegant. The agora market forum was the centre of the economic and daily life of the Roman city. The commercial life of the community was conducted on these premises. The International Festival of Jerash is held annually at this piazza.

Moving out of the agora forum, we entered the Cardo Maximus, the criss-cross main arterial road of the city running north and south - nearly two thousand feet in length - and the other east and west. The roads are still paved with the original stones that bear the ruts worn by thousands of chariots. On both sides of the main boulevard, closely spaced colonnades of the more elaborate Corinthian columns create grace in its urban design. It is incredible that so many of the columns are still standing. On the other side of the columns are the remains of early retail outlets.

A plethora of religious monuments mark Jerash. The remains of Greek and Roman temples and Christian churches are scattered over the area. The magnificent monument built to Artemis, the tutelary goddess of the city, dominates the site. We climbed the expansive and seemingly endless stairway that measures some sixty feet wide to the top of the hill. Amazingly, from the Cardo Maximus roadway at the foot of the stairway, we could not see any of the innumerable columns that stood on the slopes of the hill. Yet as we slowly and steadily climbed the stairs, an increasing number of columns gradually came into view. An architectural illusion, they appear to be sprouting out of the ground. Still further up, stands the colonnaded temple of Artemis built on a massive platform of stone blocks. The impressive layout is characteristically simple. One can imagine legions of worshippers climbing the majestic route and paying homage to the protector of the city of Jerash. We also paid homage to the connoisseurs of creativity.

BAALBEK'S ROMAN MAGNIFICENCE

"Our eyes did not know where to rest: everywhere there were marble doorways of a prodigious height and breadth; windows or alcoves surrounded by the most wonderful sculpture, curved surfaces covered with exquisite ornament, pieces of cornice, entablatures and capitals scattered like dust beneath our feet; coffered vaults over our heads; everything around us was a mystery, confusion, disorder, masterpieces of art, debris of time, unfathomable marvels. Hardly had we glanced with admiration on one side than a new wonder attracted us on the other...We resigned ourselves to look and to admire, without taking anything in beyond the colossal power of man's genius and the strength of the religious idea that had been able to move such masses and accomplish such masterpieces."

Lamartine, French poet's impression on his visit to Baalbek in 1822-1823.

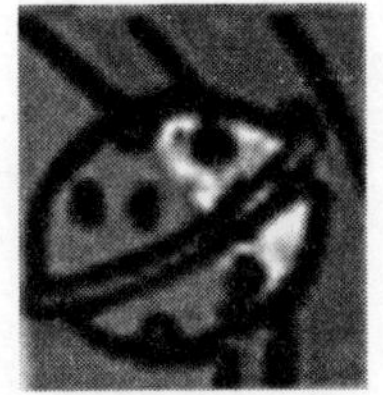

"Where else in the Arab world, could one see majestic peaks capped with snow for much of the year, rising hoary above terraced mountain slopes dotted with the red roof-tops of countless villages nestled among orchards or vineyards, set against a stark blue sky, and directly overlooking the sparkling waters of the Mediterranean?" Gushes a Lebanese historian about the physical attributes of Lebanon and few would begrudge him that. Kamal Salibi, renowned historian at the American University of Beirut, writes in *A House of Many Mansions: The History of Lebanon Reconsidered.* It is this geographical reality that has given rise to the most common of phrases describing Lebanon, "you can ski on the slopes of Mount Lebanon in the morning and swim in the Mediterranean in the afternoon of the same day."

Our trip to Baalbek, the magnificent marvel built by the Romans in the Bekaa valley began in the morning in the coastal city of Beirut. In no time, we were climbing the slopes of Mount Lebanon and passing through towns and villages whose names musically roll off one's tongue: Aley, Bhamdoun, Chatura, Sofar, Zahle…and the scenery is as lovely as described by Salibi. In a short while, we were descending the mountain slopes and entered the vast Bekaa valley, once the granary of the Roman Empire and today marked by the presence of Syrian sentry posts. Syria lies across the Ante-Lebanon Mountains, on the other side of the valley. We passed the renowned vineyard that produces the excellent Lebanese Kfara wine.

Baalbek, the magnificent remains that have defied the decay wrought by time, was originally named after the Phoenician god, Baal. The Greeks, under Alexander the Great, later gave the name Heliopolis (City of the Sun) to the expanding metropolis. However, Baalbek reached its zenith with the construction of grandiose buildings under the Romans. A principal city of the Roman Empire, many a Roman emperor sought to add to the glory of Rome by beautifying and expanding Baalbek. Pompey, Julius Caesar, Nero, Hadrian, Septimus Severus, Caracalla, Constantine and Julian the Apostle all left their mark on Baalbek. Baalbek was the architectural gift to the gods by a long line of Roman rulers.

We entered the massive sacred complex through the Propylaea, the monumental entrance with a grand staircase leading to four surviving columns and a portion of the remains of thick blocks of stone wall that bear witness to the splendour that once adorned the place. Past the Propylaea, we found ourselves in the midst of a gigantic hexagonal courtyard that originally had thirty columns decorating its outer edges. Niches and elegant columns, now in various stages of ruin, dot the entire perimeter. Priests meditated here prior to crossing the threshold to the colossal temple of Jupiter. There were underground stables and storerooms. A sacrificial altar and two ritual basins with detailed relief carvings are still visible. The sacred courtyard is an arena cluttered with architectural remains.

At the top of a staircase, we stood on the raised plateau that is home to the remains of the temple of Jupiter; six slender columns with a finely decorated cornice. It exudes elegance and is dramatically imposing. One has to imagine the spectacular dimensions of the temple 88 metres long and 48 metres wide, completed in 60 AD, that stood on a podium raised in gratitude to Jupiter visible from a great distance in the expansive Bekaa valley, it must have been an overwhelming sight for legions of worshippers. We stood humbly mute before this architectural feat that speaks eloquently of the 'silence of elegance'. Another observer in the early nineteenth century was similarly affected. Lamartine wrote of his impression upon seeing the temple of Jupiter. "Silence is man's only language when what he feels goes beyond the ordinary range of his impressions'. We silently gazed at these six columns, measuring with the eye their diameter, elevation and the wonderful sculpture of their architraves and cornices." An early eighteenth century traveller and archaeologist Robert Wood left his memories of Baalbek recorded in both English and French in a richly illustrated book *The Ruins of Baalbec*, otherwise called *Heliopolis*, published in London in 1757. The nineteenth century

Scottish artist and traveller David Roberts preserved for posterity his extensive drawings of Baalbek.

My first visit to Baalbek was in 1952 as a toddler when my father was posted in Damascus. My next visit was in 1970 when we were living in Beirut. The visit of which I write was with my husband and daughter in 2001. Half a century has gone by. I was deeply conscious of my periodic visits to this site through my lifetime. Yet as I stood there, I was solemnly reminded of the comment, "Time span so brief that no visible changes emerge." The most vivid evidence of the passage of time is recorded in photographs that have been taken in the same spot after long intervals. Sometime within the past centuries, a large block of the detailed cornice of foliage and lion's head that graced the soaring stone columns of the temple of Jupiter came down to rest on the distant ground beneath. I have photographs taken at this site that document my own passage in life: my childhood, my youth and my transition to middle/old age.

We then proceeded to the extraordinarily intact temple of Bacchus. Its dimensions, though marginally smaller than the neighbouring temple of Jupiter, are still larger than the Acropolis in Athens. On a raised stone block platform, the colossal tribute to the god Bacchus, is a memorable construction that has stood the test of time extremely well. The construction is proportional and harmonious. We were standing before an architectural frame of aesthetic grace and breathtaking vision. The entrance has been honoured by Henri-Paul Eydoux in *In Search of Lost Worlds* as, "one of the most sumptuous gateways of antiquity". One of the grand columns that surround the solid stonewalls of the temple of Bacchus leans precariously against this wall. It moved from its base during an earthquake in an earlier era. One would have thought that the weight of the leaning column would have brought down the ancient wall. Not so. Many travellers have documented their presence within the premises in the form of graffiti on the walls.

As in Palmyra in Syria and Petra in Jordan, travellers through the ages have all been mesmerised by man's efforts to honour a Supreme Being. Architectural magnets of such allure and inspiring dimensions remain permanent draws for any traveller in the Middle East.

A CULINARY EXPERIENCE AT PEPE'S FISHING CLUB IN BYBLOS

"Pepe Abed, known as the 'Pirate of Byblos' runs the 'Fishing Club', one of the most famous spots in all Lebanon. It opened its doors in 1963 and has been the favourite of many celebrities, from Marlon Brando to Brigitte Bardot to Frank Sinatra."

The Golden Book: Lebanon

The purpose of our visit to Byblos, an ancient city a little to the north of Beirut, was to engage in a culinary excursion to Pepe's Fishing Club restaurant. The secondary goal – unabashedly – was to take in the harbour city of 'layered civilisations'. I wanted my family to savour the memorable weekend lunches that I remembered from the late 1960s. I remember it as if it was yesterday, the innumerable succulent Lebanese *mezze* (appetisers, more than a generous meal in itself) laid down before us in a setting that was off a picture postcard; a mini, ancient port with a tower from the period of the Crusades guarding the entrance to the harbour with colourful fishing boats and tourist cruising boats docked within and the azure blue Mediterranean waters. As we parked in front of Pepe's, I was delighted and reassured to find that it was much as I remembered with no glaring changes. After all, the entire exercise was to rediscover a setting and repeat a memorable meal. Happily, I was not disappointed in either.

Byblos is one of the oldest continuously inhabited cities in the world. Excavations have revealed that there was a Neolithic community living on the premises seven thousand years ago. Some three thousand years ago, Byblos was a major trading port in the area. Cedar wood and oil was sent to Egypt in return for gold, alabaster, papyrus rolls and linen. For the Phoenicians, Byblos was a strategic trading post in their command over the Mediterranean Sea maritime commerce. Much later came the familiar wave of rulers in the region in the form of Persians, Greeks, Romans, Byzantines, Arabs and the Crusaders. Byblos fell from fame following the exit of the Crusaders, leaving a legacy of past glory and a most picturesque setting.

'Byblos' is also the origin of a few words in English and other European vocabularies. The Greeks called the place Gebal Byblos after the Greek word for papyrus, *bublos*, because papyrus was shipped from Egypt to Greece via the Phoenician port of Byblos. A collection of sheets was called *biblion* or book, and from the Greek ta *biblia* or 'the books', the English word 'Bible' was derived. Byblos is also the origin of the oldest known text written in the linear Phoenician alphabetic script that was the precursor of the modern Roman alphabet. The word 'Phoenetics' also found root here.

On my last visit to Byblos in 1969, I had tramped through the grass-covered ruins that exposed, here and there, a wall, the edge of a well, a burial pit. We were told of the remains of an aqueduct that had supplied the ancient community with water. There was ample evidence of a rich urban fabric that underlay the commercial city. An elegant row of Roman columns, some with their capital intact, graced the hillside. In the distance and beneath a vast mound, lay the necropolis.

What impressed me then was the vivid evidence of numerous civilisations that had made this small area bordering the harbour their home, each building on the remains of their predecessors' constructions. The inhabitants of today have also built alongside a Roman wall or used building stones utilised by past generations. It somehow comes together naturally. All the mortal remains of competing civilisations have long since gone, yet vivid the evidence still coexists. As in many other historical sites in Lebanon, the unique crossroad of the ages, different epochs and civilisations are superimposed one on top of the other.

This time, we simply strolled through the city, past the remains of Crusade's castle that once dominated the city's medieval ramparts and past churches built over centuries. We were fast heading for the highlight of the day, our Sunday lunch at 'Pepe's Fishing Club.'

Monsieur Pepe Abed is an institution in Lebanon; his fame spreads far and wide. Born in Mexico to Lebanese émigrés, Pepe Abed returned to Lebanon in the early 1960s and opened his restaurant. He is also the Honorary Consul of Mexico to Lebanon. Today, he is in his late eighties and a larger than life character. He reminds me of Anthony Quinn in his role as 'Zorba the Greek'. Just as he had managed the restaurant all those decades ago, Pepe Abed was still there in his white admiral's hat and as debonair looking as I recall from my youth. With my husband and daughter standing next to me, I made the introductions and told him that I was a second-generation customer of his (notwithstanding a thirty- year gap) who had the pleasure of dining at his table with my parents. I was proud to be able to share once again the experience with a third generation customer – my daughter. We took a few pictures, literally for 'old time's sake'.

Pepe Abed introduced us to his second wife, an elegant, classic beauty. As he took us around his place, he twice mentioned that she looked like Sophia Loren. He was not exaggerating. She fulfilled his image – and ours. He showed us his collection of semi-precious stone jewellery that he had designed. He also opened the door to his one room museum of ancient artifacts collected off shore. There was a Phoenician urn and some ancient stones, a salt-encrusted vase and ship anchor. The man who had sailed the 'seven seas' in his time, also has a passion for underwater archaeology. UNESCO has declared the mini-museum a World Heritage Site.

The other world heritage collection assembled at 'Pepe's Fishing Club' are the immense and impressive assortment of photographs (mostly in black and white) that adorn the walls of the restaurant. On the walls are photographs of Ava Gardner, Brigitte Bardot, Claudia Cardinale, David Niven…JFK, Jackie and their two young children; of the President of Lebanon, General Emile Lahoud, now and when he was still a Captain, and any number of photographs that trace the years of Jacques Chirac of France and a multitude of others. We spent considerable time exploring this fascinating historical documentary of luminaries.

A year later, as I wrote this piece in New Delhi, I read about Pepe Abed in the pictorial guide-book *The Golden Book: Lebanon.* I suddenly spotted, in a photograph of the famed walls that formed the backdrop to the historical lineup of diners at Pepe's, a colour photograph of Pepe Abed and my father! What a touching surprise. My father died in 1986. Like much in Byblos, the past and the present somehow just come together naturally.

The restaurant itself is partly nestled into the caverns of the remains of a twelfth century building. The eating area is an open-air terrace with a vine-covered trellis that overlooks the blue waters of the ancient harbour. One cannot dream of a more beautiful atmosphere. This is the venue and the tables that have attracted global celebrities throughout the second half of the twentieth century and it continues to do so today.

Eating at 'Pepe's Fishing Club' is a pure gastronomic joy culminating with decadent desserts *a la Libanaise.* In the company of our Lebanese host, a gourmand whose knowledge and appreciation of Lebanese cuisine is of the highest order; it was a memorable feast.

TRIPOLI : AN ARABIAN AMBIENCE

On Time
"And an astromer said, 'Master, what of Time?'
And he answered:
You would measure time the measureless and the immeasurable.
You would adjust your conduct and even direct the course of your spirit according to hours and seasons.
Of time you would make a stream upon whose bank you would sit and watch its flowing.
Yet the timeless in you is aware of life's timelessness,
And knows that yesterday is but today's memory and tomorrow is today's dream..."

'The Prophet' Khalil Gibran

The highway on the drive north from Beirut to Tripoli in Lebanon (65 kms from Beirut) is completely built-up. Global representatives exist in the form of McDonalds and Burger King, Benneton and Spinneys Supermarket. Also to be found are Lebanese clothing outlets, fast-food outlets and any number of restaurants serving Lebanese culinary delights. Only upon nearing Tripoli does one come across the barren and desolate mountains that once characterised much of the route from Beirut to Tripoli some thirty years ago – the last time I had made this journey. In those days, there was no highway linking the two cities. We made the trip via a meandering Mediterranean coastal road. We drove up hills and down to the coast and the acquamarine Mediterranean Sea. We skirted the lovely Jounieh Bay and looked up at the famed Casino de Liban. I confess a preference for the older route. I now reflect that was a more refined time when life was about the quality of the journey and not how fast one got there. As the Taoist saying declares, 'the journey is the reward'.

Clusters of date palm trees along the coastal route reminded me of the large grove of palm trees to be found in Palmyra, Syria. According to various references in historical texts, the cultivation of dates goes back at least four thousand years. They are not only of historical and religious importance but also carry many medicinal and nutritional benefits. Aside from sugar, the main component of the date fruit, other major ingredients include cellulose, iron, vitamins A and B, phosphorus, calcium, magnesium and large quantities of minerals. The breaking of the month-long Ramadhan fast with a glass of water or juice and a date is customary all over the Muslim world.

Representatives of all Near East civilisations have passed through Tripoli through the ages. The ancient city's name is appropriate to its configuration, for there was a federation of three seaports connected together – Arcadus, Sidon and Tyre - in the fourth century BC. While Tripoli has not been extensively excavated, as much of the ancient site lies buried beneath the modern city, periodical findings have revealed layer-cake evidence of the late Bronze Age,

Iron Age, Greek, Roman, Byzantine and Fatimid habitation. In the ninth century BC, the Phoenicians established a small trading station at Tripoli. Its strategic position has always been in its natural port, offshore islands and access to the mainland interior. Tripoli was well-located both for maritime trade and the Near Eastern caravan trade to its hinterland. African gold and ivory, slaves, corn and cattle mingled with Asiatic metals and Egyptian textile in a sprawling commercial trade.

The Phoenicians, original inhabitants of ancient Lebanon, were more traders than calculating colonialists. They travelled westward and established an empire and correspondingly, a civilisation. Their realm stretched from the eastern Mediterranean coast of present-day Lebanon and Syria to the northern coast of the African continent, including Egypt, Libya, Mauritania, Tunisia and Morocco; the southern coast of Spain, Italy, Greece and Turkey; and the island of Cyprus. They had important settlements in Sicily, founded towns such as Barcelona in northeastern Spain and the town of Marseilles in southern France. More sailors than soldiers, Herodotus recorded that some Phoenicians sailed in ships down the Red Sea at the bidding of Pharaoh Necho II (609-593) to circumnavigate Africa, a feat which they accomplished in just under three years, stopping each year between seed-time and harvest to gather provision before continuing their journey.

The city of Carthage in modern Tunisia is the finest and largest of all Phoenician towns and cities, and also the most revealing owing to architectural and literary evidence. Carthage was founded in the ninth century BC as a commercial halt for traders in the western Mediterranean. This gem of all Phoenician cities fell to the Romans in 146. I had the opportunity to see this fabled city in the winter of 1976 and ramble through its extensive ruins that lay on hills overlooking the calm blue Mediterranean. It was Hannibal of Carthage who crossed the Alps to conquer Italy. Hannibal's fame in ancient warfare lies in his introduction of a new weapon – the elephant.

"As explorers, in antiquity, the Phoenicians were second to none, as colonisers to few, save perhaps the Greeks...Their prowess as doughty fighters was shown, not only in Carthage's long drawn-out struggle with Rome, but also in the resistance that Tyre and Sidon put up against Mesopotamia and other conquerors and in the services their navy rendered to Persia. But all these things pale before their highest and most enduring memorial, the alphabet. This is where they impinge most strongly on all subsequent civilisations of Old World origin. All Indo-European and Semitic tongues – indeed all subsequent alphabetic scripts – have employed the medium developed by the Phoenicians and rapidly adopted by many other nations round about them, including the Greeks." (Donald Harden in his authoritative *The Phoenicians.*) Yet the Phoenicians left little in the way of written records and what we know of them comes largely from the accounts of foreigners or from their enemies and commercial rivals.

Kamal Salibi in *A House of Many Mansions: The History of Lebanon Reconsidered* credits geography rather than history for the similarities that the ancient Phoenicians and the present-day Lebanese people share. The Lebanese of today are known to live by their wits, flexibility, resilience and a profound sense of *joie de vivre.* Salibi incisively states: "Judging by what ancient Greek literature has to say about the Phoenicians, the urban Lebanese of today do not appear to be much different in character. Like the ancient Phoenicians, they are free-wheeling and rugged mercantilists; adventurous and footloose, yet staunchly attached to home grounds; free-spending and willing to take on any gamble, yet essentially thrifty; keeping an open mind and adapting to changing circumstances with typical Levantine facility at one level, yet doggedly set in their traditional ways at another; socially playful to the point of irresponsible levity, yet serious, highly alert and efficient, thought somewhat unconventional, when it comes to real business, where they have a marked tendency to live by their wits." Salibi continues, "Countries are created by history, but their territories belong to the realm of geography, where history is merely a bird of passage…the unity of the land in terms of natural and human geography always remained." There is ample food for thought in this comment. It reads like a research paper title in academia.

Both the Phoenicians and the Greeks valued Tripoli's naval port facilities. The Roman General Pompey took control of the city in 64-63 BC. The city flourished with the construction of innumerable buildings. An earthquake and tidal wave heavily damaged Tripoli in 551. After 635, the city emerged as a commercial and shipbuilding centre under the Omayyads. Under the Fatimids, Tripoli became a seat of learning. The Crusaders took control of the city in 1109. In the process, the renowned library, Dar ul-Ilm and its one million hand-written manuscripts were burnt down.

In a historical clash of civilisations, the Crusades, according to the military historian Paul K. Davis in *Encyclopedia of Invasions and Conquests: From Ancient Times to the Present* says, "were actually one long protracted conflict between Christian Europe and the Islamic Middle East over the land and holy sites of modern-day Palestine. It was the several aggressive attempts by European nobility, at the behest of successive popes, to reinforce the Latin Kingdom or regain territory lost to Islam, that give the illusion of multiple invasions. Battles would continue to be fought, cities would be won and lost, but the great Christian victories of the initial invasion would not be repeated."

Famed landmarks have been targeted throughout history; churches, mosques, palaces, temples and others have been lost to the ravages of time or destroyed in warfare. Dr. Lowry Burgess, professor of art at Carnegie Mellon University elaborates: "Surely, every time a culture confronts another one that it doesn't understand, part of its initial instinct is to obliterate the other completely. It's kind of a human instinct that goes back into the dimness of time." Yet others have been destroyed for their symbolic meaning. In the recent past, one is reminded of the destruction by the Taliban of two of the most famed sculptures in Buddhism, which they deemed 'offensive to Islam'. Carved from the sandstone cliffs of Bamiyan in Afghanistan in the third and fourth centuries and once gilded in glimmering gold, these 53 and 36 metres high statues had even escaped the destructive wrath of the Mongol leader Genghis Khan.

Despite a commonly-held perception of Genghis Khan as an historical strongman who sanctioned genocide of his conquered people and the sacking of the intellectual Abbasid capital Baghdad, Paul K. Davis in *Encyclopedia of Invasions and Conquests: From Ancient Times to the Present* offers an interesting alternative viewpoint. "Genghis was one of those leaders who occasionally arise who is equally adept at conquest and administration…From his conquered subjects, he took not only military tactics and hardware, but also adopted an alphabet, a written language, and whatever cultural accomplishments they could offer. His domination of Central Asia brought about a Pax Mongolica that allowed the reopening of the Silk Road, bringing ideas and trade from the Middle East and beyond."

The Mamluk Sultan Qalaoun defeated the Crusaders in 1289. Tripoli became a part of the Ottoman Empire for over four hundred years from 1516 to 1918 while retaining its prosperity and commercial importance. It is the long Muslim rule that gave birth to the distinctive Arabian ambience of architecture and lifestyle that is so unique to Tripoli.

A midday stroll through the Old City, much of which dates to the Mamluk era (fourteenth and fifteenth centuries), and its *souq*/ bazaar, is living testimony to the presence of bygone ages and its peoples. A Roman period column has for its roof a tarpaulin covering. The walls of an Ottoman building are joined by a modern construction that houses a shop selling kaftans and Oriental tablecloths. Through a maze of narrow alleys dotted with old *hamaams*, *khans* and mosques, we walked through the vegetable market, past the fish section and entered the spice market. Here are living symbols of everyday life; tailors, jewellers, perfumers, tanners and the famed Tripoli soap makers that have maintained their working traditions over the past 500 years. The following quotation has captured the precious link between Art and Man, 'Each of the fingers of the artisan is like a key to unlock livelihood.' The symbiosis between the distant past and the routine present remains uninterrupted. On the edge of the *souq* is a traditional coffeehouse that has entertained a male clientele over generations – drinking Turkish coffee, smoking the *shishah* (waterpipe) and tackling the infinite problems of the world at large.

I came across two anonymous poems to the *shishah* in *Bridge of Turquoise* by Roloff Beny, the celebrated album on Iran commissioned by Queen Farah Diba in 1978:

"The waterpipe takes pleasure at thy lips
And in thy mouth its reed has turned to sugar cane;
'Tis not tobacco smoke which wreathes thy head
But clouds which turn about the moon, and turn again."

"Then from the hookah
learn the Way of Love:
fire in its head,
smoke in its heart
and tears upon its skirt."

A lack of time prevented us from visiting the formidable citadel of Tripoli. An original Fatimid fortress, it was expanded by the Crusaders in the twelfth and thirteenth centuries and then modified by the Mamluks and the Ottomans. It is an example of cumulative architectural evidence that remains today. It also has common features of most buildings and monuments of previous eras, each one built on the remnants of past structures. Tripoli remained a county under the Crusaders and a separate province under the Mamluks and Ottomans. Tripoli ranked number three in importance under the Mamluks after Damascus and Aleppo.

Leaving Tripoli, we moved eastwards into Mount Lebanon crossing into the Kadisha valley, a natural gorge that is home to the

Lebanese Christian Maronite community. Rich in waterfalls, the mountain-scape is both rocky and barren in places while green groves carpet fertile valleys and pastureland. Monasteries dating from the twelfth and thirteenth centuries are built into the rocks and decorated with frescoes. The Syrian Christian Maronite sect is principally concentrated in northern Lebanon. The Maronites have long traditional ties with the Vatican Roman Catholic Church. Available evidence indicates that the final exodus of the Maronites into Mount Lebanon occurred at some point between the tenth and eleventh centuries.

At an altitude of more than two thousand metres, we came across the fabled cedar trees of Lebanon. These ancient trees descend from an immense primeval forest of cedars and other trees such as cypress, fir and oak that once covered most of Mount Lebanon. There are known to be twelve trees over one thousand years old and some four hundred that date more than one hundred years. The imposing and slender cedar trees can reach sixty metres in height. The trunks can reach between twelve to fourteen metres in circumference. They stood regally before us. The cedar tree is the national emblem and can be found on the flag - a cedar tree on a horizontal strip of white, bordered by strips of red. The cedar is the noble and majestic symbol of Lebanon.

The cedar tree is an historical entity often mentioned in the Bible and ancient texts. It has played an important role in the culture, trade and religious practices in the ancient Middle East. Serious exploitation of the forest began in the third millennium BC. Over the centuries, Assyrians, Babylonians and Persians made expeditions to Mount Lebanon for timber. The Phoenicians made much use of the famed cedar for shipbuilding of their large merchant fleets. According to Donald Harden in *The Phoenicians*, "The inner sanctuary, for example, of Solomon's temple was panelled with cedars from floor to ceiling and its ceiling was of cedar beams and planks forming recessed panels." Nebuchadnezzar boasted on a cuneiform inscription:

"I brought for building, mighty cedars, which I cut down with my pure hands on Mount Lebanon." Prized for its fragrance and durability, the length of the great logs made cedar wood highly desirable. The Egyptians used cedar resin for the mummification process and pitch extracted from these trees was used for waterproofing. Cedar wood was widely used by the Egyptians for temple and palace building. This highly prized material for construction reached the ancient Achaemenian capital built by Darius the Great in Shush, the Khuzestan province of modern-day Iran. In 520 BC at Shush, foundation tablets recovered from the palace of Darius record the following: "The cedar beams have been taken from a mountain called Lebanon. The Assyrian people brought them to Babylonia. From Babylonia, the Carians and Ionians brought them to Susa..."

BEIRUT : JEWEL OF THE MIDDLE EAST

"One can be permitted a romantic tone when speaking of his country, especially if that country is Lebanon. The Hebrew psalmist, the Arab poet, and the traveller have sung the beauty of Lebanon from all lands…"

Elie A. Salem, Chairman of the Middle East Programme at the American University of Beirut

The lines above appear in the Introduction by Dr. Salem to the book *Beirut: Crossroads of Cultures*, published in 1970 in Beirut a few years before a civil war ravaged Lebanon and altered forever a city dear to many the world over. There are places that touch the heart – as does Paris - and Beirut falls into that category; a city with emotional drawing power. After all, Beirut, in its golden halcyon years of the 1960s and early 1970s, was known as the 'Paris of the East'.

"Beyrout, the ancient Berytus, is well worthy of being the capital of this beautiful country. Her terraces filled with flowers; her houses with their slender arches and flat roofs, surmounted with embrasures of stones or balustrades of wood; the picturesque rocks which surround her shore; the palms towering toward the sky; the lovely colours of her walls; the minarets of her mosques; her atmosphere always bright and serene; her sky ever clear and open – all blend together into one grand and ravishing tableau," enthused a young Englishman who arrived in Beirut by steamer-boat in 1856.

In 1992, Samir Khalaf, former Dean of the Sociology Department at the American University of Beirut, returned to Beirut from the United States with his family after an absence of eight years. Two decades before his return, he had been my professor at the University. He writes of his return from exile in 'Beirut Reclaimed'. "Our intention was to test the waters, so to speak, and reconnect with family and friends. We harboured no illusions other than the faint hope that, by exposing our two boys to the few yet unravaged features of Lebanon – its captivating scenic beauty and geography, the warmth and compassion of family and friends, its prehistoric sites, colourful folklore, delicious produce and cuisine – we might rekindle their longing for their country's threatened and defiled legacy."

A cruel reminder of changed times came as I was writing the preceding sentences in Tehran in 2001. I had the BBC television news on and the top story was about a Lebanese Cessna plane that had been shot down by the Israelis with the pilot still on board. I listened to yet another unfolding tragedy in Lebanon; peace has eluded this beautiful country for so very long.

For those of us who knew Lebanon and Beirut in its Golden Age, a sweeping feeling of loss and sadness overcomes one. Similar feelings of loss had once overwhelmed a sixth century poet, "Here am I, the wretched city, lying in ruins, my citizens dead...you who pass me by bewail my fate, and shed a tear in honour of Berytus, that is no more..." Many centuries later in 1909, a British traveller in the Middle East described Beirut as "the door to Syria, a chromatic Levantine screen through which...foreign influences entered..." That man was T. E. Lawrence. In the mid-1990s, Michael Asher while retracing the footsteps of Lawrence wrote in *Lawrence: The Uncrowned King of Arabia*', "Beirut was then one of the most vibrant cities in the Middle East: When I arrived there in his footsteps, ninety years on, however, it was a shell of a place, its famous 'Downtown' quarter reduced to rubble – a maze of shell-shocked buildings without interiors or roofs. Though the war between Muslims and Christians had long since ceased and Israeli troops had pulled out of the city, they were still fighting the Palestinians in southern Lebanon, which made it impossible for me to follow that part of Lawrence's 1909 route." The Lebanese civil war seared the country from 1975 to 1991.

Lebanon is often known by another name – the Levant. The name is derived from the old French word levant (rising) signifying the sun rising over the land bordering the eastern Mediterranean. In that context, Le Levant covered both Syria and Lebanon. Beirut, because of its geographical location at the western edge of the East for the Arab world and the eastern edge of the West for Europe, was always a city of traders and merchants; commerce till 1975 was the city's byword. Lebanon was also a successsful melting pot of religions and sects, a hybrid; there were Muslims (Sunnis, Shi'ias and Druze). There were Christians (Maronites and Orthodox). There were Armenians and Palestinians. At one time, they all lived happily together but certainly, not 'ever after'. This carefully balanced mosaic exploded in 1975.

Sandra Mackey's *Lebanon: Death of a Nation* is superb in its analytical insight into the complexity of Lebanon. If there is one book to read on today's Lebanon, this is it. It is written with pathos and understanding. Lebanon was not what it was perceived to be. "The Lebanese mosaic was partly a culmination of Lebanon's entrapment between East and West. Because they have always been at the crossroads, the Lebanese are rich in mix and essence. This is a large part of their charm. But at the same time, they are tormented by their own complexity…Over thousands of years, the Lebanese developed a culture that perhaps only they can truly understand – a culture in which the trunk is Arab and the branches pure Lebanese…In its simplest terms, war came because 'every village, every patch, every bend in the road housed another family, another clan, another way of looking at the world.'…Lebanon is dead – or at least the Lebanon of which the myths of the Golden Age were spun…Ras Beirut, a false representation of Lebanon, was all that Lebanon wanted to be, not what it was in reality. Yet this small area within this small country lying at the end of the Western world and at the beginning of the Arab world portrayed for a painfully short time how rich intercultural life could be… The artificial serenity of the Golden Age deluded the Lebanese and everyone else into believing that Lebanon held the secrets of communal tranquility. But it was only adjustment, not cooperation, that allowed communal groups to coexist."

Once someone challenged the unwritten code of cooperation, the thin veneer of stability cracked. And the idealised view of the city ceased to exist.

In *Murder, Mayhem, Pillage and Plunder: The History of the Lebanon in the 18th and 19th Centuries*, Mikhayil Mishaqa documents the memoirs of several generations of the Mishaqa family. Mikhayil Mishaqa lived from 1800 to 1888 in Mount Lebanon; in Damietta Egypt; as a merchant; in Hasbaya (Lebanon) as financial comptroller to the Shihab emirs; and in Damascus during his later years as a physician and consul to the United States. Originally in Arabic, Wheeler M. Thackston, Jr, translated the book into English. In the Introduction, Thackston observes, "In the small, pluralistic society of the Lebanon, localism, kinship and clan loyalties were the primary societal bonds. Confessional adherence to the sect into which one was born was inevitable, for no one could exist without such a tie, but religious affiliation appears to have been of less importance overall and certainly less a factor than liege loyalty." It was the beloved national poet Khalil Gibran who wrote, in 1934, in 'The Garden of the Prophet,' "Pity the nation divided into fragments, each fragment deeming itself a nation." His words were sadly prophetic.

Kamal Salibi has succinctly captured the dilemma of Lebanon when he says, "To create a country is one things; to create a nationality is another…Greater Lebanon, no less than Mount Lebanon before it, was truly a statue of gilded bronze standing on feet of clay". (*A House of Many Mansions : The History of Lebanon Reconsidered.*)

The shattered mosaic that was Lebanon has been vividly captured in an American cartoon. The American Marines were on a peace-keeping mission in Lebanon. It shows a lieutenant standing before a map of Lebanon with a pointer in his hand, telling his helmeted squad: "OK, Marines – We're faced with Druze and Shia Muslims being backed by the Syrians against the Christian Phalangists. The Druze and Shias are divided among themselves, as are the Christians. The Israeli pullout is leaving a gap that the 'Lebanese army' probably can't fill and the PLO is creeping back in…Nobody likes us, and it's all preceded by 2000 years of bloodshed. Any questions?"

The city of Beirut was founded on a narrow strip of coastal plain wedged between the Mediterranean Sea to its west and the Lebanon mountains to its east. Throughout history Beirut has held its own. It has been destroyed and ravaged repeatedly, yet the phoenix has risen, again and again, from the ashes. Today, can Beirut arise from the rubble once more?

Ancient Beirut lies buried beneath the port area, making excavations impossible. Beirut is a city with layers of history beneath it. The ancient name for Beirut was Biruta – a Semitic word for 'wells'. The first positive evidence for the existence of the city of Beirut goes back to eighteenth century BC. Reference to Beirut was found on a stone sphinx of the Egyptian twelfth dynasty discovered during construction work in Beirut in 1925. Such is the marvel of the city; there are constant reminders from the past of the presence of peoples from any number of civilisations. Beirut's ancient past came to a close with the end of Persian rule. As the city passed into Roman rule in the fifth century BC, the Graeco-Roman cultural synthesis took over Beirut and to this day innumerable Roman ruins remind us of the long shadow of the Roman reign. The Roman Empire encouraged the maritime trade route and Beirut's location was ideal for its sea-faring Phoenicians. Beirut prospered in its western orientation. The Roman Empire crumbled but its eastern half remained as the Byzantine Empire, Christian in faith, Greek in language and Eastern in orientation. Lebanon was part of that cosmopolitan empire.

The Arabs conquered Lebanon in 640 AD. Henceforward, the outlook was land-based and the focus was inland and eastwards. The cities of Aleppo, Damascus and Edessa now attracted the region's flourishing trade and culture. The Omayyads made Damascus their capital. The Abbasids founded Baghdad as the capital of their Empire. The Fatimids had Cairo as their capital city. In all this period, Beirut was relegated to the western outskirts of the respective empires.

Beirut once again came to the forefront in the Middle East with the coming of the Christian Crusaders in the late eleventh century. Their arrival on the western shores of the Levant brought other Muslim players to Beirut's - and the region's - defence. For two hundred years the Muslim Arabs fought the foreign Crusaders. Saladin consolidated his rule by fighting the Crusaders and reestablishing Damascus as the capital of the Ayyubid Empire and uniting an Arab Empire that stretched from Egypt to Aleppo in northern Syria. The last Crusader left the Mediterranean shores in 1302. The Mamelukes, the founder of the Circassian slave dynasty in Egypt once again made Cairo the capital of their Arab Empire. The defeat of the Mameluke sultan by the sultan of Constantinople in 1516 brought an end to Arab rule of the Middle East. For the next four hundred years, the Ottoman Empire ruled the region from Constantinople. The defeat of the 'The Sick Man of Europe', Ottoman Empire, at the end of the First World War brought Lebanon into the French Mandate in 1920. Beirut once again served as a primary port for the French rule over Greater Syria. Lebanon acquired independence in 1946.

Lebanon has historically been at the crossroads of culture, at the confluence of Islam and Christianity and Arab and Western civilisations. Lebanon has also traditionally had a Mediterranean orientation. A certain French affiliation since the period of the French Mandate has characterised Beirut. Charles Malik in *Beirut – Crossroads of Culture* observes that "There is much truth in the reflection that Arabic is the language of the emotion and instinct, French the language of culture and thought, and English the language of international commerce and politics; much as were Syriac, Greek and Latin, respectively, in the days of Christ. You curse and love in Arabic, you enjoy Racine and Victor Hugo in French, and you conduct your international political and commercial transactions – and these days the technology of space – including of course, these days the jargon of the moon, in English." Most educated Lebanese to this day are trilingual – speaking with immense fluency - Arabic, English and French.

A passionate patriot and, at one-time, Lebanon's representative at the United Nations, Charles Malik has presented a persuasive argument on the unique role of Lebanon in history, "Lebanon is literally at the centre of the world, both spatially and temporally. The circle with the smallest radius that can be drawn from any centre on the globe to include the following ten cities is the circle that can be drawn with Beirut as its centre. The ten cities included in this circle are these: Athens, Istanbul, Antioch, Damascus, Baghdad, Jerusalem, Alexandria, Cairo, Mecca and Beirut itself. Can you think of any other ten cities anywhere in the world that have had as decisive an impact upon history as these ten cities? And Beirut is absolutely at the centre of them all, more than any other city…" The same vibrant crossroads of cultures dramatically diverged in 1975 in a civil war that tore the country apart.

However, there has always been a flip side to Lebanon's unique charm. The Lebanese sociologist Samir Khalaf in *Beirut Reclaimed* has aptly captured it. "There was, of course, a darker side to Beirut's image as a resort and commercial centre. It had exacerbated further the lopsidedness of the Lebanese economy. The country became virtually a nation of services, middlemen, agents, idle renters and hotelkeepers. As a 'merchant republic', the Lebanese were too eager to please and serve others, with all the cruel ironies that such ingratiation and servility often do to society's self-esteem and national character. Beirut embodied at times the most lurid features of an open bazaar and an amusement park where the impulse for fun and profit were unabashedly released." The 'peaceful cultural mosaic' that was Lebanon exploded and ceased to exist with the onset of the civil war.

My association with Lebanon and particularly Beirut goes back to the period when Beirut was very much a living symbol of that crossroads of cultures – the late 1960s and early 1970s. Today, with the benefit of over thirty years of hindsight, I find myself agreeing with Sandra Mackey's portrayal of Beirut as a city with an Arab soul and a Western veneer. "It was Ras Beirut with all its glitz and glitter that most symbolised the 'Golden Age' of Lebanon, the period when the good life was the birthright of the privileged among the Lebanese and when Beirut's foreign guests dipped in the pool of grace, ease, and plenty. Ras Beirut was truly multicultural, smoothly blending timeless Arab traditions with the tempo and technology of the multinational society that came to represent the illusion that Easterners believed was Lebanon. Yet in this charming amalgam of Arab character and Western patina lay the roots of Lebanon's destruction."

Beirut is not a city with architectural or town-planning artistic merit, either then or now. In 1969, the city was a jumble of densely packed buildings and winding narrow streets. There were few high-rise buildings - our apartment in the Shell building, owned by the Emir of Kuwait, was one of the few and thus a city landmark. Bahije Makdessi, a Lebanese engineer, built the Shell building (named for the petrol station that lay at its feet) in 1959 during a construction boom period in the city. The only broad boulevard was the Corniche Avenue skirting the city's Mediterranean coast. In 1999, many more tall buildings broke the skyline. Even more bullet-scarred buildings with no roof and no walls littered the city. Beirut appeared more concentrated, more shrunken. The Champs-Elysees of Beirut, Rue Hamra, had diminished both in splendour and size. Some 1990s built sleek highways now crossed the city but otherwise the same winding narrow streets and the broad Corniche Avenue still existed. Beirut never had wide-open spaces, squares or any semblance of modern town planning. Haphazard constructions both then, and more so now, are visible everywhere.

Assem Salaam, Professor of Architecture at the American University of Beirut, wrote in 'City Planning in Beirut and its Outskirts' in *Beirut : Crossroads of Cultures* "...before listing the various attempts at town planning in Beirut, that Lebanon on the whole has almost no tradition in this field. The piazzas of Italy, the squares of London, the crescents and circles of Regent's Park and Bath, the street architecture and terrace housing of Paris and the monumental conceptions of Italy and France, are all unknown to Lebanon. Whatever little tradition exists is in details such as the crowded *souqs* and the pedestrian walkways in Tripoli, Sidon, Byblos or Tyre."

Beirut's perennial charm lies not in the city's physical infrastructure but in its unique location. And charm is that quality that exists in absolute terms, either it is present or it is absent. And charm does not present itself to logic. An aerial view of the city confirmed - then and even now - the unique attraction of Beirut. "Taking a bird's eye view of Beirut of 1969, like the tourist who is looking at the city from the window of an airplane, we come to the conclusion that the city has intrinsic charm resulting from its natural setting and configuration, from the lack of imposed uniformity in its buildings, and from the enthusiastic freshness of its elements". So wrote Raymond Ghosn, Dean of the Faculty of Engineering and Architecture at the American University of Beirut in 'Beirut Architecture' in *Beirut: Crossroads of Cultures.*

Kamal Salibi, a professor of history at the American University of Beirut, writes of the attractive vista that presented itself to another visitor to Lebanon in the 1960s. Salibi writes, "Travelling around the country in the 1960s, the American geographer Joseph Van Riper, of the State University of New York at Binghampton, remarked that people must have always arrived to settle in the Lebanon not only in search of social or political security, but because it was 'such a nice place in which to live.' (*A House of Many Mansions: The History of Lebanon Reconsidered*)

A young English traveller in the 1850s, an American geographer in the 1960s, Samir Khalaf in the early 1990s and myself in 1969, in 1978 and some twenty years later in 1999, cannot make light of the glorious setting that is Beirut. Nestled between the blue Mediterranean and the slopes of Mount Lebanon, Beirut lies spread on the narrow strip of land that is Lebanon. Through the ages, much has changed and, of course, Beirut bears its many visible scars inflicted by the bloody civil war. Yet one cannot fail to be seduced by the lure of Lebanon.

My first exposure to Beirut was in the late 1960s. My father was the Ambassador of Pakistan to Lebanon. I started my postgraduate studies in Sociology at the American University of Beirut (AUB). I have since then seen universities all over the world yet I have not seen a campus with a setting as magnificent as the one that is AUB. It possesses a distinctive beauty. Seen from the Mediterranean shore, the campus rises gently over the slope of the city. In between the cypress and pine trees, the main building, College Hall, stands tall with its clock tower and its roof capped in orange tiles. Dotted about are faculty buildings built in neo-Arabesque style architecture, all with the orange tiled roofs. Within the campus, leafy lanes provide shade over meandering pathways that open into open squares. Here and there are wooden benches on which to dream and ponder the meaning of life.

The Protestant American mission was established in 1866 and the Syrian Protestant College that later, in 1920, evolved into the American University of Beirut (AUB). The founder, the Reverend Daniel Bliss, chose the location of the new campus himself. Bliss's journals describe his many horseback rides through the cactus and sand of undeveloped Ras Beirut. "We rode everywhere through the city, looking as we rode. Finally we saw the site where the College now stands…and immediately decided that we had found the finest site in all Beirut if not in all Syria." And Archie Crawford, Vice-President of International College in Beirut, provides an early description of AUB. "I went up, for five Lebanese pounds, with three friends, on one of those early planes, for a ride over the city, in 1923. What a thrill it was. I was particularly struck with the lack of grass and trees, the only large green area being the campus of AUB." ('Foreign Communities in Beirut' in *Beirut – Crossroads of Cultures*).

Until the mid-1970s, AUB was a pivot and a beacon of academia in the Middle East. It has produced generations of political leaders, bureaucrats, social scientists, engineers and doctors in the region. In 1948, at the first meeting of the United Nations convened in San Francisco, there were more graduates of AUB among the participants than any other single university, some nineteen in all. John Bagot

Glubb in *A Short History of the Arab Peoples* recognised AUB's unique role, "...a Syrian or Iraqi diplomat would mingle easily with the Americans in the United States, if he had been educated in the American University of Beirut." It was said that among the establishment or educated elite in all Arab countries aged over forty-five that it would be a good guess that the individual was AUB educated. The Jordanian cabinet has a majority of AUB graduates. The Lebanese Parliament and cabinet also has a large number of former AUB students. Among the Gulf countries, many older technocrats belong to the AUB family.

In Tehran, at a meeting of the Professional Women's Group, I was to present my book *Gender and Development.* It was mentioned that I had an MA in Sociology from the American University of Beirut. After the talk an Iranian woman who was also a member of the Group, approached me. We knew one another but not about each other. She grasped me by the arm and exclaimed that she, too, was a graduate of AUB and had received her degree in education in the late 1950s. The rapport between us was instant.

Fayza Hassan, wrote an article on 'Americans in Egypt' in *Al-Ahram*, the renowned weekly newspaper in Egypt, stating, "The American University in Cairo was then a very small and rather young institution in no way comparable to the American University of Beirut which has had a seminal effect on the Arab world since the nineteenth century." George Antonius in his classic book *The Arab Awakening* describes the role of AUB and its regional influence. "Thus came into being an institution which was destined to play a leading part in the country's future. When account is taken of its contribution to the diffusion of knowledge, of the impetus it gave to literature and science, and of the achievements of its graduates, it may justly be said that its influence on the Arab revival, at any rate in its earlier stage, was greater than that of any other institution."

Arthur Goldschmidt Jr., in *A Concise History of the Middle East*, calls AUB, established by American Protestant missionaries in Beirut, "the crowning institution." He adds, "Legend has it that the first Arab nationalist party was a Beirut secret society founded around 1875 by five early graduates of the American University...The commitment of students and alumni of the American University of Beirut, in both the nineteenth and the twentieth centuries, has nurtured the ideas of Arab nationalism and spread them among both Muslim and Christian speakers of Arabic."

I returned to Beirut in 1978. Living in London, I was on a mission to Sudan for the World Fertility Survey (WFS), a United Nations affiliated research organisation for fertility and family planning in developing countries. I decided to revisit Beirut before returning to London. I sent a telegram (there was no fax or email in those days) to a friend in Beirut. She never received it. As we started the descent over the shimmering blue Mediterranean waters, I was thrilled to be returning to Beirut. I took a taxi to my friend's apartment on Rue Commodore. Well before reaching her place, the taxi suddenly stopped on the Airport Road, the driver rushed out and grabbed my suitcase from the boot and before I could cry out in shock, he had ushered me out and into his friend's taxi who, I subsequently discovered, was going my way. Only much later, I saw - but did not accept -his rationale; what was the point of two taxis going in the same direction? My suitcase just about made it too.

I cried when I saw the city. Entire blocks were black skeleton buildings. Just as on television when they show wartime Berlin, you could see through some of the buildings. Jagged and torn iron rods hung between floors. The pavement of the famed Corniche Boulevard that hugs the coastline was home for thousands of refugees from the south. It was a shambles of slums. Before coming to Beirut, I knew there was a civil war going on but stupidly or wishfully took no notice of it. Reality hit me hard.

After twenty-one years, I was once again on Middle East Airlines (MEA) now approaching Beirut on a flight from Tehran. In 1999, my husband and I were coming to Beirut for him to present his credentials as Ambassador of Bangladesh to President Emile Lahoud of Lebanon. Beirut from up above still looked as beautiful as it did when I first saw it in 1969. My level of sentimentality knew no bounds. It was my husband's first visit to Lebanon but he had heard so much about the place that he - I hope - shared my rising excitement as we landed at Beirut's new airport. I related, for the umpteenth time, my hazardous taxi ride on my last trip to Beirut as we drove on the new airport road.

We drove to the old Rue Commodore but the new Commodore Hotel. The new Commodore Hotel is the old Commodore Hotel done anew. In the old days, Commodore Hotel was a favourite centre for foreign journalists. A vivid description of the old Commodore Hotel is provided by the then UPI and *New York Times* Beirut bureau chief Thomas L. Friedman. He covered the civil war and is today a regular columnist for the *International Herald Tribune*. He wrote in *From Beirut to Jerusalem:* "The home of all good Beirut fixers – not to mention all good Beirut reporters and crooked taxi drivers – was the Commodore Hotel. Every war has its hotel, and the Lebanese wars had the Commodore. The Commodore was an island of insanity in a sea of madness." I don't know if that reputation is intact today. However, the 'new' bar is designed with the journalist and newspaper in mind. The carpet is woven with newspaper designs and old black and white photographs of newspapermen on the job grace the walls. Friedman's assessment of Lebanon's fallout is the following: "But how could a city go from being a vision of heaven to a vision of hell practically overnight? Because it was too good to be true, because Beirut in its heyday was a city with a false bottom."

I was on familiar territory. I revisited my old bookstores on Rue Hamra; Librarie du Liban and Four Steps Down. I saw the old Wimpy, in its day the first fast food outlet on Rue Hamra. The main street of central Beirut now looked somewhat rundown. I looked down Rue Abdel Aziz and, in the distance, I could see the orange tiled roof of the American University of Beirut. I made my way down the crowded streets looking for familiar shops. I walked past the American University Hospital where I worked as a volunteer on morning coffee-rounds. I went into 'Bargain Box' where, more than thirty years ago, I used to hand over unwanted clothes and books during my summer holidays. Nothing much had changed here. Well-meaning individuals still give and youngsters still do a good deed.

I crossed Rue Bliss and went through the door of the Bliss entrance to AUB. As I entered the campus, I looked above at the familiar writing on the wall. "That they shall have life and have it more abundantly." I gulped in emotion. Yes. I have had 'life' and I have had it 'abundantly' for which I am most grateful. I climbed down the steps and stood before the rebuilt College Hall. The College Hall houses the main administrative offices of AUB and the office of the President of the American University of Beirut. It was completed in 1873. A bomb blast destroyed College Hall during the civil war in 1991. A massive fund-raising among AUB graduates worldwide resulted in a new College Hall that was completed in 1999.

I sat in the Milk Bar, the university cafeteria and observed, over a cup of coffee, the students of today. In my time; there were no cell phones, fewer girls in *hejab* and more foreign students. Otherwise, so much looked the same. I located the only remaining professor from my time at AUB, Dr. Samir Khalaf who is now Director of the Centre for Behavioural Studies. We met again after twenty-six years and exchanged news. I asked him about my other professors and he presented me with his book *Beirut Reclaimed.* With immense pride I was able to return the gesture by presenting him with a copy of my book *Gender and Development* published by the American University in Cairo Press. After all, in my eyes he was still my professor and I was still his student.

I entered the bookshop Khayat as I had many times, many decades earlier. I stood there and gazed around; I was simply looking. A small black and white television was on. Books lay about everywhere; piled on the floor, stacked on shelves, falling all over the place, as if they had been lying around since the last time I was there. Obviously, information technology had not reached Khayat. An elderly couple sitting behind an old desk asked me if I was looking for anything special. I replied that I was 'just looking'. There must have been something about the way I was 'looking' that prompted them to repeat their offer to help. I then told them that I was an old AUB graduate retracing my path in the neighbourhood and that I had once been a frequent customer of theirs. Such warmth and hospitality then followed. I was offered a chair and a cup of Turkish coffee. We reminisced about old times and bit our lips over the tragic years that the city had passed through. We lamented the passing of those days. They insisted I stay and meet their children and grandchildren. and I so wanted to share this moment with them. However, I had to meet my husband at Commodore Hotel for an appointment elsewhere and I most regretfully rushed out.

A deeply moving, poignant and loving memoir to AUB and Beirut is Ann W. Kerr's book *Come with Me from Lebanon* (1994). As a young American, she arrived at AUB in 1954 to pursue her studies. She met her husband Malcolm Kerr at AUB. He was the son of AUB professors. In 1981, Malcolm Kerr was offered the post of the President of AUB. It was the pinnacle of his life's career and desire. The achievement was similar to what Sir Ronald Storrs said when he became Governor of Jerusalem: "There is no promotion after Jerusalem." Kerr was the first AUB graduate to become President of his alma mater. In the midst of the civil war, Malcolm Kerr was gunned down on his way to his office room at College Hall on the AUB campus in 1984. He lies buried beside College Hall under a massive banyan tree that he used to climb while growing up on the AUB campus. A tablet notes: 'He lived life abundantly.' He began and ended his life at AUB.

Ann Kerr succumbed early to the charm of Lebanon. Reflecting on her arrival in Beirut in 1954, she writes in *Come with Me from Lebanon*, "For me it was not just the Frenchness nor the Arabness nor the Armenianness that made Lebanon so appealing, but rather the collage of them all in a cultural and linguistic blend of charm and style and color. I was happily unaware of the precariousness of the political and religious underpinnings of this collage and of the tragedy the instability portended. Along with the appeal of the blend of cultures was the physical beauty of the country in its variety of seascapes and mountain vistas, added to the genuine warmth and hospitality of the people who lived there. In the few weeks since my arrival, I had become completely smitten with this lovely place."

On a trip to Beirut with her daughter in 1977, Ann Kerr writes of the lure of AUB and Beirut that touched a second generation. "Steeped in the family lore of Beirut and as susceptible to its seductive charms as her parents, Susie relished the beauty of the campus and the hospitality of friends much as I had twenty-two years earlier...The air still smelled of sun-warmed pine needles and sea breezes, and, as always, the brilliant aqua-blue of the Mediterranean formed a backdrop for the entire length of the campus."

On a tour of the city, I gave a running commentary to my husband on the buildings and sites that existed or that no longer existed, given the span of thirty years. We drove past Hotel St. George's. In the late 1930s, Antoine Tabet, a French-trained Lebanese architect, designed the renowned Hotel St. George's on the promontory of Minet el-Hosn in Beirut. It was the watering hole for regional journalists and the rich and famous were to be found spending time on its famed terrace overlooking the blue Mediterranean. Now it stands forlorn, covered in canvas, as it awaits total reconstruction - a skeletal symbol of its past glory. The bullet-scarred buildings are painful to see. They stand there without walls or roof afflicted by markings like a bad case of measles, tragic reminders of the urban warfare that tore the city apart. Beside state-of-the-art glass and chrome shopping malls, I spotted shattered buildings full of shattered lives.

I found the most striking symbol of Beirut's long history in the old downtown and newly reconstructed centre of town. 'Soldiere' is the long-term 2.5 billion dollar project envisioned by Prime Minister Rafik Hariri that aims to bring life back to the war-ravaged district. What used to be the narrow streets of the commercial heart of Beirut is today a purpose-built, reconstructed area. It is meant to symbolise the resurgence and resilient spirit of Beirut. The beautiful, late nineteenth century classical façade architecture of the buildings adds to the distinct feeling of a Disneyland-like setting. The buildings have not yet grown roots in the area but appear superimposed and speak of the intense desire of the Lebanese to recreate bygone days. Someone once said 'in life, the past may haunt you but it shall not return to comfort you. That is nostalgia.' These words reverberated in my head.

In the heart of the symbolic resurgence, is a thriving café full of young Lebanese yuppies. In the long summer evening, it was a picture of leisure and enjoyment. At the edge of the terrace is a steep drop and on the land below rows of Roman antiquity columns stand majestically. These remains of a past civilisation came to light during excavations for the current reconstruction of Beirut. Another glance reveals a three-storeyed building with no roof and few walls and with a tree growing on the third floor. These three structures coexist in a bizarre way as testimony to the civil war that is the hallmark of the twentieth history of Lebanon. Everyone speaks of "before the war" and "after the war".

Today, Beirut can still manage such events as an art exhibition of water-colours by Mohammed Machnouk titled 'Beirut…A Love Story' and 'Beirut…A Morning Beauty'. It was Virginia Woolf who said, "One cannot think well, love well, sleep well; if one has not dined well." Beirut can also still prove a culinary feast that few cities can beat. One dines superbly well in Beirut with its vast array of Mezee (starters) dishes; items ranging from warm fresh bread, succulent aubergines, crisp cucumbers, *hummous* (mashed chick peas drenched in olive oil, garlic and lemon juice), *tahini* (mashed sesame seed paste with the same aromatic and delicious oil, garlic and lemon garnishing), cherry tomatoes that pop in the mouth. For the main course one can opt for fresh *hammour* fish or tiny grilled birds the size of a child's fist (delicious and to be eaten with bones and all), chicken or lamb. Who can resist a sweet baklava or two washed down with an Arabic coffee? Indoors or outdoors, the ambience is always just right. Undoubtedly, Lebanese cuisine ranks as one of the foremost global culinary efforts.

Once again we had a superb authentic meal, a Japanese sushi lunch at a trendy new restaurant where you need to book a table on weeknights. A dinner of mouth-watering pasta in a just-opened Italian restaurant in the reconstructed downtown area of central Beirut was also partaken of. It was packed with Lebanese having a night out on the town. We were in another world. Suddenly, I remembered that the adjacent building was the former Opera house. Today, it is a ghost of a structure. The blackened shell of the once opulent building awaits reconstructive and cosmetic surgery. Until then, it is partly covered by boards on which are printed sketches of life within the Opera house – ballet dancers, artistes, opera singers, and the like. This is surrealism.

The commercial, financial and recreational hub of the Arab world in the Golden Age "before the war", Lebanon "after the war" is losing its educated nationals. The Lebanese are emigrating en masse. According to the Social Affairs Ministry, 895,000 people emigrated during the 15-year civil war that broke out in 1975. The same number fled in peacetime between 1995 and 1999. A staggering 277,000 people left for good in 1999 alone, an amazing statistic in a country of just 3.5 million.

Phoenix (Greek) from which the name Phoenicia (the ancient name of the Lebanese territory) derives, was the term used for the date palm. It was also the name for the magnificent 'bird of Arabia' that as it aged, set itself on fire then reemerged in full youthful vigour from its own ashes. Somewhere between a turbulent past and a promising future, Beirut may once again rise like the phoenix from the ashes, as Beirut has arisen many a time in the past. This time it shall be a phoenix in a different form for the ashes that gave birth to the new phoenix have been mixed with the blood and tears of a people that once belonged to a Golden Age. For Lebanon is the land of perpetual rebirth.

In remembering Beirut, the words of the American singer Grace Ray always come to mind. "Precious memories flood my soul."

BOSRA'S HIDDEN AMPHITHEATRE

"Here a most extraordinary site greets you: a classical theatre more spectacularly and authentically preserved than virtually any other around the Mediterranean, described as 'the most perfect of all Roman and Italian theatres."

Rey-Coquais, 'Bosra', *The Princeton Encyclopedia of Classical Sites*, 1975

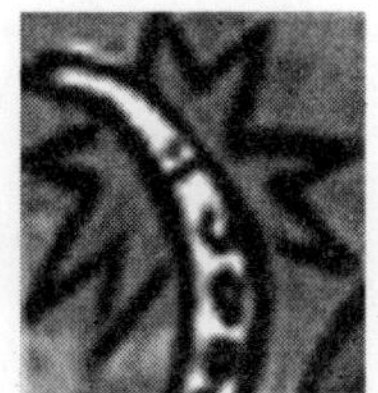

We were heading south from Damascus towards the Jordanian border, our destination Bosra, 140 kms south of Damascus. The topography soon changed to rich red-brown soil raked with stones and basalt chips. Boulders with layers of pink, grey and cream ripples could be spotted amongst the patches of olive tree farming. We soon entered the vast and inhospitable Hawran plain. This black basalt, stone littered, treeless and windswept plain is a harsh and unattractive sight. As a result of relatively recent volcanic activity, the sombre and grim Hawran plain produces the unique blocks of basalt stone so widely used in Syrian architecture.

En route to Petra in Jordan, the purpose of our stopover at Bosra was to see what has been called "one of the most beautiful and well-preserved Roman amphitheatres in the world…possibly, the best preserved Roman theatre in existence." Entering the parking lot at Bosra, we were surprised to come across an imposing citadel but the renowned amphitheatre was nowhere in sight. In the midst of the Hawran plain, we saw no hills or inclines behind which the sought-after construction could be hidden. I had a sinking feeling of despair. I was the instigator of this stopover and my family would - not for the first time - accuse me of following a wrong trail. Well, one certainly cannot win them all.

However, we were assured that we were in the right town and that the extraordinary amphitheatre could be found within the formidable fortress located in the middle of Bosra. Obviously a fact but to the naked eye, it appeared to be a fable. Once reassured, we went on to explore the rest of Bosra, a town where numerous civilisations have left their mark.

Earliest reference to Bosra is found in the archives of the Egyptian pharaohs Tutmose III and Ahkhenaton some 1300 years BC. Bosra has also been referred to in the Bible. It was, along with Petra in modern-day Jordan, one of the leading Nabataean cities in the first century BC. The Romans, under the emperor Trajan, made Bosra the capital of the province of Arabia in the first century AD. As an imperial capital and crossroads on the caravan route, the city flourished with elaborate city planning taking effect. Bosra played an important role in the days of early Christianity. It was also the first city in Syria to adopt Islam. The square minarets are the oldest in existence in Syria. Its location served as an important halt on the way to the holy cities of Mecca and Medina. Under various Muslim dynasties, Bosra continued to prosper. Under the Ottoman Empire, the vitally important Damascus-Hejaz railway line passed through Bosra.As alternative trading and religious routes emerged, Bosra gradually diminished into a town sidelined to obscurity.

We walked through the recently excavated extensive remains of the Roman baths of the early third century. The guide explained at length the classical sections and sequence of the Roman bath in the order of practice and comfort: *apodyterium* dressing room, *frigidarium* cold room, *tepidarium* warm room and finally the *caldarium* hot room. Brick pillars and vaults supported the paving stones of the baths and heated air passed underneath. Some centuries later in the 1370s, the Hamaam Manjak was built by the Mamelukes during the heyday of the city's role in servicing the Haj traffic to and from the holy city of Mecca. It has been described as "a masterpiece of medieval architectural engineering." These complexes also served as vital community social centers; a venue for rest and relaxation.

We saw the badly ruined remains of what was once the cathedral of Bosra. It was one of the earliest Byzantine Christian churches, dedicated in 512 AD by Julianos, the Archbishop of Bosra. We sighted a number of mosques, or rather the remains of mosques. The Mabrak mosque is where the Holy Prophet was supposed to have rested on his journey as a merchant in the region. Legend also has it that this is where the camel that carried the first copy of the Holy Quran to Syria knelt down and rested. The Fatima mosque is named after the daughter of the Holy Prophet. The Fatimids built it in the early eleventh century. A minaret survives along with some of the original arches. We excused ourselves from further exploring the vast plain of architectural remains of innumerable peoples and started walking towards Bosra's Star attraction.

We were walking towards an Arab fortress similar to many others we had seen in the region; all of them formidable and imposing. Having crossed the walkway over the wide moat, we entered dark and broad corridors or halls. We kept walking up an incline looking at the massive blocks of stone that formed the walls. Syria Tourism describes the military ramifications of this construction: "On a semi-circular front, great square towers built of enormous blocks of stone (some of the corner ones are more than five metres high), project from the blind ramparts. A deep ditch, the first line of defence, is crossed a six-arched bridge. An iron-bound gate, series of vaulted rooms, twisting passages, rampart walks, and all kinds of defensive works, give an impression of the military quality of the castle…"

We kept moving in darkness, natural light provided by shafts open to the sky and defensive openings on outside walls. As we continued our upward walk, these openings disappeared. We must have been well inside the citadel. Suddenly, we were high up on the top rampart of the citadel in the open-air, looking down on the right at the tiny cars and people below.

A glance to the left and there, below a sharp drop, was the Roman amphitheatre. We were standing on the broad edge of the top of the amphitheatre, looking down at the stage from a dizzying height. There was the awesome amphitheatre and it is magnificent. Incredible is its near-perfect state of preservation, as it was probably built in the mid-second century AD. It is also unique in that it has been built free standing and not, as in Petra, built into the side of a mountain or natural slope to support its massive proportions.

The stage is forty-five metres long and eight metres deep. The amphitheatre can hold some fifteen thousand spectators spread over thirty-seven tiers. It is still in use every summer during the Bosra Art Festival. Ross Burns in *Monuments of Syria: An Historical Guide* tells us: "The acoustics are excellent, a voice at normal conversational level rising from the stage can be heard at any point in the theatre." Evidence of other stagecraft has been found. The auditorium probably had a retractable cloth roof covering that provided shade in the summer and warmth in the winter. The stage may have had a wooden roof.

We gingerly made our way down the steep slope of large blocks of stone that form the sides and seats of the amphitheatre. It was a long and careful trip down to the stage. Once on stage, we had to gaze far above us to locate the edge of the citadel and the top of the amphitheatre. Around us, on the stage, were decorative Corinthian columns "giving some indication of the richness of the treatment, once ornate with coloured marbles, statues, windows and sculptured friezes like the façade of a fantastic palace," enthuses Burns.

The two structures - equally impressive - are closely linked; the Ayubid fortifications fit like a jacket around the earlier Roman built amphitheatre. The Omayyads started the first outer transformation of the amphitheatre. The Seljuk dynasty added more towers. The Ayyubids built the final and greater part of the fortifications in the early thirteenth century in response to incursions by Crusaders. Architecturally, the present two-in-one construction is both ingenious and brilliant.

. Happily, we had found what we were searching for and I had the last word.

PALMYRA : "THE BRIDE OF THE DESERT"

"If you are going to see one thing in Syria, make it Palmyra."

'Middle East', Lonely Planet, 1994

The family's trek to Palmyra in 1969 originated in Beirut, where my late father was posted as Ambassador of Pakistan to Lebanon. It was hot, dusty and the car journey from Damascus, a distance of 210 kms, seemed never-ending. I do not recall there being any air-conditioning in the car either. The relentless elements had, over time, carved patterns and created contours on the ancient tablelands. The vast, arid and barren landscape did nothing to break the monotony of the journey. Ahead appeared yet another range of desert mountains. How much longer? And then we went down an incline and there, as far as the eye could see, lay the 'Bride of the Desert', an ancient architectural showpiece, its vast scale evoking its fallen splendour and magnificent desolation. Palmyra is a poignant and moving site, a reminder of the transient existence of human glory.

Henri-Paul Eydoux, eminent French archaeologist, declared: "He finds himself in a world of marvels – a gigantic architectural décor in an immense, motionless setting ...few civilisations flowering in the arid lands have attained such heights." A vast necropolis of Roman funerary towers that broke the desert landscape lay before us. One was five-storeys, about one hundred feet high, a family mausoleum. Like watchtowers housing burial catacombs, the overwhelming feeling was one of solitude and silence amidst the desolate desert. There were also underground tombs – such as that of the Three Brothers - vast and deep, with numerous chambers coming off the main corridor.

Tourism in the late 1960s was not the global package tour phenomenon of today. We stayed at Hotel Zenobia; a small hotel built in the long bungalow style, having much character and a splendid view of the ancient Palmyran city lying at its doorstep.

The principal attraction at Palmyra is the Great Colonnade of 1500 decorated columns that line the main thoroughfare that leads to the temple dedicated to the Roman god Bel. The pre-eminence of Bel gave rise to the credo that there was a trend towards monotheism.

Henri-Paul Eydoux speaks of one dedication that described the god Bel as ' a god who is one, unique and merciful.' We saw some 150 remains of the original 1500 columns, in various stages of ruin while a few stood in all their original glory and others were half to a quarter intact. We walked through the Triumphal Arch, the agora market place and the amphitheatre. The ruins are immense and impressive.

The name Palmyra - city of palms - goes back only to the beginning of the Christian era. The city was classically known by its Semitic name, Tadmor - city of dates - from far back in antiquity. Pliny the Elder, the Roman historian in the first century AD, has graphically sketched Palmyra: "Palmyra is a city famous for its situation, for the richness of its soil and for its agreeable springs; its fields are surrounded on every side by a vast circuit of sand, and it is as it were isolated by nature from the world, having a destiny of its own between the two mighty empires of Rome and Parthia, and at the first moment of a quarrel between them always attracting the attention of both sides."

Palmyra was founded more than two thousand years ago as a caravanserai, a halting-post in a palm-fringed verdant oasis in the midst of a hostile desert. As a caravan city, it was closely allied to the Roman Empire. Strategically located at the crossroads of international trade between the East (China, India, Central Asia, Persia) and Europe, excavations have yielded rich evidence of its commercial heritage; aromatic herbs from Kashmir and China, fabrics from India, China and Turkistan and pearls from the Persian Gulf. Palmyra was a cosmopolitan city based on trade and communication, a central link in the caravan land-routes that transported silk, tea, spices, precious stones and other commodities across continents. This was an era prior to the discovery of any sea-route from China and India to the West. Palmyra was "an essential stopping place for the caravans that wanted to follow the shortest route between the Indian Ocean and the Mediterranean," notes Fabio Bourbon in *Archaeology and its Splendour.* In time, sea-routes strengthened and eventually cancelled the time-consuming and costly caravan land-routes.

The word 'caravanserai' originates from a Persian word meaning a 'hostel for travellers'. Caravanserais were complex constructions, often built like a fort housing travellers and traders, their goods and their means of transport (horses and camels). For security, a single door served as both entrance and exit. The fortress-like walls were built around a courtyard with its life-giving water-well. Rooms around the courtyard housed travellers and provided stables for their animals. A room for prayers was also set aside. Many of the important and large caravanserais were provided for and maintained by rulers as a means of controlling vital trade routes and as convenient venues for the collection of taxes. Caravanserais were to be found all over the Middle East: Arabian peninsula, Anatolia, Central Asia, Iran, Syria, Turkestan, Yemen. Some were built as staging-posts en route to the Holy Places of Mecca and Medina notes Yves Thoraval in *Dictionnaire de Civilisation Musalmane.*

Roger Stevens observes in *The Land of the Great Sophy* (Iran), "Along the edge of the great deserts *ab-ambars* or water storage tanks, tunnel-vaulted buildings flanked by high wind-towers, eerie in their isolation and, all too often, desolation, are more frequent than either. But on the old trade routes the standing feature of the landscape generally encountered every twenty miles or so is the caravanserai... They were for the most part in operation for travellers at the time of Curzon's visit in 1888 and it is only in the present century, mainly since the arrival of the motor-car, that they have fallen into decay." According to Arthur Upham Pope, the renowned Iranologist, "Never was the Persian facility for practical planning better demonstrated." Travelling by road in this region of vast desert and scrubland, one can see little evidence of habitation until one comes across an isolated mud-walled ruin that pierces the ground like broken teeth yet speaks of a once thriving transient community of travellers.

Desmond Stewart in his book *Early Islam* captures both the substance and spirit of caravanserais. "Great caravans travelled though Central Asia to Baghdad en route to North Africa and Mediterranean ports as far distant as Spain. Ships of the empire plied distant waters carrying merchandise between Far Eastern lands – India, China, Ceylon and the East Indies – and Persian Gulf and Red Sea ports. The vessels arriving at Baghdad's docks brought with them the varied resources of the world. From China came silk, ink, peacocks, porcelain, saddles and spices; from India rubies, silver, sandalwood, coconuts, ebony and dyes. Other cargoes included grain and linen from Egypt, glass and fruit from Syria, silk and other textiles from Persia; perfumes from Arabia; pearls from the Persian Gulf. Slaves and gold came from Africa; drugs, trinkets from Byzantium; leather from Spain; furs, amber, ivory and swords from as far away as Russia and Scandinavia. This international traffic in goods, and the payment it entailed led to a new profession – banking. An enterprise that reached a degree of sophistication that was not to be attained in the West for another three centuries. Two kinds of currencies were in use: the Persian dirham used in the East and the Byzantine gold denarius in the West." And Palmyra was a key staging post between the two worlds.

By the second half of the third century AD, with Rome's powerful hold over its colonies declining amidst anarchy and invasions, Palmyra rose to its zenith of prosperity under Queen Zenobia (266 - 272 AD). Today, Palmyra is synonymous with Queen Zenobia whose fame has come down through the ages along with that of the Queens Cleopatra, Hatshepsut and Nefertiti of Egypt.

The Roman historian Trebellius Pollio generously endowed Queen Zenobia with the following: "She was the noblest of all the women in the East, and the most beautiful...She had a dark skin, black eyes full of fire, teeth as white as pearls, a wonderfully lively countenance, and was of unimaginable gracefulness...Usually travelled on horseback, but could equally well march three or four miles on foot with the troops. She drank with her generals, but never took too much. She used vessels of gold set with precious stones that had belonged to Cleopatra. She kept royal state...She appeared in public as a Roman emperor, a helmet on her head and clad in a purple mantle with fringes decorated with pearls that left her arms bare..." Exercising greater independence, Zenobia soon founded an empire in the heart of the Syrian Desert that extended from the Mediterranean Sea to the Tigris River and from Asia Minor to Egypt. She created a cultural milieu in Palmyra, the most vibrant in the Middle East. The pinnacles of fame and power attained by Queen Zenobia soon reached the ears of the new Roman emperor Aurelian who regained control of Palmyra as a Roman vassal city and deposed Zenobia in 272 AD. Captured, Queen Zenobia was paraded through the streets of Rome in golden chains as the symbol of royal booty. She died in Tivoli near Rome.

This was the rise and fall, the zenith and collapse of the Palmyran civilisation. Palmyra was reduced from being the capital to a mere Syrian frontier stronghold. It never recovered its leading position, as Aleppo and then Damascus became centres of commerce and culture. Much later in the seventeenth century, Arabs came and built a fortress on the highest mountain peak and transformed the Roman temple of Bel into a citadel whose broken-down walls housed a community of Palmyra residents as late as the 1930s.

Some decades later...

Thirty years later, my husband was posted as Ambassador of Bangladesh to Iran and also accredited as Ambassador to Syria. I felt that I could not let go of the second opportunity of a lifetime to visit Palmyra. For my husband and our daughter, it would be their first. What would it be like to see this immemorial sight after the insignificant interval of thirty years of my lifetime?

This time, in 1999, we set out from Damascus in an air-conditioned car and made the drive in no time – so it appeared to me – since anticipation accelerates speed. My daughter, in clear terms, thought otherwise. There were occasional built-up areas along the way. I was on the lookout for the particular mountain that, once crossed, would reveal the Palmyra plain. We made the incline, took the dive, and then, once again, there lay before me the unforgettable sight. Majestic ruins preserved in the hot desert sun with a triumphal arch gracing columns silhouetted under the clear and deep blue sky. There it was, just as I remembered it; truly a poet was needed. A calendar of decades had simply slipped by.

We climbed the massive blocks of the tallest funerary tower - quite a feat given my husband's and my aging knees - and followed the indomitable Italians before us into the large Tomb of the Three Brothers. We then moved on to stroll amongst the sprawling remains of the once prosperous metropolis. My husband wrapped his head with a *keffiyeh*, the Arab head-dress popularised by Yasser Arafat, as a sunscreen. A guide gave us a worthwhile tour of the grand temple of Bel, pointing out the wine-presses, water aqueducts and the evidence left by inhabitants through the ages; an Ionic column decoration here, an icon painting there, Arabic inscriptions and the many wall-engravings depicting palms, the symbol of Palmyra.

As we drove by the Triumphal Arch, I suddenly came across a faded and dilapidated signpost – Hotel Zenobia. It still existed! We made a sharp left and entered the premises of the hotel where we had stayed thirty years ago. This time, my husband and our daughter had replaced my parents, my sister and brother as I sat once more under the shade-giving tree and drank coffee, intoxicated by the view of the spectacular open-air museum laid out before us. The French aphorism – *plus ca change, plus c'est la meme chose* (the more it changes, the more it remains the same) came to mind.

I asked the waiter if the manager was on duty. He seemed perturbed, I think he expected a rebuke of some sort and I re-assured him that I simply wanted to meet the manager, which I did at length. I told the manager that I was an old customer of thirty years ago – surely, before he was born. He laughed and replied, " Yes, Madame, I am twenty-four years old but you must have been a baby". I was most flattered at the gallantry of the young man but corrected him.

"No, I was at university!" We were both happy! After all, an Austrian saying declares: "At 20 you have the face the Lord gave you, at 40 the face that life gave you and at 60 you have the face that you deserve."

I then asked him about the history of Hotel Zenobia. We were standing in a building more than one hundred years old. It had originally been built as a caravanserai for a Palmyra Bedouin nomad family. Syria became a French protectorate (1920-1946) following the collapse of the Ottoman Empire at the end of the First World War. A French military post was stationed in the building and, to add spice, a Madame Margot de Andria alleged to be a French spy, had resided here. The building became a hotel, run by a French company, from 1920-1938. Subsequently, Palmyra residents, the al-Assad family, ran it as a hotel. In 1990, the Orient Tours and Company took over the management of Hotel Zenobia.

The original thirteen rooms facing the Palmyran ruins remain intact. We had stayed in one of them thirty years ago. Some additional rooms had recently been added to the back of the bungalow. Among the historical and notable personalities who had graced the rooms of Hotel Zenobia was T.E. Lawrence. After a long interval, I saw *Lawrence of Arabia* (made in 1962 with Peter O'Toole as T.E. Lawrence). It remains for me a superb film of immense historical interest with intelligent dialogue, splendid settings and brilliant characters. It must rank as one of the finest films ever made. Seeing it again after decades, my interest in one of the legendary figures of the twentieth century was rekindled.

I bought *Lawrence: The Uncrowned King of Arabia* by Michael Asher in Cairo and read it in Tehran. Occasionally, one comes across a book that one simply cannot put down where one relishes each and every page, not wanting it to end. This biography belongs to that rare category. Asher is a British Arab desert explorer and someone who, from childhood, hero-worshipped Lawrence. Yet in his search for the truth behind the man, Asher finds his hero to be somewhat flawed. For "Lawrence was both masochist and misogynist, a constant creator of myths and mysteries about himself. Yet this tormented, physically unimpressive man was also one of the authentic heroes of the twentieth century."

More recent guests at Hotel Zenobia have included President Jacques Chirac. Unfortunately, we were leaving Palmyra early next morning for Krak de Chevaliers - the King of Castles – and could not see the rooms where Lawrence had stayed. Krak de Chevaliers is the formidable Crusades fortress constructed in the Middle Ages: "An engine of intimidation" as described by a contemporary English traveller. T.E. Lawrence unabashedly wrote that it was "the best preserved and most wholly admirable castle in the world." He described another remote and daunting Crusades castle in Syria, the Qal'at Saladin, as "the most sensational thing in castle-building I have ever seen." *The Crusades: Islamic Perspectives* by Carole Hillenbrand reveals the excursions of the Christian Crusaders through the Levant as seen through Muslim eyes, an insight not often explored.

Agatha Christie had occupied suite number two for nine days in 1938. Agatha Christie's husband, Max Mallowan, renowned British archaeologist, worked for years in Mesopotamia, the land between the Tigris and Euphrates rivers, a vast cradle of civilisation that is, today, largely within the national boundaries of Iraq.

Inicidentally - and to digress - we had seen the rooms where Agatha Christie had stayed at the Old Cataract Hotel overlooking the Nile in Aswan in Upper Egypt. It is named the Agatha Christie suite and she wrote her famous novel *Death on the Nile* there in 1937 that was, subsequently, filmed on site. My daughter saw the film for the first time and I for the second and delighted in having seen all the sites of the film. The Old Cataract Hotel, full of historical and physical richesse, celebrated its hundred years in 1999. Aswan's flagship hotel owes much of its unique charm to its location over the rocks of the First Cataract of the Nile. Distinguished guests at the Old Cataract Hotel have included Winston Churchill, King Farouk of Egypt, Tsar Nicholas II and Aga Khan III and his Begum.

The Aga Khan chose to be buried in a mausoleum on a hill in Aswan. He died in 1957 when my father was posted in Paris and my parents presented official condolences on behalf of the Government of Pakistan to the young French-born Begum Aga Khan. We had the honour of meeting, in 1997, the graceful and gracious Begum Aga Khan who was clad in a French chiffon sari. She died in the south of France in May 2000 at the age of 94 and was buried beside her husband at Aswan. Such are the ties that create the legends of love. The late President Francois Mitterand was a regular guest at the Old Cataract Hotel. His last stay was a few months before his death when his daughter Mazarine accompanied him. His regular suite has been named the Francois Mitterand suite.

A gem of an anecdote goes like this: Lord Benbrook, a regular guest at the Hotel Cataract, who, arriving at the Terrace to find his favourite table taken, approached the intruder thus: "I am sorry, but this table is reserved." The occupant, an American, asked: "Since when?" Benbrook politely replied: "Since 20 years."

Hotels such as these are historical jewels whose very air and ambience breathe charm and character and constitute pages from history. Today, these hotels are one in a thousand and most others are a thousand and one. If only I had known that Hotel Zenobia was still there after thirty years, we would never have stayed the night at the twenty-year-old 'five star' Palmyra Chams chain-hotel. Already under renovation, the elevators were inoperative and the bathroom door did not lock. The narrow double bed in the large room had an enormous spotlight hanging over it that dominated the room and in the dark looked like a UFO in flight. How I regret not knowing of Hotel Zenobia's existence. However, we did make it back there for dinner and lingered over the view of Palmyra in the moonlight.

A welcome impression in Palmyra after the long interval was the fact that 'new' urban settlements and the supporting tourism infrastructure have been kept apart from the ancient settlement. The 'new' town of Palmyra is distinctly separate. The hostels, hotels, cafés, restaurants, snackbars, carpet and curio shops are all grouped together and do not infiltrate the *raison d'être* of a visitor's odyssey to Palmyra. "…The city is the sort of accessible ruin that used to give ruins a good name – it is as it remains; a starkly crumbling trace of history and not a theme park; a continuation of the landscape by other means," Nick Coleman in an article on Syria entitled 'On the Ramparts where Ancient Struggles with Modern'.

Amongst the limestone mountains in Cappadocia (Goreme) in Turkey, early Christian chapels, monasteries and sanctuaries were carved deep into the rocks in the first century AD and adorned with beautifully painted frescoes and much gilded work. Earlier, the Hittites had carved living quarters in the soft contours of nature. I first visited Cappadocia in 1976 while travelling from London and then again in 1998 en route to Iran. I was appalled at the litter of campsites, Coca-Cola stands, souvenir stalls, beer-houses and other features of global tourism that had encroached on the mountains by my second visit. It was a sorry sight. Measures must be taken to prevent the 'support system' of tourism from blighting heritage sites.

A trek to the top of the highest mountain in Palmyra to see the sunset, where the remains of the Arab-built citadel lie, is mandatory. Hardy trekkers and back-packers make the long and arduous climb on foot. Us comfort-seeking creatures sought the facility of a car-ride. On the climb-up, we had an aerial view of the sprawling city of Palmyra. An annual Palmyra festival celebrated in May attracts Syrian, Arab and international entertainers. A recently laid-out racecourse for camels and horses comes alive. A few ancient funerary towers are spaced here and there in the distance. A small, square, white-painted building, which appeared to be newly built, caught my eye as it was highly incongruous in the setting. Clearly visible was 'W.C.' written in large letters across the front façade; a sight for sore eyes but a boon for the bladder.

Some one hundred viewers of the sunset - all tourists - stood in small groups at the base of the formidable fortress at the top of the mountain, mercifully silent, waiting for sundown. It was a golden setting. There was nothing around us, not at the height we were at. Down below in the Palmyra plains, a vast terrain undisturbed by man, it was as if time had stood still. The sense of timelessness of Palmyra was strong at that moment; a dreamlike scene of unmatched serenity that wrapped us in its silence and beauty.

"The desert is so huge and the horizons so distant, that they make a person feel small, as if he should remain silent. There is the absolute timelessness of the desert...You do not even have to understand the desert; all you have to do is contemplate a single grain of sand and you will see in it all the marvels of creation." Paulo Coelho in *The Alchemist.*

A quotation in a travel-guide came to mind. "Arabian sands are a source of intense fascination from time immemorial. Ripples of sand and sand-dunes are bathed in glorious gold with the setting sun." The desert is *terra incognito.* Man has, from far back in time, roamed the immensities of the desert; its barren hills, deep hues and unending sand.

ALEPPO : "THE MILKY WHITE"

"The day will come when one must part from you, city of Aleppo.
It is most appropriate that there will be no joy then
For the truth is, beauty can be found here
In her well-built grandeur.
There are all sorts of merchandise to be found here.
The grace of wealth and goods is beyond counting.
But more than this, her water and air are enchanting
As are her river and her buildings."

Nabi, eighteenth century Ottoman court poet

Flying into Aleppo from Damascus, the barren beige landscape gave way to checkerboard patches of fertile cultivation. The soil appeared a rich reddish brown. I took it to be a positive indicator of the historical prominence and current prosperity of the city. Aleppo is Syria's second capital. Legend has it that the Prophet Abraham milked his cow on the hill that dominates the city. Hence we have Aleppo's Arabic name Halab al-Shahba, Aleppo : 'The Milky White'. The Syrian name for Aleppo is 'Halab'.

The kingdom of Aleppo existed in the reign of the Akkadians around 3000 BC and the city boasts a history that long predates the advent of Islam. Aleppo has witnessed the sweep of history, every civilisation in the Middle East has added to its rich legacy; the Hittites, the Egyptians, the Sumerians, the Aramanians, the Cananites, the Persians, the Macedonians, the Seljuks, the Romans and Byzantines. The Arab conquest of Aleppo in 637 lasted approximately 900 years until the Ottoman Turk reign from 1516 to the end of the First World War. A period of French mandate followed. Syria gained independence in 1945.

Today's international boundaries situate Aleppo in northern Syria, close to Turkey to its north, Iraq to its east, Lebanon to its southwest and Jordan to its south. The city's unique strategic location has historically lent itself to its position as a thriving commercial centre at the crossroads between the Middle East, Asia, the Mediterranean and Europe. In ancient times, Aleppo reigned as a major commercial entrepot for regional and international trade – a prominent halt along the fabled Silk Road connecting the East and the West. Testiment to its international standing, innumerable remains of caravanserais dot the city. These stopovers provided necessary facilities to travellers and traders and were sources for the exchange and replenishment of stocks and products. It was a halt for weary merchants and their transport, be it camels or horses. Today's transport is more likely to be a massive four-wheel-drive vehicle. The transit complex could house a bazaar, water reserves, a mosque, a *hamaam, a madrasah*, offices, storage and accommodation The caravanserais of yesteryears were the equivalent of today's hotel/ motel, garage, petrol-station, bank, café, restaurant and travel agency.

Aleppo has always prided itself on being in the midst of culture and commerce. The number of signboards and billboards that appear in Cyrillic, Armenian and, to a lesser degree, in French impresses upon one the traditional cosmopolitan character of the city. European travel literature has mirrored the cosmopolitan element that is so apparent in this city. Aspiring and established entrepreneurs from Europe - Amsterdam, London, Marseilles and Venice - mingled with Armenian, Jewish and Muslim merchants. The Armenian presence in Aleppo is pronounced; Armenian villages of eastern Anatolia (Turkey) were early sources of immigrants to Aleppo. Bruce Masters remarks in 'Aleppo: the Ottoman Empire's Caravan City', in *The Ottoman City between East and West: Aleppo, Izmir and Istanbul* that "Although there were clearly many more Greek Orthodox Christians in the city at any time during the seventeenth century, the Armenian community of some three hundred households in 1620 was by far the most influential Christian community in the city with many of its members holding positions in the Ottoman administration." Aleppo's cosmopolitan culture attracted people from far and wide and the city's population reached its peak of about 120,000 inhabitants in the second half of the seventeenth century. Aleppo ranked as the third largest urban centre in the Ottoman Empire, after Istanbul and Cairo.

The Arab period saw the city flourish in terms of architecture, with the building of innumerable mosques, *madrasahs, hamaams* and *souqs*. A fortress on the central hill of Aleppo was built by Sayf-al-Dawla in 944. The Aleppo citadel stands in the centre of the city, 160 feet high. It was attacked by the Mongols in the middle of the thirteenth century and then again by Tamerlame at the end of the fourteenth century. The Mamluks added on to the indomitable citadel of Aleppo in the thirteenth century. Earlier civilisations dating back 5000 years had already built an edifice on the site. The citadel today, surrounded by a dry moat, rises abruptly from the midst of the teeming city. It is said that architecture is 'the printing press of the ages' and 'that buildings record the state of the society in which they were erected'. An unfortunate testimony to our twenty-first century is the sea of plastic bags and litter that is to be found within the moat surrounding the citadel.

We crossed the bridge over the moat and then crossed the first line of defence, the exterior thick wall of the massive citadel. The colossal wooden door with metal bars threatened to close behind us. We climbed up and down stairs and over the remnants of walls. There were towers that gave us a birds eye view of the city and, in the depths of the towers, cold, dark and damp caves. There were elaborate *hamaams*, built separately for men and women, for steam baths, cold baths, rest rooms and tea-rooms. Aleppo's *hamaams* are renowned and about sixty of them are to be found throughout the city, some dating back eight hundred years. An enormous hall has been restored with an Arab interior complete with ceiling and walls painted in rich colours on panelled and carved woodwork. One could easily spend a full day exploring the many nooks and crannies that would reveal hidden surprises. It is undoubtedly a striking example of Arab military architecture. However, we had to move on.

Aleppo's status as a major commercial transit city attracted the first Europeans. At the end of the fourteenth century, Venice had appointed a vice-consul at Aleppo. The French and then the English in the second half of the sixteenth century followed suit. Yet the city also had to endure the Mongol invasion by Hulagu in 1260 and Tamerlame in 1401 when the city was pillaged and scores of people were killed or sold into slavery. In 1348, the bubonic plague decimated the population. Yet, again and again, Aleppo rebuilt itself and, each time, regained its primary role as a regional commercial hub.

By the time Ottoman rule had established itself in Syria in 1516, Aleppo was recognised as a thriving commercial centre. According to 'The Ottoman Conquest and the Development of the

Great Arab Towns' by Andre Raymond in *Studies in Arab History*, "Until the middle of the eighteenth century, Aleppo remained the main market of the whole East, astride two commercial streams: the stream of manufactured goods going from the West to the East and the stream of Eastern products and raw materials moving from the hinterland to Europe…The bulk of its trade with Marseilles was more important than the trade between Marseilles and Egypt: in 1786-1789 the sales and purchases between Marseilles and Egypt were worth 4.2 million French pounds, while for the same period the trade between Marseilles and Aleppo and Alexandretta (in Syria) was worth 5.6 million pounds." Chevalier d'Arvieux wrote, "Aleppo is undoubtedly the largest, the richest and the most beautiful town of the whole Ottoman Empire after Constantinople and Cairo. The splendour of Aleppo is not confined to mosques only, but it is just as striking in the *khans* and bazaars, where goods from all the parts of the world can be found."

It is important to note that the Ottoman sultans regarded themselves as custodians of the Sunni Islam faith. The Haj pilgrimage passed through much of the Ottoman lands. The two major gathering centres for the pilgrims were Damascus for the Arab and Asian Muslims and Cairo for the northern Arab and African Muslims. In convoys consisting of thousands of people, humans and animals moved towards the Hejaz in present day Saudi Arabia. The pilgrims had to purchase food, tents, mounts and other necessities en route to sustain their three or more month journey to the Holy Places. At a strategic crossroad, Aleppo was a key supplier of goods and services to the Haj pilgrims.

In these mass gatherings, commercial exchanges within the sprawling Ottoman Empire were both extensive and intensive. There was a large market within the empire for the transfer of foreign goods. Bruce Masters notes that "French consular reports indicated that in 1812, the volume of trade between Baghdad and Aleppo was at least four times as great as the volume of trade between France and Aleppo.

This trade all carried on camel back consisted of imports to the city: Iranian cloth and tobacco, Indian cotton cloth, spices and indigo and coffee from Yemen and exports from it: European imports, especially sugar, silk cloth and soap." Another authority cites that in the Middle Ages 'one day's sale in Aleppo equalled a month's in Cairo.'

Masters also notes, "The other great institution of Aleppo's trade was the caravan. The caravans were of two types: the large trans-desert caravans and smaller teams of camels, mules or donkeys. The first could range up to 2000 camels in size and plied the routes to Baghdad and the Hijaz, the latter serviced Anatolia, the Syria coast and Egypt. The largest caravans to the Hijaz set out during the annual pilgrimage, although merchants sometimes organised smaller caravans specifically for the transport of coffee…"

The eleventh century Persian poet Manuchehri wrote the following verse on the caravan trail.

"O Traveller, strike and fold the tents of dawn:

Already from this caravanserai the scout moves on

Ahead, the drummer beats the morning drum,

The camel-drivers pack their mounts, and would be gone."

Our next visit was to the famed covered souqs of Aleppo that extend some ten kilometres and are located at the base of the citadel. The majority of the bazaars belong to the fifteenth and sixteenth centuries. Many regard the Aleppo *souqs* as only second to Istanbul's Kapah Carsi (Covered Market). I have sauntered through Kapah Karsi but my absolute favourite *souq* in the Middle East is Khan-al-Khalili in Cairo. Masters provides a descriptive account of Aleppo's bazaars. "Aleppo's markets were roofed and relatively cool in summer and, by all accounts, remarkably clean all year round. Rubbish was collected by yet another guild that sold it to the operators of the city's public bathhouses. The market was served by numerous fountains, public baths, mosques and a large public lavatory, all maintained as beneficiaries of yet other pious foundations." We also found the souqs "remarkably clean". These commercial passages are truly a living museum of popular traditions.

Mark Twain, in 1867, in *An Innocent Abroad* described the bazaar at nearby Smyrna (present-day Turkey) as follows; "...business is chiefly carried on in great covered bazaars, closed like a honeycomb with innumerable shops no larger than a common closet, and the whole hive cut up into a maze of alleys about wide enough to accommodate a laden camel, and well calculated to confuse a stranger and eventually lose him...". The oriental splendour of all the central markets in the Middle East has been covered in his comments.

A renovated section of the central souq caters now exclusively to tourists. All the souvenirs one may want from Aleppo, Syria and even Iran, Turkey, Lebanon and Egypt can be found here; Iranian block-printed tablecloths, Turkish rugs, Lebanese glassware and Egyptian papyrus prints are some items sold among the range of products. This is the artisans' modern retail outlet, under one roof for the sake of convenience. Much of what we saw we had already burdened ourselves with on earlier postings or visits to these countries. No more knick-knacks or purchases of international trivia that appears so necessary at the time.

So we strolled into a 'real' *souq*, a never-ending tunnel of bright lights further illuminated by the sunlight that glimmered through the roof-openings and vaulted window-openings and with everything under the sun to buy. We entered the cloth market and my eye was caught by rolls of Syrian brocade in deep, rich colours of red, blue, green and gold. Where else would I find such exquisitely woven and patterned textiles? I succumbed to temptation and we acquired a blue and gold brocade tablecloth – an essential for survival! However, it was reassuring to know - and it marginally eased feelings of guilt - that Aleppo has always been known as a major silk trading centre. Iranian silk from the Caspian Sea region of Gilan, Turkish silk from Antioch and Bursa and silk from distant China had frequently changed hands in the textile *souq* where we had been bargaining for our purchase.

The *souqs* are named after their trade. Thus we have the cloth-market, the gold market, the silver market, the shoe market... Then there is the spice market where the various aromas from sacks of colourful spices waft by leaving a fragrant trail. Then there is the bazaar that stocks sweatshirts with "Harvard" printed across the front, Tex-Mex T-shirts, bland coloured track suits, shiny polyester dresses and trousers, and pink and yellow frilly nylon dresses that no child, I think, would like to be caught wearing. This *souq* is visually representative of today's international interaction.

A visit to the Aleppo Museum was a disappointment and somewhat sad, not for its content but its form. The museum, built in 1965, looks as old as its years; unkempt and ill maintained. Built in Soviet block style architecture, the vast complex is a sorry sight. That late afternoon, we were the only visitors. A central courtyard displayed one of the museum's stunning possessions, a large and brilliant Byzantine period floor mosaic of animals; goats, panthers, rhinoceros and elephants, all in motion. We walked around it a couple of times and marvelled at the artist's ability to capture the realistic movements of the animals. Yet, there it lay on the ground totally unprotected from the elements. The authorities plan to build a shelter over it. However, they admitted that the masterpiece has been lying exposed for long years.

Once again, I mused over the ongoing debate about whether cultural treasures should be left at natural sites or whether the Louvre, the Berlin Museum, the British Museum, the New York Metropolitan Museum or the Hermitage in St. Petersburg or any other cardinal repository of international heritage should return foreign treasures and masterpieces to their countries of origin. That day I realised, sadly, that there was an argument for the leading museums of the world to house treasures such as this magnificent piece of neglected and forsaken art.

In contrast, we had a delectable dinner of Syrian/Allepine cuisine in a beautifully restored sixteenth century palace. Beit Wakil (Wakil's House) is located in the old district of Aleppo in a narrow alley paved with cobblestones. A recent private initiative to restore some of the old houses has resulted in the opening of a number of restaurants that have combined age-old architecture and tradition with modern amenities. Another 'new' restaurant named after the empress of Austria 'Sissi' looked most inviting as we walked by it. Adjacent to it is an Armenian school for girls.

Beit Wakil viewed from the outside is plain and simple. Once inside, a magical world from an oriental story comes into existence. The in-house brochure did justice to it; "The beautiful courtyards with breathtaking relief and tracery work of their walls, the marble fountains among the jasmine and lemon trees, the unique Liwan with its majestic arch and coloured marble flooring, the elegant arabesque woodwork of the wall cupboards, the hand-drawn wooden ceilings with cornices, the famous central qua'a (room) with its suspended dome and coloured arabesque glass windows, the stone-built cellars and the limestone caves below with a labyrinth of tunnels, one of which links the palace to the Citadel of Aleppo" are just a few of the many elements which distinguish Aleppo masonry art and Arab architectural design.

To add to ambience, steep steps lead down to cold and dark underground rooms. Carved into the stones are recesses for water and small well-like holes for storing food. Long shafts allow air and light into the caves. These underground rooms were obviously built for habitation. I was reminded of visiting similar structures in Famagusta, Cyprus, where entire communities had lived in such caves in the sixteenth and seventeenth centuries and again in the twentieth century when civil war erupted between Greek and Turkish Cypriots in the 1960s.

Beit Wakil combines a fine restaurant with a hotel consisting of sixteen rooms. I asked about the occupancy rate, with the thought that it might be fine to dine in a sixteenth century palace but perhaps not to spend the night there, the manager replied that except for one vacant room (that he showed us), all the rooms were occupied. He led us upstairs, along wrought-iron balconies overlooking a courtyard and into a small but comfortably furnished room with Syrian woven fabrics and a newly attached bathroom – perfectly cosy and inviting.

Hotel Baron is a historical institution in Aleppo and well known among travellers throughout the Middle East. Our *Lonely Planet Guide Book on the Middle East* (1994 edition) describes the Hotel Baron as follows: "There's only one place in the middle-range category – the Baron Hotel. The hotel was opened in 1909 by two Armenian brothers and soon became one of the most famous in the Middle East. The place still has loads of character although sadly it is becoming increasingly rundown…If you can't afford the stay there, the least you should do is to have a beer in the bar." Thinking that conditions in 2001 must have further deteriorated - erroneous as we found out - we had hotel reservations elsewhere (disappointing as we found out). However, after the Aleppo museum visit, our friendly and resourceful Armenian guide had made an appointment with the owner/manager of Hotel Baron, another Armenian. We ended up spending more waking hours at Hotel Baron than at Hotel Chams where we only went to sleep the night.

Over a cup of hot and frothy cappucino in the bar/salon, where dark wooden beams crisscrossed the ceiling, the afternoon spent with Mr. Armen Mazloumian was a memorable journey into bygone times. We entered a period of history that no longer exists but for a structure that has welcomed a parade of personalities through its doors. The chairs we sat on dated to 1916 and so did some of the furniture in the adjacent dining room.

This is the true story. In 1856, Mr. Mazloumian's great grandfather had travelled from Turkey to Jerusalem on business with the East India Company and the Levant Company. In Jerusalem he found accommodation for travellers that provided separate rooms for sleeping 1-3 persons, with - though not attached - clean washroom and toilet facilities nearby, a dining hall and separate salons for socialising. These convenient and clean arrangements are primitive by our standards but were luxurious at the time. One has to remember that the only public accommodation at that time – the mid-nineteenth century – was the traditional caravanserais. On his return journey, he stopped in Aleppo and opened the first Hotel Ararat in 1860. Mount Ararat can be called the symbol of Armenia. A novelty feature - then as now - was the bell-gong that was rung to announce meals. Once the very senior Mazloumian had died, his two sons continued the hotel business.

A French-Armenian architect built the Hotel Baron and it opened its doors to the public in 1909. It was actually the second Hotel Ararat and became Hotel Baron in 1916. Before I could ask Mr. Mazloumian how Hotel Baron had got its name, he provided the answer. The word for 'sir' in Armenian is 'diar'. He speculated that as the Armenian staff at the hotel called his grandfather 'diar', the European guests began calling the owner 'baron' as a term of respect in lieu of 'sir'. And so the Hotel Ararat became Hotel Baron in 1916, during the time of the French mandate in Syria. And the street on which it stands took the same name – Baron Street.

The Visitors' Book dates back to 1933. It is kept in safe storage. The Swedish royal family stayed at Hotel Baron in 1937. Hitler's senior officials were guests too. So was Lady Gertrude Bell, Lady Edwina Mountbatten, Charles Lindbergh, Kim Philby posted as a journalist in Beirut, Yuri Gagarin the Soviet astronaut, Julie Christie…William Saroyan the American-Armenian author, David Rockefeller, Agatha Christie, T.E. Lawrence (of Arabia)… but sadly not us. I had read the brilliant book *Lawrence: The Uncrowned King of Arabia* by Michael Asher and I marked the page where Asher wrote, "As he lay in his bath in the Baron's Hotel in Aleppo, he cannot have avoided the conclusion that his own fear had defeated him." We saw the room that T.E. Lawrence had once occupied. It was a heady feeling.

We were taken on a tour of Hotel Baron. Agatha Chrisite had occupied room 203. It was however now also occupied, so we were shown the duplicate Room 202 instead. The hotel, at the time, was under selective renovation in order to modernise the amenities, yet retain its Old World charm. The ground floor was built in 1909. The second floor was added in 1937. There are 45 rooms in all. Eight rooms have the original furniture. In one of the rooms, we saw a free-standing wooden cupboard and twin large enamelled white sinks with old-fashioned taps and faucets. Here were items totally functional yet objects that I had not seen for a long time. The geometric patterned tiled floor in black and white or multi-coloured was very similar to the flooring in my aunt's house – now demolished – in Karachi, Pakistan. The spacious corridors had some framed and faded posters of the London/Istanbul/Baghdad Simplar Orient/Taurus Express Train. The poster picture was of the Ctesiphon Arch outside Baghdad that I had first seen in 1973 and then again in 2000. It was a stroll down memory lane.

Lingering on our way out, we walked into the adjacent salon. In a show-cupboard were some ancient pieces of pottery, a black and white picture of Hotel Baron in 1911 and a letter from T.E. Lawrence written from Hotel Baron on April 1, 1914 that appeared in the book *Home Letters,* a compilation of his letters published after his death. Then there was a medium-sized framed profile sketch of Lawrence that was presented to Mr. Mazloumian by Colonel Dick Clarke, the British Defence Attache posted in Damascus from 1994-1997. I asked Mr. Mazloumian how Colonel Clarke came to own this portrait. Apparently, Colonel Clarke bought it and then presented it to Hotel Baron. Mr. Mazloumian insisted that it looked more like Peter O'Toole than T.E. Lawrence! I replied that it is only our generation that knows of Peter O'Toole and for the younger generation, it would be irrelevant. He laughed and agreed. Behind us, quietly seated in a deep armchair, I glimpsed a young girl smiling.

A dedicated and passionate owner runs an incredibly historical hotel. There is more than sole commercial viability to the continued existence of the Hotel Baron. Only a keen sense of the past can justify an investment in the present for the future of this family-run hotel. We left Hotel Baron mesmerised by the long and extensive voyage through history and ready to hit any trail before us, armed with two gifts of modern carry-bags with 'Hotel Baron' discretly printed on them. These bags accompanied us on many other travels within the region.

DAMASCUS : "BY RIGHT THE ETERNAL CITY"

"If Paradise be on earth, Damascus must be it; if it is in heaven, Damascus can parallel and match it."

Ibn Jubayr, Spanish Muslim geographer and traveller visited Damascus in 1184.

"She measures Time not by days, months or years, but by the empires she has seen rise and crumble to ruins."

Mark Twain in *Innocent Abroad*

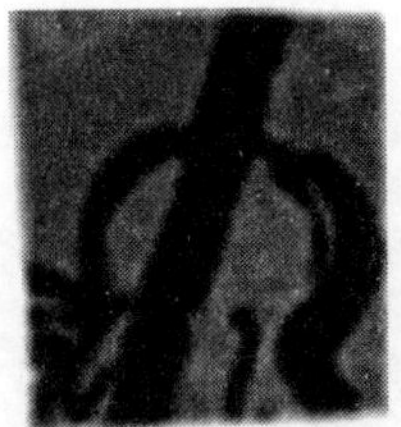

As the plane flew into Damascus from Tehran, I noticed the many domes and minarets of mosques jutting out even in the sparsely settled areas below us. Well, we were entering a city known, amongst many other epithets, as the 'City of Mosques.' The old city of Damascus can boast some two hundred and fifty mosques alone. The aerial view of Damascus is truly a city of domes. There are old mosques, new mosques and mosques in the making. Neither are the mosques showpieces but active centres for prayers and gatherings.

Damascus is the first city that I lived in abroad. Born in East Pakistan, now Bangladesh, I accompanied my parents to Damascus in 1950. My father was on his first diplomatic post in Damascus and he was setting up the Embassy of Pakistan mission. My next visit to Damascus occurred some twenty years later, when my father was the Ambassador of Pakistan to Lebanon. We then made frequent trips across the Bekaa Valley to Syria. Another thirty years were to pass before I touched the soil of Syria again. This was when my husband was Ambassador in Iran and concurrently accredited to Syria in 1999. A number of nostalgic visits to places I had visited earlier or had missed earlier followed. My last visit to Damascus - a city known as the city most continuously inhabited in the world – was in May 2001.

Following the Iran Air flight path on the video screen before us, I was suddenly struck by the fact that over past decades, I had visited each and every one of the cities shown on the screen: Amman, Ankara, Baghdad, Baku, Beirut, Cairo, Damascus, Esfahan, Tiblisi and Yerevan. Some had been visited and some had been lived in. Some of the places had even changed their parent country; Baku, Tiblisi and Yerevan in the early 1980s had been part of the Soviet Union. Today in the twenty-first century, they are to be found in independent Azerbaijan, Georgia and Armenia. The trip to Damascus seemed to mirror my life in the region; an area fondly lived in and visited often over decades. If I am a long-term traveller in the Middle East, I have only followed with equal enthusiasm the footsteps of any number of travellers before me.

Sham/Dimashq has the reputation of being the oldest city in the world. Mark Twain supporting the claim pointed out, "Though another claims the name, old Damascus is by right the Eternal City." According to accounts, thirty-three successive civilisations have left their traces in Damascus. The city has always been in the path of the great sweep of history. It was first settled in 6000 BC. Yet recent discoveries suggest habitation as long ago as 8000 BC. Little is known of the identity of those inhabitants. In 2000 BC, the Amorites established a small principality. Damascus, a focal point of the Armaean kingdom was documented in the Old Testament. In 64 BC, the Romans made Damascus part of their empire. Damascenes became the mercantile middlemen of the Roman Empire; marketing and distributing products between the Orient and Europe. One of the ten most prominent cities of the empire, Damascene products such as swords, glassware and textile were renowned all over the Roman Empire. A Jewish traveller Moshe Bassola from Italy wrote in 1522: "Damascus is a great city, twice the size of Bologna…It is surrounded by very strong walls and fortifications, and by a moat. There is also a very strong citadel. All kinds of crafts and wares may be found there, more than in Venice…In particular, the manufacture and commerce in silk are extensive…Women also earn much money, and in general, anyone who is willing to work hard in commerce can keep his family in plenty, even if he has little capital, since there is profit in everything…"

Damascus is often credited with being the site where Arabic numerals were invented; the zero in mathematics, algebra, alchemy, astronomy, logarithms and physics. Bertrand Russell in his *History of Western Philosophy* wrote: "It is instructive to consider some of the words that we derive from Arabic, such as: algebra, alcohol, alchemy, alembic, alkali, azimuth, nadir and zenith…These words would give a good picture of some of the things we owe to the Arabs." Significant developments in agriculture, language of trade and urban development, philosophy and metallurgy also took place in Damascus, a city always at the forefront of thought and culture.

Arabs from the Arabian Peninsula took control of Damascus in 635 AD and mass conversion to Islam took place. The first few decades of Arab rule were the Golden Age of the city; for a brief period its empire stretched from the shores of the Atlantic to the Indus River basin and from the south of France to western China. The Omayyad dynasty took control of the city in 661 under the fifth Caliph al-Moawiya, thus ending one thousand years of western rule. This signalled the artistic and cultural apex of the city. Damascus' reputation as a jewel in Islamic heritage remained intact. At the time of its demise in 750, the Omayyad Empire extended from the Pyrenees to Samarkand and the Punjab. After this, under Abbasid rule, Damascus became a provincial town as they made their capital Baghdad. Subsequent Arab dynasties gave rise to other capitals in the region - Aleppo, Cairo and Mosul. Elaborating on Islamic cities in *The Islamic City: A Colloquium*, Hourani and Stern argue that Islamic civilisation is largely urban-based with its prolific mosques, *madrasahs*, *souqs* and *hamaams* contributing towards the metropolises' power and prestige.

Devastating foreign excursions into Damascus by the Crusaders in the eleventh and early fifteenth centuries and the Mongols periodically in the twelfth, thirteenth and fourteenth centuries brought chaos and destruction in the ancient city. Under the Crusaders, the Kingdom of Damascus in an armistice agreement had to provide revenue from agricultural lands in a three-way split. "One third for the Turks, one third for the Franj (Westerners), and one third for the peasants," notes Ibn al-Qalanisi the Damascene chronicler of the eleventh century. Hulagu devastated Damascus in the thirteenth century. Tamerlane attacked the city in 1399. During the Ayubid dynasty, particularly under the Kurdish ruler Saladin in the late twelfth century, Damascus regained its regional prominence and enjoyed a brief period of renaissance. Contemporary European travellers noted that the city was considerably larger than either Paris or Florence. A third golden age for Damascus occurred from 1260 to 1277 under the rule of Bahri Mameluke. Damascus remained a principal city of the Ottoman Empire from 1516 to 1918.

The city emerged as a primary centre for the early twentieth Arab nationalist movement. Fakhri al-Barudi was one such Damascene nationalist and man of letters who espoused the concept of one indivisible Arab national homeland extending all the way from the Indian Ocean to the Atlantic shores. In poetic terms he wrote:

"The countries of the Arabs are my homelands:
From Damascus to Baghdad;
From Syria to the Yemen,
to Egypt, and all the way to Tetuan."

Following the Ottoman defeat in the First World War, Syria passed into French control. The French mandate lasted till Syria attained its independence in 1946.

Damascus was a primary rendezvous in the region for Haj pilgrims on their way to the Holy city of Mecca. Situated at a good distance from the sea and from the extensive hinterland to its east, Damascus nevertheless made good use of its location as a staging post for the annual pilgrimage. According to Ross Burns in *Monuments of Syria: An Historical Guide,* "The pilgrimage was a 'gigantic enterprise' particularly important to the economy of Damascus, especially under the Ottomans whose claim to most of the Muslim world meant that a great deal of the empire's credibility and its claim to the Caliphate depended on escorting the pilgrimage safely to Mecca and back each year. Up to 30,000 pilgrims would converge on the assembly point in the Midan quarter to join the consolidated caravan for the six-week journey across the desert to Mecca…" In one of the neighbourhoods, the travellers would buy their food supplies, clothes, tents and animals, thus contributing to Damascus' thriving economy. The Haj was a powerful stimulus for trade within the empire.

On the mode of caravan travel, Philip Hitti provides a detailed description in *Capital Cities of Arab Islam*, "In the Peninsula (Arab) the one-humped, long-suffering, undemanding camel was, of course, the main means of transportation. It could carry five hundred pounds, cover twenty-five miles a day, and survive for days on a minimal supply of food and water. The camel was an indispensable member of the Arabian caravan…Caravan trade was a more complicated business than appears on the surface. Besides finances, training, and experience, it involved knowledge of geography and of facilities for supplying water and relaying mounts. Guides and guards were necessary, so were alliances – at least forms of understanding with tribes whose territories lay en route. Passage often entailed payment of tolls, taxes, or bribes. Escorts were reinforced on passing through a hostile territory. A caravan might consist of hundreds of camels and scores of merchants…Merchants counted on up to a hundred per cent profit to meet expenses and ensure the proper yield on their investment." The scale of the operation is evident in a statement by Bertrand de la Brocquiere who was in Damascus when a caravan came in from the desert. He observed that it took two nights and three days to offload that caravan.

In *The Arab Awakening,* George Antonious notes the impact that the building of the Hejaz railway, begun in 1908, had on the region. "But the most important result, and one which Abdul-Hamid (the Ottoman Sultan) had perhaps not envisaged was the speeding up of communications for travel and therefore for ideas in the western Arab province. Before the operation of the line, it would take a quick caravan not less than forty days to travel from Damascus to Madina; while the sea-journey from Syria to the Hejaz took from ten to fifteen days, according to the sailings which were infrequent and capricious. With the railway, the two cities were brought to within five days of each other; and this abbreviation was destined, as we shall see, to make an incalculable difference to the fortunes of the Arab movement when at last if found an opportunity for breaking into open revolt." The improved transportation system had a long reaching impact on communication within the region and on subsequent political developments.

"The Umayyad mosque along with the Dome of the Rock in

Jerusalem is one of the great monuments to the ingenuity of early, Islam," remarks Ross Burns in *Monuments of Syria: An Historical Guide.* Equally categorical, al-Adrissi in 1154 declared, "In Damascus, there is a mosque that has no equal in the world." The Omayyad mosque ranks fourth after the sanctuaries of Mecca, Medina and Jerusalem. The ground beneath the Omayyad mosque first saw a Semitic temple, then a Christian church and then in 708 the Caliph al-Walid commissioned its construction that was completed in 715, the year of his death. The original wooden octagonal dome was destroyed in a fire in 1893.

The Palestinian geographer al-Maqdisi visited the city in 985 when Damascus was ruled by the Fatimid caliphate from Egypt. He has left us a vivid description of the famed mosque. "The walls of the mosque, to a height of two men, are faced with multi-coloured marble, and from there to the ceiling with mosaics bearing representations of trees and towns and displaying inscriptions, all the ultimate in beauty, elegance and artistry. Hardly a known tree or town does not figure on the walls. The column capitals are covered with gold; portico arches are ornamented with mosaics...The *mihrab* and its surroundings are covered with carnelian and turquoise stones of the largest possible size. To the left of it is another *mihrab*, reserved for the use of the sultan who, at a cost – I was told – of 500 dinars, renovated it."

The Omayyad mosque is best approached from one end of the ancient Souq al-Hamidiye. Here too exists one of the most characteristic features of Islamic cities, the covered street designed for the comfort of shoppers to protect them from the fierce glare of the sun. The bazaar provides every commodity for sale under one roof. This is the horizontal precursor of today's multi-storeyed shopping mall. When I first visited Souq al-Hamidiye some thirty years ago, gaudy coloured lingerie of every description and size was hung up for display. This apparel is still displayed on hangers that sway in the breeze creating a rainbow of colours. We made a stopover for al-Hamidiye's famed icecream at an icecream parlour-cum-restaurant. A vintage outlet, we were told that Jordan's King Abdullah had been a customer the past week.

"There's no doubt about it - walking the length of the shady and sinuous al-Hamidiyeh Souk, mingling with vibrant humanity going about its wordly business, and then bursting out into this space, at different times sacred to so many faiths and religions - is one of the greatest experiences to be had in any city on earth" is the level of enthusiasm recorded by Dan Cruickshank in *Around the World in 80 Treasures.*

Out of the Souq, a soaring Roman arch built in 1195 semi-circles the hustle and bustle of a busy market. This arch is all that remains of the Temple of Jupiter. Near the Souq al-Hamidiye are the traditional warehouses for the receiving, storing and dispatching of goods and also the rest houses for traders and travellers. Today Damascus is still divided into quarters; Christian, Kurdish, European and upperclass and bazaar. The population is mostly Arab but a melting pot exists in the form of Afghans, Armenians, Kurds, Persians, Turks and Turkomans. Most of the Jewish population immigrated to Israel in 1948.

The 'Barada Panel' gold-painted mosaic tiles bring to mind the mosaic decoration of the Dome of the Rock in Jerusalem. The mosaics depict the - now dry - Barada River in Damascus along with an abundance of trees, fruits and palaces. These mosaics once adorned much of the walls of the inner courtyard of the Omayyad mosque. What we see is both sumptuous and shimmering. The beautifully detailed arabesque decorated columns are engraved with Islamic inscriptions.

The football-field size courtyard of the Omayyad mosque has lost none of its impact or splendour in twelve centuries. Its size is some 50 metres by 122 metres. The flooring is of white marble put in place in the late nineteenth century to replace the earlier eleventh century stone or baked tiles. The hot sun brilliantly reflected off the marble creates a visual impact. Within the complex, lies the shrine of Imam Hussein. Following his death at Kerbela, his head was supposedly brought to Damascus by Caliph al-Moawiya and displayed in the mosque. Particularly, for Shi'ia Muslims, it is a major pilgrimage site. Also within the complex lies the tomb that reputedly holds the head of John the Baptist.

The Beit Khalid al-Azem is a perfect example of Syrian-Arab architecture. It belonged to a former Prime Minister and follows the Arab/Turkish pattern of two distinct zones of residence; *haremlek* for the women and family social occasions and *salamlek* for men and male social gatherings. There is also an area for staff and services that is known as al-Khadam. The inner courtyard had, in its midst, shade-giving trees and fountains splashing over colourful Arabic mosaic tiles. "...that feeling for water which unites all Islamic landscape from the Alhambra to Delhi," writes Bernard Lewis in the highly attractive book *The World of Islam*. There were stone basins. The interior rooms had their roof and walls decorated in Arabesque wooden panels with shelves and niches for objects of art. The salons were located on the ground floor during summers and moved upstairs during winters where richly patterned Persian carpets provided warmth. Here one comes across the significant influence of Ottoman architecture and décor. I was reminded of the seat of the Ottoman Empire (Sublime Porte) at the Topkapi Saray royal complex in Istanbul.

We frequently drove past the impressive Tekiyeh Suleimanieh built by the prolific Ottoman architect Sinan, the same genius who built the massive Suleimanieh mosque in Istanbul. Tekiyeh Suleimanieh was always on the 'wrong' side of the road as we were driving from one destination to another and, unfortunately, we never made the stop. Work on it began in 1445 and continued till 1450. It was built as a meeting station for the caravans of pilgrims heading to Mecca for the Haj. This multi-domed complex with dual minarets consists of two symmetrical wings; one provides a *madrasah* and the other a prayer and rest house.

The Maristan was build by Nur al-Din in 1154 to serve as a hospital and medical teaching centre. According to Amin Maalouf in *The Crusades through Arab Eyes*, a contemporary classic, "The medical care then available in Damascus was among the best in the world." The indomitable twelfth century traveller Ibn Jubayr described the hospitals he found in Damascus. "Each hospital has administrators who keep the records, which list the names of the patients, the expenses required for their care and nourishment, and various other sorts of information. The physicians come every morning to examine the patients and prescribe the remedies and diets that can cure them, depending on what is required for each individual". The Maristan is today the Museum of Arabic Medical and Scientific History.

Saladin's tomb lies alongside the complex of the Omayyad mosque. The founder of the Ayubid (1186-1260) dynasty, Saladin established Damascus as his capital. Damascus enjoyed a brief period of renaissance during Saladin's reign. The Ayubid Empire extended to Egypt, Palestine and Yemen. The inscription on Saladin's tomb reads: "Oh Allah, be satisfied with this soul and open to him the gates of paradise, the last conquest for which he hoped." Built originally in 1193, the mausoleum was restored with funds provided for by Kaiser Wilhelm II of Germany during his visit to Damascus in 1898. In a small area just outside the Omayyad mosque complex, it is an unassuming tomb of a man known for his humility and generosity of spirit. Born in Takrit (modern-day Iraq) he was sent by the Damascus ruler to Egypt in 1169. Saladin overthrew the last Fatimid Caliph in Cairo and assumed the seat of power. He then marched on Damascus in 1174 and took both Damascus and Aleppo and established the Ayubid dynasty. In 1187, Saladin retook the Holy city of Jerusalem from the Crusaders yet allowed tens of thousands of Crusaders to entrench themselves at Tyre (present-day south Lebanon). In this regard, Amin Maalouf observes in *The Crusades through Arab Eyes*, "Of course, there is no reproaching the sultan for the magnanimity with which he treated the vanquished. In the eyes of history, his repugnance for needless bloodshed, his strict respect for his commitments, and the touching nobility of his acts of compassion are as valuable as his conquests. Nevertheless, it is incontestable that he made a serious political and military error."

The ancient and renowned Hamaam Nur al-Din is to be found at the end of the long and cavernous *souq* and it still functions as a public bath. It is one of the oldest in Damascus and was founded between 1154 and 1172 in order to provide an income for one of the *madrasahs*. The domed chamber dates from the Ottoman period. My husband made a three-hour session at this ancient and still functioning bathhouse. I would guess that it is the same *hamaam* that Dan Cruickshank wallowed in and wrote about in *Around the World in 80 Treasures*. "It's located near the souq…we enter through a small door and find ourselves in a splendid cubical, domed space." All over Damascus a liberal sprinkling of baths, mosques, *madrasahs*, gates, fortresses and fortifications are to be found. In a lived-in, not a museum, city, antiquities may also be a part of or serve as a backdrop to modernity.

Ibn Maymoun, a Sufi astronomer, philosopher and physician born in Cordova in 1204, held the prestigious post of special physician at the court of Saladin. "Sufis attempt to create through a life of self-denial and piety, an individual link to the Creator through gnosis or knowledge as opposed to the more communal basis of Sunni mainstream Islam." A definition of Sufism by Ross Burns in *Monuments in Syria: An Historical Guide*. Al-Ghazzali was a great Sufi mystic and theologian of his age. Born in Andalusia, Spain in 1165, he travelled east and eventually settled and died in Damascus in 1240. The Perfect Human Being would possess the following characteristics according to members of a philosophical society, Ikhwan as-Safa in the ninth century. "The ideal and morally perfect man should be of East Persian derivation, Arabic faith, of Iraqi education, a Hebrew in astuteness, a disciple of Christ in conduct, as pious as a Greek monk, a Greek in the individual sciences, an Indian in the interpretation of all mysteries, but lastly and especially a Sufi in his whole spiritual life."

A short ride away from Damascus is the ghost town of Quneitra. Here we found not ancient but modern history. The Israelis occupied Quneitra in the 1967 Middle East war. In 1974, in a cease-fire agreement, Quneitra, a part of the Golan Heights, was returned to Syria at a high price. The town was bulldozed and razed to the ground. A sign left behind expressed the 'scorched earth' policy. It read: 'You wanted Kuneitra; you shall have it in ruins'. The sight before us was appalling; the entire town lay in ruins. Most houses were of one-storey whose roof simply 'sat down', so to speak; as a result of bulldozers attacking the walls, the roof simply caved in, often split in two but not shattered. The two-storey hospital was a hollow shell with blackened inner walls and a bullet-scarred exterior. There was a pervasive eerie feeling of abandonment. Quneitra is a sobering sight of wartime ferocity. I was reminded of the empty shells of homes that we saw in divided Cyprus in the late 1960s. Pope John Paul II had paid an historic visit to Quneitra a week before us.

Yet this same man-scarred landscape is endowed with immense natural beauty. We passed through blue-sky country, windswept and biblically pastoral. Stretches of farms and orchards yielding apples and pears, vineyards and gnarled olive trees lay as far as the eye could see. An American journalist I.F. Stone once quipped that "If God is dead, He died trying to solve the Arab-Israeli conflict." It is a cruel statement but one that reflects the possibility that the 'cradle of civilisation' – the Middle East – could also become its grave.

AFGHANISTAN : A FORGOTTEN HERITAGE

"Kabul is a most bustling and populous city. Such is the noise in the afternoon, that in the streets one cannot make an attendant hear...The great bazaar is an elegant arcade, nearly 600 feet long and 30 broad...There are few such bazaars in the East and one wonders at the silks, cloths and goods which are arranged under its piazzas...In May one may purchase the grapes, pears, apples, quinces and even melons of the bygone season, then 10 months old...Kabul is famed for its kababs or cooked meats...Few cook at home."

Caravan Journeys and Wanderings in Persia, Afghanistan, Turistan and Baloochistan by J.P. Ferrier, 1857

"Though only the 2nd April, the heat was intense; the centigrade thermometer stood at 35^0 in the tent, and the flies and mosquitoes left us no peace...A social feeling pervades all the members of a caravan: they have their food in common; the noble, the tradesman, the peasant, and the fakheer (beggar) sit in the same circle and eat out of the same dish, and this without the least possibility of offence being given or pride being wounded; it is sufficient that they are Muslims and pilgrims…A horse is to the Turcoman what a ship is to the pirate; it carries himself and his fortune. In his saddle, he is in his fortress; in truth, it is on horseback that he fights…"

J.P. Ferrier, Adjutant-General of the Persian army in the 1840s, wrote of his caravan of more than seven hundred people leaving Persia for Central Asia in April 1845 through a terrain that was undulating and the surface arid and stony.

In these times, everyone has seen a map of Afghanistan in the international media with the names Ghazni, Herat, Kabul, Kandahar…dotted on the map. Yet few know that these dots locate cities that can trace an artistic and cultural heritage that date centuries if not millennia. How many people know that Afghanistan is a vast, deep mine of human history, buried beneath the surface of places that carry the names – Mazar-I-Sharif, Kabul, Kandahar, Herat, Ghazni, Balkh…?

Afghanistan's history as a nation spans little more than two centuries; although in the past it has been part, or even the centre, of great empires. Zoroastrianism was introduced in the sixth century BC. Islam reached Afghanistan in the seventh century AD. Buddhism spread west from India to the Bamiyan valley where it remained strong till the tenth century AD. Local kings or invaders that have included Alexander the Great, Mahmud of Ghazni, Ghurids, Genghis Khan, Tamerlane, Timurids, the Russians and the British have ruled the land over the span of history. In 1774, the Kingdom of Afghanistan was established. The monarchy was overthrown in 1973 in a military coup. The Soviet Union occupied Afghanistan from 1979 to 1992. Civil strife continued. In October 2001, what has been declared 'The First War of the Twenty-first Century' started in Afghanistan.

Yet testament to this ancient and eclectic heritage are the vestiges of past civilisations; ruins that struggle to remain and often jolt us into recalling a glorious past. The half-minaret of Masud III (1099-1115) in Ghazni is all that is left of the elaborate mosque complex that once stood there. Somewhere in the distant past the top half of the cylindrical and fluted shaft had fallen off. Masud III's name is inscribed in tall Kufic writing at the top of the lower shaft which has an eight-pointed star base. The mosque of Bahram Shah in Ghazni was built in the late eleventh or early twelfth century. Here too only the brick minaret, star-shaped in plan, remains of the original mosque. The Ghaznavids, a dynasty of Turkish origin, ruled the region from 962 to 1001 and established the city of Ghazni as their capital.

Herat was an ancient Silk Road oasis at the crossroads between Persia, India and China, a stopover on the world's oldest highway for travellers as they crossed steppes and deserts. In an inaccessible mountain valley and standing in isolation in a narrow gorge is the surviving minaret of what was once the Great Mosque of Jam constructed in the late twelfth century. This construction took place during the rule of the Ghurids (1148-1215) whose capital was Herat. The Qutb minaret in Delhi is said to have been inspired by the minaret at Jam. The surviving brick structure soars four storeys, some seventy metres high, gradually tapering. The outer surface is extensively decorated with terracotta plaques and Kufic inscriptions from the Holy Quran. Turquoise glazed bricks create an illusion of fragile filigree work. Turquoise was the first and most popular colour used for decorative glazing in Islamic architecture.

One account for the legacy of surviving minarets is provided in *Islamic Art and Patronage: Treasures from Kuwait*. "Dozens of stone and baked-brick minarets survive in Afghanistan, Soviet Central Asia, Iran, Iraq, Syria and Turkey, sometimes independent of any adjacent building. Their inscriptions reflect a wide range of patronage, indicating that to all classes a minaret gave good value for the money...For all classes of patrons, minarets were gratifyingly visible and not as expensive as a new mosque or other building." This argument seems highly plausible; the minarets received considerable recognition without incurring extensive expense.

The Masjid-i-Jami, the Friday Mosque, in Herat "is one of the finest Islamic buildings in the world, certainly the finest in Afghanistan," states the *Lonely Planet Guide to the Middle East.* Repeatedly destroyed by different waves of armies at the crossroads of a nation, the current mosque was built in 1498. It has been in a long and slow process of restoration since 1943, interspersed with repeated bouts of destruction by modern warfare.

One of the brilliant masterpieces of Islamic art is known in artistic circles as the 'Herat Bucket'. The artist Masud ibn Ahmad created it in 1163 in the eastern province of Khorasan whose once great cities are now divided between Iran, Turkmenistan and Afghanistan. At the time, Herat was part of the Persian Empire. Today, Herat is one of the major cities of Afghanistan. David Talbot Rice in *Islamic Art* has described the 'Herat Bucket': "It remains unsurpassed in the story of Islamic metalwork." According to Dr. Mikhail Piotrovsky, a member of the Russian Academy of Sciences and the Russian Academy of Humanities "It is beautiful in form, in rich colouring, calligraphy and figure composition. It is a fine sample of the different techniques used in the Islamic metal craft casting, engraving and inlay...The inscriptions on the bucket bear the most interesting information about the world in which it was created, about the masters, customs and owners, about the role of the middle class in the Islamic society. Images on the girdles of the bucket are extraordinary in their artistic value and in exceptional information." The bucket was used to carry water during bathing and is eighteen cm. in thickness. Such buckets were used for visits to the *hamaam* bathhouses. "It was ordered by one named individual for presentation to another, 'the pride of merchants', apparently in connection with the pilgrimage to Mecca," notes Barbara Brend, lecturer at the British Museum and British Library in *Islamic Art.* It today forms part of the Hermitage collection in St. Petersburg, Russia.

This jewel of Islamic art points to Herat as a principal centre for metalwork, much in vogue in its day. At the close of the fifteenth century, Herat was still producing huge vessels, like cauldrons in shape but intended to contain water in mosques. Azizallah Shaykh Vali, a master craftsman, made a brass jug covered in gold and with silver inlay in Herat in 1494. An inscription around the neck refers to the days of the reign of Sultan Husayn Bayqara who is effusively referred to as the Sultan of the Turks, Arabs and Persians. This magnificent object of art was sold at Sotheby's, London, in 1989. A tenth century copper bowl found in Iran has engraved on it in Arabic Kufic script 'He who talks much, errs much'.

It is also worth noting that some of the first Persian carpets were woven in Herat. Herat, Samarkand, Yazd, Tabriz and Kabul were renowned Timurid cities for fabric weaving. A magnificent masterpiece of a 'Rug with Overall Pattern' made in Afghanistan in the sixteenth century is featured in *Islamic Art and Patronage: Treasures from Kuwait.* "Identified with the city of Herat, a famous centre of artistic activities under the Timurids, Herat became renowned for the high quality and intricate floral designs of its rugs during the sixteenth and seventeenth centuries."

In the years 1414-1416, the ruler of the day, Shah Rukh, had his dynastic pride set into the ancient citadel of Herat in the form of inscriptions "which celebrates the pure lineage of the Timurids, praising Shah Rukh and his five sons with all the poetical resources of the fifteenth century," declares Barbara Brend in *Islamic Art.* Also in Herat, the architect Qavan ak-Dub built Shah Rukh's queen, Gauhar Shad, a *madrasah* and a mosque in the 1420s. Both the ruler and his consort were eventually buried under the dome chamber of the *madrasah.* In more recent times, the Russians blew up parts of the mosque as a defensive measure, a common fallback in warfare. A Women's Garden that once surrounded the fifteenth century tomb as a sanctuary and cool retreat is today a field of mud. The Masjid-i Hauz-i Karbuz in Herat was constructed in 1441 and the "*mihrab* in the covered 'winter' mosque, is faced with fine tile mosaic of the best quality commissioned by the Timurid rulers," from the UNESCO commissioned book *The Art of Islam*,

Set in the foothills above Herat at Gazur, Gah is the shrine of the eleventh century mystic Khwajeh Abdullah Ansari. The main building was constructed at the command of Shah Rukh. Late in the fifteenth century, the ruler Husayn Bayqara built the royal burial grounds within the shrine complex. Certain features used in its construction and embellishment, such as the use of portal bays and the arched ivan as a screen, would be transferred to Mughal architecture in India. The finest manifestation of Mughal architecture, with its origins in Central Asia, is the resplendent Taj Mahal at Agra.

The Islamic art of the book peaked and reached exquisite heights in the fourteenth century. There was deep reverence for the pen and the written word. There were men of pen and men of sword, the former being a highly esteemed class of secular and literate men distinct from theologians and those well versed in religion. Ibrahim ash-Shaybani eloquently stated the many virtues of the art of writing (a skill today highly endangered with the arrival of computer technology). "...the language of the hand, the idiom of the mind, the ambassador intellect, and the trustee of thought, the weapon of knowledge and the companion of brethren in the time of separation." The art of cursive epigraphy is a master skill as much appreciated then as now. Few would argue with the remark by Qadi Ahmad who, aware that most of his compatriots were illiterate wrote, "If someone, whether he can read or not, sees good, writing, he likes to enjoy the sight of it." A finely detailed inlaid brass pen box from Syria or Turkey, dating to the early thirteenth century, has engraved on the lid: "Do not write with your hand except that which will delight you to see on

Judgment Day.' And who can disagree with the sentiment expressed by the seventeenth century Sindhi writer Tahir ibn Hasan : "Everyone, who lives through the Water of Life of the pen, will not die, but remain alive as long as life exists."

Arabic is the language of Islamic scripture, the Holy Quran. Arabic was also, since the seventh century, the language of law, philosophy, science and theology. According to Bernard Lewis in *Islam and the West*, Arabic was "a classical language, the medium of a body of literary, philosophic, and scientific writing which was regarded as exemplary and authoritative not only by the Arabs themselves but by other Muslim peoples; a practical language, widely used in government, society, and commerce. It was thus the equivalent in the medieval Islamic world of Latin, Greek, and Hebrew in the West..."

Arthur Goldschmidt Jr. in *A Concise History of the Middle East* has recognised the primacy of the Arabic language. He argues "...Arabic Civilisation, emphasises the importance of Arabic in the development of the culture. Not only because of its prestige as the language of the Quran and of the conquering elite, but also because of its capacity for assimilating new things and ideas, Arabic became the almost universal language of arts, sciences, and letters between 750 and 1250."

The paramount prominence of the art of writing in Islamic arts cannot be overstated. In addition to the highly aesthetic and religious role of calligraphy, another perspective is presented in *Islamic Art and Patronage: Treasures from Kuwait.* "Thus the extraordinary coincidence of the needs of a faith revealed and transmitted through words and of a state trying to hold together a huge empire with very diverse people speaking many languages found its most consistent expression in an Arabic script becoming identified with Islam wherever it occurred." Arabic became the lingua franca of a vast and diverse empire.

The art of the book included bookbinding (which included gilded leather book covers), illustration, illumination and calligraphy. It was through the medium of calligraphy that the sacred words of the Holy Quran were copied and handed down from generation to generation. Different forms of calligraphy developed over time: Ghobar, Kufic, Naskh, Nastaliq and Thulth. Herat and Shiraz were major schools of the highly developed and appreciated art of calligraphy. The Herat school of calligraphy is credited with the formation of the Esfahan school that prospered under Shah Abbas I. The Reza Abbasi Museum in Tehran has an extensive collection of calligraphic works by masters of the twelfth to fifteenth centuries.

In *Calligraphy and Islamic Culture*, Annemarie Schimmel, a German authority on Islamic calligraphy notes "The Timurid masters in Samarquand and Herat and the Safavid architects in Isfahan and elsewhere invented delightful ornaments consisting of the names of God, His Prophet, and the First Imam 'Ali' or of pious formulas, which were inserted in colorful tiles in the overall pattern of vaults, entrances, and domes…Cursive epigraphy reached its apex in the inscriptions on mosques and minarets. The use of tiles enabled the artists to produce highly intricate, radiant inscriptions of flawless beauty; here, Timurids and Safavids found unsurpassable solutions." Having seen the sublimely beautiful mosques in Esfahan and Yazd in Iran, Samarkhand in Uzbekistan and the Hanifah mosque in Baghdad, I would have to concur with Schimmel.

Given the absence of the reproduction of the human form in Islamic art, floral and geometric patterns were designed to achieve levels of immense complexity and beauty. According to Peter Mansfield in his elaborate study of *The Arabs*, "Islamic art tended towards the elaborate development of abstract ornament – the delicate geometric patterns which can be seen at their finest in the mosques and palaces of India, Persia, Egypt or Andalusia. The Arabic script itself, usually in the form of Koranic quotations, was incorporated into the designs to achieve at its best an effect of exquisite harmony."

The principles of geometry and rhythm appear in repeated pattern in various media; stone, leather, brass, wood, paper, tiles, bronze and marble.

The art of illumination of books is an art of ornamental painting using gold. Early Qurans were plain in format and, over time, were illuminated till they reached heights of perfection. Many manuscripts have splendidly illuminated margins representing animals, birds and floral scrolls. Various geometric patterns, sometimes interlaced, were devised. The format could be vertical, horizontal, circular or star-like in format. Favourite colours were gold, red and blue. Tinted paper in pale pink, pale gold or deep cream added to the enchantment of the page. An exquisite all-over illuminated page of the Holy Quran in Naskh script is on display at the Islamic Art Museum in Tehran. It is signed in 1828 by Ziya-al-Saltaneh, the daughter of Fathalishola. Another masterpiece at the same museum is the unsigned Holy Quran in Ghobar script of the fourteenth century. There are thirty matchbox-sized separah (chapters) of the Holy Quran. Each chapter is leather bound and the calligraphy is miniscule. Bernard Lewis declares categorically in *The World of Islam*, "In each of its four main aspects – calligraphy, bookbinding, illumination and illustration – Persian artists reached the peak of perfection." At a later stage, the illuminated art form was transferred to other objects such as textile, painting and tiles.

A magnificent illuminated manuscript, made in Herat in 1494-1495, is ranked as "the most perfect pages of Persian illumination since it balances complexity with clarity" (Brend in *Islamic Art*). It is part of the Nizami collection and is to be found at the British Library in London. Another miniature masterpiece, also painted in Herat and dated 1495, depicts Sufis discoursing in a garden. It is taken from the Mir Ali Shir Navali collection. Today, it is to be found at the Bodleian Library in Oxford.

At an auction in Paris by Drouot Richelieu in 1998 of the personal Ottoman art collection of a grandson of Sultan Abdul

Hamid II (1876-1909), one of the outstanding items out of a collection worthy of the finest museum was a "very rare Persian manuscript, 297 folios, unedited, illustrated with 33 miniatures. A precious document, splendid for its content and for the originality of the illustrations," stated the auction catalogue. Another precious item on auction was The 'Chronicles Tawarikh of Tabari' dating from the late fifteenth century, probably from Herat in the Khorasan province of present-day Iran. This masterpiece was leather-bound in the Ottoman style of the sixteenth century. It must have fetched a price at auction far beyond the conservative estimate of $20,000 to $25,000. At the same auction, a ceramic water pitcher from Bamiyan, in today's Afghanistan, of turquoise blue transparency and dated the eleventh century, was estimated at $3500 to $5000.

The Mongol Khan Tamerlane (1370-1405), born near Samarkhand, wanted to reconstitute the empire of his forefather Genghis Khan or 'Universal Ruler' (1167-1227), the founder of the Mongol Empire, the largest land empire in the early 1200s. Tamerlane, founder of the Timurid dynasty, was a fifth-generation descendant of Genghis Khan. By the age of 25, Tamerlane had already conquered Iran, Iraq, Armenia, the Caucasus, a part of Syria and the Asia Minor While Mongols are traditionally known as destroyers who ravaged much of the cultivated land and savaged the captured population, contrary to popular belief latter day Mongols were significant patrons of the arts. Many Mongols converted to Islam including the Ilkhanid rulers of Persia at the end of the thirteenth century. The Ilkhanid ruler Oljaitu established his new capital at Sultaniyieh (near Qazvin and en route to Tabriz in present-day Iran) and endowed it with many mosques and monuments including the still-standing massive mausoleum at Sultaniyieh. As pointed out by Arthur Goldschmidt Jr. in *A Concise History of the Middle East* "...the Mongol era proved the old adage that captive Persia always subdues its conquerors." In order to expand and beautify his new capital at Samarkhand, Tamerlane recruited artisans from cities he had conquered in Iran and Syria. The Mongols established a Pax Mongolica that stretched from China to Poland.

One Mongolian scholar theorises that the reason for Genghis Khan's negative image is because 'his history was written by his enemies'. Since the Mongols were not scribes, no documentary evidence has come down through the ages. The only comprehensive chronicle of his times *The Secret History of the Mongols* was a thirteenth century account of Genghis Khan's life. And that too was lost for centuries till it surfaced in the early 1800s, rediscovered by a Russian diplomat in China. Since the 1980s, one Francis Woodman Cleaves produced the first authoritative modern version of *The Secret History of the Mongols.*

While Genghis Khan's legacy is his famed power to destroy, a 2003 study refers to his incredible reproductive power. *The American Journal of Human Genetics*, in an article 'The Genetic Legacy of the Mongols', estimates that Genghis Khan has more than 17 million direct descendants living today; one in every 200 people is related to him. The study goes on to state that in Mongolia alone as many as 200,000 of the country's two million people could be Khan descendants, giving new meaning to the idea of a nation as a family.

My late father, husband and I visited Ulan Bator, capital of Mongolia in July 1981. We flew Aeroflot from Moscow to Ulan Bator crossing nine time zones, as far East as Hanoi. This was during the period of the Soviet Union and 'independent' Mongolia appeared as the Sixteenth Republic of the Soviet Union in all but name. Ulan Bator was grey and grim. The strongest memory is of the pungent and rancid smell exuded by every food item. Mare's fermented milk *kumees* is a national delicacy. However, for us it fell into the category of 'Highly Acquired Taste'. The positive memorable experience was witnessing an extraordinary equestrian event in the vast arid plains of Mongolia.

"One branch of the Timurids made itself master of Northern India and founded the great Mughal empire; from being uncouth nomad warriors, they transformed themselves into protectors and promoters of one of the most refined and resplendent civilisations that has ever existed," notes the Florence-born, Swiss, Islamic art scholar Titus Burckhardt in *Art and Islam: Language and Meaning.* Burckhardt further informs us that "A European traveller of the sixteenth century, who visited Samarqand, the then Timurid capital, has described the extraordinary scenes when Turco-Mongol chieftains were having immense mosques and universities erected while themselves living in their tents set up in the midst of gardens. The buildings described are largely still extant; with their facings in mosaics and ceramic tiles they are among the most beautiful monuments of Islam."

Tamerlane's grandson Baysunghur established the most famous fifteenth century atelier in Herat. A progress report now preserved at the Topkapi Museum in Istanbul is a record of projects under the head of the atelier Jafar Tabrizi (active 1412-1431). The report addressed to Baysunghur mentions " twenty-two projects that are underway – manuscript designs, architectural works, tents and other objects – and includes the tames of twenty-three artists – painters, illuminators, calligraphers, binders, rules, and chest makers – who worked individually or in teams". The leading role that Baysunghur played in the domain of arts is recognised in a contemporary doctoral dissertation (Harvard University, 1985) by Thomas W. Lentz titled *Painting at Herat under Baysunghur ibn Shahrukh.* Another Timurid descendant, Husayn Bayqara, (died 1506) continued the royal patronage of arts in Herat that had been destroyed by Genghis Khan in 1220.

Herat remained a major cultural metropolis; Herat artisans were to be found in Shiraz and Tabriz in present-day Iran and throughout the Ottoman Empire. Herat also attracted the cultural elite of the region; the Persian poet Nour Eddin Djami, the Herat-born poet Mir Alisher Noavoi and Behzad, the master Persian calligrapher and painter of miniatures. Djami was born in Djam and died in Herat. "His master of the Persian language and the riches of his style made him the last of a line of great Persian poets in the tradition of Saadi,

Nezami and Hafez," declares Yves Thoraval in *Dictionnaire de Civilisation Musulmane*. One of the cultural icons of Central Asia, Navoi was a master of ghazal love poems and a vizir minister of Husayn Bayqara. Behzad's brilliant miniature drawings enriched the manuscripts of *Boustan* and *Golestan* of Saadi and the *Khamseh of Nizami.*

The Safavid dynasty in Persia has its origins in Herat. In the sixteenth century, the Safavids under Shah Abbas established the most famous, innovative and grandiose urban complex at Esfahan, known in its day, as 'Esfahan-e-Nesf-e-Jahan' or 'Esfahan is Half the World'. Shah Abbas's father Tahmasp was a governor of Herat. Tahmasp then moved his capital to Qazvin - in modern-day Iran - in 1548. Esfahan, in the Persian heartland, was established in 1596.

An eloquent summary of the presence of Islamic art in global artistic heritage is offered in *Islamic Art and Patronage: Treasures from Kuwait*, a superb publication on one of the finest collections of Islamic art, that of Sheikh Nasir Sabah and his wife Sheikha Hussah Sabah of the royal family of Kuwait. "The eloquence of Islamic art – its ability to 'speak' to the observer in a purely visual language – is therefore considerably wider in scope than European art with its concentration on narrative and the human form and focus on figural painting and sculpture. Long before European artists developed to a high degree the notion of beauty inherent in abstraction, mathematical order, visual and physical texture, and color, these aspects of artistic imagination were central to the production and patronage of art in Islamic lands. What is relegated to the subsidiary realm of 'decorative arts' in the European imagination and academic curriculum is therefore a major focus of artistic energy in the Islamic world."

Herat has always held its own regarding its strategic importance. "The position of Herat on the line of advance from Persia and Turkistan, towards the Indus, has made its possession essential to the success of any invasion of India from that quarter and we accordingly find that from the time of Darius to the present, its occupation has been a prelude to any attempts of the kind by successive conquerors...Herat is at the present time the asylum of all the fallen greatness of past centuries. Here is to be seen the descendants of Genghis Khan, of Tamerlane and Nadir Shah...There is not a position of more importance in a strategically and commercial point of view and the fertility of the soil is great...The great roads from all the principal countries of Asia meet. Persian, Turkestan, Afghanistan, India and Sistan merchants gathered here." (J.P. Ferrier in 1856).

Today, all traces of so many epicentres of glorious origins are lost in the obscurity of the ages.

Kandahar found itself a place on the world's map as early as 550 BC. It was a part of the Persian Achaemenian Empire under Cyrus the Great and his successors. At its greatest extent, the Achaemenian Empire stretched from present-day Libya to the Indus Valley and to Turkey to the west. There is some evidence of a remarkable culture that thrived around 2000 to 1900 BC. in the northern plain around the present-day town of Balkh. The city of Balkh can claim a mosque dating to the tenth century whose stout brick columns support rectangular capitals and arcades rich with elaborately carved stucco work. Balkh was part of the Abbasid Empire (750-940) whose capital was Baghdad.

The Barmecides of Persian origin from the city of Balkh, dominated the upper echelons of the Abbasid administration, particularly during the reign of Harun-ur-Rashid. Some three generations of Barmecides served the empire as bursars, tax collectors, provincial governors, military commanders, tutors and' ministers. The father of Maulana Jalaluddin Rumi, the Sufi poet and dervish, emigrated from Balkh and settled in Konya (in modern-day Turkey). Interestingly, Bernard Lewis points out in *The World of Islam* "...although it is true that not all Islamic mystics were Persians, it is also true that neither the Arabs, the Turks nor Indian Muslims produced mystics of the stature of the Persians Sanai, Nizami, Jalaluddin Rumi, al-Ghazali, Farid ad-Din Attar and Hafiz." Lewis argues that Shia'ism led naturally to mysticism and it was Persia that produced the most eminent of all Islamic mystical writers. Balkh was once known as the 'Oumme el Belad' (Mother of All Cities). According to a Chinese visitor in 663 AD, Balkh had three of the most beautiful buildings in the world.

A once glorious city in Afghanistan, Furrah ancient – and almost forgotten - past was built even before Alexander's expeditions. "Furrah is one example of the difficulty of stating anything certain about the geography of Central Asia; a place may today be the centre of a flourishing population, and in four - and - twenty hours a desert. The Afghans have become so used to sudden and forced displacements that they never attach themselves to the soil. Their tent is their country...nothing there is certain; nothing is durable; everything is liable to impromptu changes – men as well as things," observed Ferrier. This observation reminds me of the regional dictum: 'My brother and I against our cousin. My cousin and I against a stranger.'

The 1994 edition of the *Lonely Planet - Middle East*, notes that it was not possible to visit the Kabul citadel known as Bala Hissar since it was used by the military. It was possible, however, "to walk the entire length of the often crumbling walls...It took about five hours to walk the full length of the walls."

In an highly informative article 'Afghanistan, the Daunting Land: Political and Cultural Complexities Make a Mission Harder', Souren Melikian art and culture columnist in the *International Herald Tribune* laments the current status of the ancient cities in Afghanistan. "Herat, the great Persian metropolis wrested from Iran in the mid-19th century with British backing...Ghazni, 120 kilometres (75 miles) southwest of Kabul. This city part-Persian and part-Pashto speaking, was once the great capital of the eastern Iranian world under the sultans of the Ghaznavid dynasty in the eleventh and twelfth centuries. It is the hometown of a famous twelfth century Persian poet, the Sufi mystic Sanai...Kabul itself, which had been undergoing an intellectual renaissance in the early 1970s, is now devastated – its fine archaeological museum a half-destroyed empty shell…Kabul is one of the oldest Persian-speaking cities in the world…"

An exhibition took place in Barcelona, Spain in 2001 that revealed the ancient artistic creativity of Afghanistan dating back thousands of years. 'Afghanistan: A History of Millennia' unveils three thousand years of Afghan art and archaeology with two hundred and thirty objects on display, as well as films, photographs, books and music. The exhibit contains pieces on loan from private collectors and museums in Russia, the United States, Germany and France. The objects on display reflect Hindu, Greek, Roman and Chinese influences. Materials such as wood, ivory, clay, silver, bronze and glass were employed to make busts of Buddhist saints, ornate human and animal figurines, arrow heads, ink wells, cooking utensils and jewellery pieces including foot long silver bracelets. Souren Melikian in another article 'Painting the Portrait of a Mysterious Culture' in the *International Herald Tribune*, referring to the exhibition on Afghanistan's cultural heritage in Barcelona and the 'Herat Bucket' in particular, (on loan from the Hermitage Museum in St. Petersburg), advises "it alone justifies a visit."

The exhibition was conceived following the destruction by the Taliban government of Afghanistan in 2001, of the two colossal sculptures of the Buddha, dating from the third and fifth centuries, carved into the mountain-side of the Bamiyan valley. Spanish organisers "wanted to offer an alternative view of the Central Asian nation." The exhibition also travelled to the Musee Guimet (Museum of Asian Art) in Paris in 2002 but we missed it by two months. One of the great Buddhist centres of the region, Bamiyan could boast 'more than 10 monasteries and more than 1000 priests' according to a Chinese priest who visited Bamiyan in 632 AD. Souren Melikian writing in the *International Herald Tribune* in her article 'Painting the Portrait of a Mysterious Culture' notes, "A whole Persian romance in rhyming couplets was composed by Onsori, an eleventh century poet from Balkh, under the title 'The Red Buddha and the White Buddha' – the names given to the two giant Buddhas in Bamian province blown up last March by the Taliban." Sadly, this place had witnessed another tragedy in the distant past. Shar-I-Gholgola is the ruined city in the Bamiyan valley. The name means 'city of sighs', the sighs being those of the inhabitants after Genghis Khan massacred the population.

Another artistic offering comes from the internationally renowned Iranian film director Mohsen Makhmalbaf. His film, *Journey to Kandahar*, released in 2001, was widely acclaimed. It documents the life of an Afghani girl living in Canada who returns to Afghanistan to help her sister who has threatened suicide. Makhmalbaf has captured the trauma and tears of this war-torn nation. Following the making of this film, Makhmalbaf wrote a thirty-two page economic, political and historical analysis of Afghanistan. He titled the essay 'The Buddha Was Not Demolished in Afghanistan; He Collapsed Out of Shame.' It is a deeply poignant indictment of Man's inhumanity and callousness.

GLOSSARY

Abbasids	Arab dynasty, capital Baghdad (750-1258 AD)
Ab-ambar	Water storage tank (Persian)
Al-Khadam	Service area in Arab homes
Arabesque	Decorative floral motifs
Ayubid	Muslim dynasty of Kurdish origin, capitals Cairo and Damascus (1169-1260 AD)
Caravanserai	Resthouse-cum-warehouse (Persian)
Chenar	Deodar tree
Chinoiserie	Chinese design motifs
Cupola	Rounded dome forming a ceiling or roof
Denarius	Ancient Roman silver coin
Dirham	Monetary unit of Morocco and the United Arab Emirates
Fatimids	Arab dynasty descended from Fatima, daughter of Holy Prophet Muhammad (909-1171 AD)
Ghalian	Waterpipe for smoking (Persian)
Hafte-rang	Of seven-colours (Persian)
Hamaam	Spacious thermal baths, also venues for socialising
Haramlek	Secluded living space for women and family members
Hejab	Head-cover
Hukah	Waterpipe for smoking (Urdu)
Imam	Prayer leader in mosques
Ivan	Pointed arch (Persian)
Keffiyeh	Arab men's headdress
Khamseen	Sandstorm (Arabic)
Khans	Resthouse-cum-warehouse (Persian)
Kufic	Angular script in Arabic calligraphy

Madrasah	Islamic theological school (Arabic)
Maidan	Large open space
Mamelukes	Slave dynasty that ruled Egypt and Syria (1250-1517 AD)
Mastaba	Funerary mound
Mehrab/mihrab	Semi-circular niche in mosques used by the prayer leader and also to show the direction of Mecca
Minbar	Stepped platform in a mosque for preaching
Nargileh	Waterpipe for smoking (Arabic)
Naksh	Designs/decorations
Omayyads	Arab dynasty, capital Damascus (661-750 AD)
Ottomans	Turkish dynasty (1300-1924 AD)
Pol	Bridge (Persian)
Ramadhan	The month of fasting in Islam
Salamlek	Living space for men and their social gatherings
Satrap	Governor-General (Persian)
Separah	A chapter (out of 30) from the Holy Quran
Stela	Slab or pillar with inscription and sculpture
Shi'ia	Worldwide Muslim minority sect
Sunni	Global Muslim majority sect
Ziggurat	Stepped monument, could be a tomb

FIVE FAVOURITE BOOKS ON THE MIDDLE EAST FOR THE ARMCHAIR TRAVELLER

"Read not to contradict and confute; nor to believe and take for granted; nor to find talk and discourse; but to weigh and consider. Some books are to be tasted, others to be swallowed, and some few to be chewed and digested."

Francis Bacon

The following five books fall into the last category.

Amin Maalouf. *The Crusades through Arab Eyes*, Schocken Books, New York, 1985.(History evoked through an alternative perspective.)

Amin Maalouf. *Ports of Call*, The Harvill Press, London, 1999.(An evocative novel that speaks of the pain and struggle that Lebanon and the region suffer to this day.)

Michael Asher. *Lawrence: The Uncrowned King of Arabia*, Penguin Books, London, 1999.(Brilliantly retracing the footsteps of T.E. Lawrence, Asher dispels some of the myth behind the legend.)

Fabio Bourbon. *Yesterday and Today: The Holy Lands: Lithographs and Diaries by David Roberts*, The American University of Cairo Press, Cairo, Egypt, 1994.(A visual treat of the ancient monumental masterpieces of the Middle East; documented in sketches of the mid-nineteenth century by David Roberts and in photographs of the same sites taken in the late twentieth century.)

Yves Thoraval. *Dictionnaire de Civilisation Musulmane*, Larousse, Paris, 1995. (The pocket book reference source for all you need to know about the Muslim civilisation.)

REFERENCES

"A man will turn over half a library to make one book."
Samuel Johnson

A Passion for Iran: A Photographic Journey, Yassavoli Publications, Tehran, 1998.

Antonious, George. *The Arab Awakening*, Librarie du Liban, Beirut, 1969.

Art and History of Jordan, Bonechi, Florence, 2000.

Atasoy, N. Bahnassi, A. and Rogers, M. *The Art of Islam*, UNESCO/ Flammarion, Paris, 1990.

Bakhtiar, R.N. *Isfahan: The Living Museum*, Forough Danesh Press, Tehran, 1998.

Bourbon, Fabio. *Yesterday and Today: The Holy Land*, The American University in Cairo Press, Cairo, 1994.

Bourbon, Fabio. *Yesterday and Today: Egypt*, The American University in Cairo Press, Cairo, 1996.

Brend, Barbara. *Islamic Art*, Harvard University Press, Cambridge, 1991.

Browne, E.G. *A Year Amongst the Persians*, A. and C. Black Limited, London, 1970.

Burckhardt, Titus. *Art of Islam: Language and Meaning*, World of Islam Festival Publishing Company Ltd., London, 1976.

Burns, Ross. *Monuments of Syria: An Historical Guide*, I.B. Tauris, London, 1999.

Carpiceci, Alberto Carlo. *Art and History of Egypt: 5000 Years of Civilisation*, Bonechi, Florence, 1994.

Cruickshank, Dan. *Around the World in 80 Treasures*, Weidenfeld & Nicholson, London, 2005.

Danzer, Gerald A. *An Atlas of World History*, Borders Group, Inc., Michigan, 2000.

Davis, Paul K. *Encyclopedia of Invasions and Conquests: From Ancient Times to the Present*, ABC-CLIO Ltd., Oxford, 1996.

Edhem, Eldem, Goffman, David and Masters, Bruce. *The Ottoman City between East and West: Aleppo, Izmir and Istanbul*, Cambridge University Press, 1999.

Esfahan Province International Exhibition Co. *Esfahan: A Gateway to Persia*, Esfahan, Summer, 1997.

Eydoux, Henri-Paul. *In Search of Lost Worlds*, Hamlyn, London, 1975.

Faramarzi, M.T. *A Travel Guide to Iran*, Yassaman Publications, Tehran, 1997.

Friedman, Thomas L. *From Beirut to Jerusalem*, Collins Publishers, Toronto, 1989.

Glubb, John Bagot. *A Short History of the Arab Peoples*, Hodder and Stoughton, London, 1969.

Goldschmidt, Arthur Jr. *A Concise History of the Middle East*, Westview Press, Oxford, 1991.

Goodwin, Jason. *Lords of the Horizons: A History of the Ottoman Empire*, Henry Holt and Company, New York, 1998.

Gray, Ann and McGuigan, J. *Studying Culture: An Introductory Reader*, Arnold, London, 1997.

Guadalupi, Gianni. *The Discovery of the Nile*, The American University in Cairo Press, Cairo, 1997.

Hafez. *Diwan of Hafez*, Booteh Press, Tehran, 1998.

Haider, Raana. *Paris; A Homage,Tara Press,New Delhi 2006.*

Harden, Donald. *The Phoenicians*, Penguin Books, Middlesex, England, 1971.

Heude, William. *A Voyage Up the Persian Gulf and A Journey Overland from India to England*, Gregg International Publishers Limited, Hants, England, 1970.

Hickman, Katie. *Daughters of Britannia: The Lives and Times of Diplomatic Wives*, Flamingo, London, 2000.

Hitti, Philip K. *Lebanon in History* (Third edition), Macmillan, New York, 1967.

Hitti, Philip K. *Makers of Arab History*, St. Martin's Press, New York, 1968.

Hitti, Philip K. *Capital Cities of Arab Islam*, Oxford University Press, London, 1973.

Hoffman, Ross, Gaetano, L. and Morrison, V. *Man and His History: World History and Western Civilisation*, Doubleday and Company, Inc. New York, 1960.

Hopwood, Derek (ed.). *Studies in Arab History*, St. Martin's Press, New York, 1990.

Hourani, A.H. and Stern, S.M. (eds.). *The Islamic City: A Colloquium*, University of Pennsylvania Press, 1970.

Kerr, Ann Z. *Come with Me from Lebanon*, Syracuse University Press, New York, 1994.

Khalaf, Samir. *Beirut Reclaimed*, Dar-an-Nahar, Beirut, 1993.

League of Arab States. *Portraits of Arab Civilisation*, Directorate of Information, Cairo, undated.

Lebanon, Bonechi, Florence, 2000.

Lewis, Bernard (ed.). *The World of Islam*, Thames and Hudson, London, 1976.

Lewis, Bernard. *Islam and the West*, Oxford University Press, New York, 1993.

Lewis, Bernard. *A Middle East Mosaic: Fragments of Life, Letters and History*, Random House, New York, 2000.

Mackey, Sandra. *Lebanon: Death of a Nation*, Anchor Books, Doubleday, New York, 1989.

Mansfield, Peter. *The Arabs*, Penguin Books, Middlesex, England, 1979.

Marsden-Smedley, Philip and Klinke, Jeffrey (eds.). *Views from Abroad: The Spectator Book of Travel Writing*, Grafton Books, 1988.

Matthews, David. *The Battle of Karbala: A Marsiya of Anis*, Rupa, New Delhi, 2003.

Michaud, R. and Barry, Michael. *Colour and Symbolism in Islamic Architecture: Eight Centuries of the Tile Maker's Art*, Thames and Hudson, London, 1996.

Michell, George. (ed.). *Architecture of the Islamic World*, Thames and Hudson, London, 1978.

Middle East, Lonely Planet Publications, Victoria, Australia, 1994.

Ministry of Information, *The Land of Kings*, Tehran, 1971.

Ministry of Tourism, *Syria*, Damascus, 1989.

Mishaqa, Mikhayil. *Murder, Mayhem, Pillage and Plunder: The History of the Lebanon in the 18th and 19th Centuries*, State University of New York Press, New York, 1988.

Municipality of Isfahan. *Isfahan*, Isfahan, 1997.

Nahavandi, Houchang and Bomati, Yves. *Shah Abbas: Empereur de Perse*, Librarie Academique, Perin 1998.

Naipaul, V.S. *Among the Believers: An Islamic Journey*, Penguin Books, London, 1982.

Quotation Finder; HarperCollins, Glasgow, 1999.

Rice, David Talbot. *Islamic Art*, Thames and Hudson, London, 1975.

Rogers, J.M.. *Mughal Miniatures*, Thames and Hudson, New York, 1993.

Roux, Georges. *Ancient Iraq*, George Allen and Unwin Ltd., London, 1964.

Saadi. *Gulistan*, Marefat Booksellers and Publishers, Shiraz.

Saba: The Art Research and Studies, No. 1, Autumn and Winter, Tehran, 1999.

Said, Edward W. *Orientalism*, Vintage Books, New York, 1979.

Salibi, Kamal. *A House of Many Mansions: The History of Lebanon Reconsidered*, University of California Press Ltd., London, 1988.

Sane, Mansour. *Fars*, Foundation of Fars Province Studies, Shiraz, 1996.

Schimmel, Annemarie. *Calligraphy and Islamic Culture*, New York University Press, New York, 1984.

Shafi, Mirza. *On Life and Living*, Palal Prokashani, Dhaka, 2004.

Thoraval, Yves. *Dictionnaire de Civilisation Musulmane*, Larousse, 1995,

UNESCO. *The Art of Islam*, Paris, 1990.

Verrier, Michelle. *Les Peintres Orientalistes*, Farhangsara Yassavoli, Tehran, 1997.

Weeks, Kent. *The Lost Tomb: The Greatest Discovery at the Valley of the Kings since Tutankhamun*, Orion Books Ltd, London 1999.

Wood, Vivian C. *Iran and Iranians*, Yassavoli Publications, Tehran, 1998.

Word, William A. 'Ancient Beirut' in *Beirut : Crossroads of Cultures*, Librarie du Liban, Beirut, 1970.

Other titles in the *Travels with a Nomad* series.

Paris, A Homage
An intimate memoir that uncovers the city's yesterday, today and tomorrow. 'Paris is a feeling... a call of the heart', writes Raana Haider as she explores in her own exuberant style, the city she adores.

India, Beyond the Taj and the Raj (forthcoming)
The author, on a journey through India, explores its diversity and researches the past and discusses the present of twenty-two cities and ancient sites in India. Raana inspires us with her writing on India's ashrams, rock-cut temples, splendid palaces, formidable forts, white washed churches and magnificent mosques.

INDEX